Social and Psychological Foundations of Economic Analysis

Social and Psychological Foundations of Economic Analysis

J. L. Baxter
Lecturer in Economics
University of Sheffield

HARVESTER · WHEATSHEAF
NEW YORK LONDON TORONTO SYDNEY TOKYO

First published 1988 by
Harvester · Wheatsheaf
66 Wood Lane End, Hemel Hempstead
Hertfordshire HP2 4RG
A division of
Simon & Schuster International Group

Printed and bound in Great Britain by
Billing & Sons Ltd, Worcester

British Library Cataloguing in Publication Data

Baxter, J. L., 1934–
Social and psychological foundations of economic analysis.
1. Economics. Psychological aspects
I. Title
330′.01′9
ISBN 0–7450–0417–2

1 2 3 4 5 92 91 90 89 88

Contents

List of Figures

List of Tables

Preface

This book represents the latest stage in research work which has been pursued intermittently since the early 1970s. At that time the author, like many others, was struck by the important role which wage comparisons appeared to play in wage claims. A failure to keep pace with the wage awards made to others seemed to give rise to deep feelings of injustice on the part of many bargaining groups, and frequently caused them to resort to actions designed to obtain the rates of pay to which they felt entitled. One looked in vain to economic theory to explain what at that time appeared to be an important source of inflationary pressures in many countries. Runciman's book on *Relative Deprivation and Social Justice*, to which the author's attention was drawn, provided valuable insights into the ways in which apparently diverse ideas from a number of disciplines could be woven together into a coherent whole, making it possible to understand events which were otherwise difficult to explain. It was only later that the present writer came to appreciate that the framework of analysis developed from Runciman's work could be extended into other areas of economics in which the standard neo-classical theory had little to say, or was not at all convincing. In particular, the approach developed helped understand the phenomenon of 'sticky' money wages, whose importance in economics has long been understood but inadequately explained.

A concern to explain the asymmetric behaviour of money wages led in turn to a re-examination of the standard treatment of consumer preferences. Looked at from the perspectives of psychology and sociology, the standard treatment is clearly deficient, as numerous researchers have pointed out. Duesenberry's work especially still stands out as a notable landmark in this area of work, despite the tendency in recent years to give greater weight to other theories of the consumption function. Even Duesenberry's work, however, does not really grapple with the issue which lies at the heart of the matter: namely, the question of what constitutes the underlying basis of utility. Economists have tended either to ignore this question, or have felt that it could more appropriately be posed to those within other disciplines in the social sciences. Inquiry into the basis of utility inevitably brings one face to face with the inadequacy of the assumptions about human motivation on which the elaborate theoretical structure of economics currently rests. The conclusion, inescapably, is that if economics is to break out of its present rigid straightjacket, it must be prepared to rebuild on a more substantial theory of motivation, and also incorporate notions such as social comparisons.

It is hoped that the present book will be of interest to a wide readership. Academic colleagues in the field of economics should be able to find something of value in the work, whatever their ideological standpoint in economics. The book ought also to appeal to students who have progressed beyond an introductory course in economics, many of whom, in the author's experience, still do not feel that economics is as relevant to their daily lives as ought to be the case. Students on management and business studies courses will welcome the attempt to bridge the gulf which presently exists between conventional economics and the courses they receive on such topics as consumer behaviour, marketing and industrial relations, which generally draw heavily on psychological and sociological theories and practice. It is earnestly hoped, finally, that numerous social scientists other than economists, many of whom have an interest in interdisciplinary studies, will find that the rather different application of familiar ideas is valuable, and even suggestive for their own future work.

Some economists may find the first major section of the book on intervening variables rather indigestible. The choice seemed to be between a potted psychology for economists and a rather more extensive treatment of motivation and social comparisons, drawing directly on the original material or other sources which psychologists themselves use. The author opted for the latter course, since it seemed important both to give an adequate account of the concepts to which so much importance is attached, and to show that the theories are supported by a good deal of research evidence. This approach seems unavoidable if interdisciplinary work is to develop and have any real standing. An attempt has also been made, however, to integrate the work from other disciplines with closely related areas of work in economics.

Since it may irritate some readers, the writer would like at this juncture to note that the attribution of male-only sex to consumers, wage-earners, etc., at certain stages in the text is not an oversight, or a deliberate snub to the other sex, but rather an effort to keep the text as simple as possible. It has to be acknowledged, however, that this convenient usage does not sit happily in a text which stresses the importance of sex distinctions in economic analysis.

It remains, finally, to thank all those who have contributed in any way to the present study. Over the years I have been working in the field, I have received constant encouragement, and no little help, from Jim Ford. Peter Earl and Peter Warr have also read either sections of the book or the book in its entirety, and provided many valuable comments and suggestions. Ultimately, however, it is the author who decides what appears in print, and must therefore accept final responsibility. I would like also to take this opportunity of thanking the various secretarial staff who have at different times shouldered the large typing burden entailed in bringing the book to press.

1 Introduction

In the introduction to his *Principles*, Alfred Marshall set out very eloquently what he took to be the central concerns of economics:

> Political Economy or Economics is a study of mankind in the ordinary business of life; it examines that part of individual and social action which is most closely connected with the attainment and with the use of the material requisites of wellbeing. Thus it is on the one side a study of wealth; and on the other, and more important side, a part of the study of man.

Marshall clearly saw man in the round, and as part of society, with interests extending well beyond those of narrow economic gain. This view of man and society has less appeal to the majority of economists today, it seems, although there are those, such as Herbert Simon (who used the above quotation in his 1976 Nobel address) who argue for what amounts to a reinstatement of those old ideas. As the problems with which economists have had to deal have become increasingly complex, and the tools of analysis progressively more sophisticated, there has been a regrettable tendency to lose sight of the principal objectives, and the true nature of our subject, and to believe that intricate economic problems are subject to purely technical solutions. Yet in many, perhaps most, instances, it is human behaviour which lies at the root of these problems, and it is only through a better understanding of this behaviour that we can hope to find solutions.

Our principal contention in the present study is that economic theory is seriously deficient in that it neglects what are often referred to as 'intervening variables', i.e., those variables which influence the response by individuals to any change in their general environment. In economic terms, the role of intervening variables can be illustrated by reference to the consumption function, which attempts to explain changes in personal consumption expenditure by changes in personal disposable income. Considerable progress has been made in establishing the precise form of this relationship, but we still have instances where the standard explanation breaks down badly. We had an example of such an occurrence in the United Kingdom in the period 1978–80, when the savings ratio suddenly increased sharply. Among the explanations offered for this sudden departure from the norm was the exceptionally rapid increase in unemployment during the period. The fear of unemployment, according to this thesis, persuaded many employees that it would be only prudent to set aside more out of their incomes in case they too lost their jobs. Changed expectations about employment, in other words, had a marked influence on consumer behaviour, with expectations fulfilling the role of a variable intervening in the normal relationship between changes in income and the associated changes in consumption. Expectations, however, are only one example of a number of potentially important intervening variables.

Much of our attention in the present study will be focused on what we consider to be another key intervening variable: motivation. It is important for economists to be able to understand what it is that energizes the individual, and gives him or her direction. In other words, we need to understand what it is that turns an inert individual into an active one and makes him act in one particular manner rather than another – we might also enquire about the factors which make the individual *continue* to act in a cerain manner, and ultimately persuade him to *stop* so doing. Since motivation is largely subjective in nature, it is perhaps not surprising that, among social scientists, it has principally been the subject of study by psychologists, but we hope to show that it ought to be accorded much more attention by economists.

Economics does not, of course, wholly neglect motivation, but it treats it in a very perfunctory manner. Consumers, we assume, are motivated by the goal of utility-maximization, and businessmen by profit-maximization. The claim is not that all consumers, or all businessmen, necessarily behave in such a manner, but that it is a sufficiently accurate representation of average behaviour for these assumptions to serve as the keystones for much economic analysis. Little in the way of hard empirical evidence is ever produced to support such contentions, however, and the suspicion lingers that the desperate manner in which economists cling to these assumptions about motivation has more than a little to do with their central role in facilitating the construction of an elaborate general equilibrium model of economic behaviour. In the present study, we shall be examining the question of motivation at some length. This enables us to highlight certain basic flaws in standard consumer theory, and, we hope, will make it much more difficult simply to go on blindly ignoring other possible approaches.

Yet another important intervening variable we shall be considering is social comparisons. Although, as we shall see, there is a great deal of solid empirical evidence showing that social comparisons do exert a powerful influence on, for example, consumer purchasing decisions, and on employees when making their pay demands, such comparisons find no formal place in conventional economic analysis. Even Duesenberry's (1949) work on the relative income hypothesis, one of the most interesting and useful attempts to explore the implications of social comparisons, is now downgraded, or omitted altogether, in some of the newer textbooks on macroeconomics. We hope to show in the present study, however, that social comparisons are an indispensable aid in explaining a number of phenomena with which economists have been grappling for some time.

The nature of many of the intervening variables with which we shall be preoccupied, and the fact that they have been studied extensively in other social sciences – principally psychology and sociology – means that we shall be drawing heavily on these fields. There are obvious dangers in an economist trying to interpret the work of those in other disciplines, but progress requires that the effort be made, and some care has been taken to tread warily. The writer is also well aware that the terms 'psychological' and 'sociological' are often used as terms of abuse when applied to economic theories, but since, as we stressed at the outset, economics deals with the activities of human beings, it cannot hope to escape entirely into a world in which only 'economic' variables count. We should therefore be very wary of economic theories which attempt to deny any role to psychological or sociological variables, and also examine closely any behavioural assumptions in economics which appear to be at odds with the theories and evidence available in the other social sciences.

At some stage, the social sciences merge with each other – indeed, we do not have to go back very far in time to find common origins and sources of inspiration – and they ought to be consistent and supportive of each other rather than contradictory. The worst sin of all, however, is simply to ignore the other's existence. Hirshleifer (1985), while advancing the case for a central role for economics within the social sciences, provides us with an admirable statement of the 'flip side':

> Thus economics really does constitute the universal grammar of social science. But there is a flip side to this. While scientific work in anthropology and sociology and political science and the like will become increasingly indistinguishable from economics, economists will reciprocally have to become aware of how constraining has been their tunnel vision about the nature of man and social interactions. Ultimately good economics will also have to be good anthropology and sociology and political science and psychology.

Unfortunately, if one does take the trouble to explore the other social sciences, one quickly becomes aware that, as in economics, there are different schools of thought. It could even be said that progress in some areas of economics is, in turn, dependent on further progress being made in these related disciplines. Even now, however, some of the different approaches adopted in a subject like psychology appear to be complementary rather than competing, awaiting only the broader framework which will enable elements of the different theories to be unified. There is, in any case, already much common ground which can be drawn upon, and indeed already is drawn upon, in certain branches of economics, like consumer behaviour. What we now need to do is bring the useful ideas into the mainstream of economics.

We shall not, in our study, be attempting to cover the whole field of economics, nor indeed be looking in depth at all the intervening variables of potential importance. We shall not, for example, be treating expectations as a separate intervening variable, although we shall be indicating at various stages in our analysis the implications for individuals' expectations. Nor shall we be treating at length the subjects of individual attitudes and perceptions, two forms of intervening variable which are almost certainly important, but would broaden our area of study excessively. Attitudes and motivation are linked – although the precise nature of the association does not appear to be agreed – and both influence individual behaviour. It will be apparent, too, that our analytical framework is of general application, and could well be extended to areas of analysis other than those covered in this book – Bausor (1984), for example, has suggested ways in which perceptions may have a bearing on expectations. Our framework seems especially useful, however, in providing close links between the important areas of consumer behaviour, labour supply and wage behaviour; and we shall also be looking briefly at its links with the managerial and behavioural theories of the firm developed in recent years.

It will be apparent from what has already been said that, from a methodological standpoint, the present study adopts a different approach from Friedman's 'mature positivist view of economic science' (Caldwell, 1982), or 'instrumentalism' as many writers on methodology have described it. In his 1953 article on 'The Methodology of Positive Economics', Friedman set out his, by now, well-known position: that the 'realism' of the assumptions on which an economic theory is based are of no consequence; what matters is the ability of a theory to yield valid and meaningful *predictions*. Furthermore, 'the only relevant test of the *validity* of a hypothesis is comparison of its predictions with experience' (emphasis as in the original).

Friedman's position has been very influential and widely adopted, but as one might expect, such a controversial stance has also had its critics. Good discussions of the issues raised can be found in Blaug (1980) and Caldwell (1982, 1984). From the point of view of the present study, one of the principal issues must be Friedman's implicit view that prediction is the sole goal of science, and that *explanation* is either unnecessary or sufficiently provided by the association between variables. Acceptance of such a stance might be understandable if economics were replete with examples of association between variables which held consistently, and were as accurate as one might reasonably desire, since this would imply that no variables of consequence had been omitted from the analysis. But how many examples of such association can we truly claim in economics; and are there sufficient for our purposes? The facts are that most associations do not exhibit the desired constancy, and there are frequently major divergencies – the association between changes in the money supply and changes in the rate of inflation is a case in point. (One thorough study by Hendry and Ericsson (1983), has even gone so far as to claim that this particular relationship has yet to be satisfactorily established in the case of the United Kingdom.)

It is one of the principal contentions of the present study that greater *understanding*, and therefore improved *explanation*, of the factors influencing the association between variables is essential to accurate prediction, and is in any case also necessary for good policy-making. Central to this improved understanding is a deeper appreciation of the complexities of human behaviour as it affects economic affairs, in particular of the prime motivational forces underlying personal behaviour. These motivational forces, as we indicated earlier, take the form of intervening variables, frequently influencing the response of dependent variables to changes in associated independent variables.

Nor is a full understanding of human activities possible without an analysis of individual behaviour *in a social setting*. Boland (1982) has identified the 'explanatory problem of individualism' as one of the two 'hidden agenda' problems of neo-classical economic methodology (the other being the 'problem of induction'). Boland defines methodological individualism as 'the view that allows *only* individuals to be the decision-makers in any explanation of social phenomena' (emphasis as in the original). As such, methodological individualism does not allow explanations which involve non-individualist decision-makers such as groups of individuals, or institutions. It is the case, of course, that the activities of firms are critical to economic analysis, but in neo-classical economics the responses of firms to changing economic circumstances take place without reference to decision-takers as individuals within these firms. The response of firms is automatic, dictated only by the axiomatic behaviour attributed to them.

The individualistic approach is often contrasted with the so-called 'holistic' approach. Methodological holism asserts that social theories must be grounded in the behaviour of irreducible groups of individuals (Blaug, 1980). In the present study we also have an interest, however, in the links and interactions between groups, as well as in the groups themselves – sometimes referred to as a 'structuralist' approach to analysis (see, for example, Kay, 1982). We believe, in sum, that a complete analysis of human behaviour must include important elements of all these approaches. It may be that, for some purposes, aggregates of individuals behave in much the same manner as individuals acting on their own. It is certainly also the case, however, as we shall see in the present study, that there are instances where group behaviour cannot be predicted by summing over a number of individuals. The approach adopted in our study therefore extends well beyond the bounds of neo-classical economics, and makes it possible to analyse and explain economic behaviour about which neo-classical economics has little or nothing to say.

The axiomatic approach of neo-classical economics may be likened to an inverted pyramid resting on its apex. A large and ever-growing body of theoretical, and to a lesser extent empirical, work has developed from the basic axioms employed, but in the shadow of this large body of work are extensive dark areas about which we know little, and about which we are likely to remain in ignorance so long as economics rests on such narrow foundations. The behavioural basis of economics sorely needs extending, in so far as we also need to consider alternative, and additional, behavioural assumptions to those underlying the neo-classical model.

The methodological approach advocated here is already reflected in a variety of research programmes, with differing emphases. These fall under a number of more general headings, such as 'economic psychology' or 'psychological economics', the latter placing rather greater emphasis on economics, the former on psychology. There is also a growing body of interdisciplinary work covering the fields of sociology and economics. Recent examples dealing with the problem of inflation are to be found in Goldthorpe (1978) and Gilbert (1986). The term 'behavioural economics' is also used to denote a broad spectrum of research covering economics, psychology and sociology. The common link between all these approaches is a concern to break down the artificial barriers between subject areas in the social sciences, and to broaden the foundations of economic analysis.

After examining in section 2 what we consider to be some of the key intervening variables with respect to economics, we go on in section 3 to examine the present micro-foundations of consumer theory, and show how they are found wanting in the light of our analysis of the intervening variables, especially motivation. In section 4 we make a logical extension of the analysis to include personal decisions as they affect the supply of labour. Finally, we round off our investigation by showing how our analytical framework can contribute to an understanding of wage behaviour, helping explain why it is that wages tend to be inflexible in a downward direction, and are subject to continuous upward pressures. We shall find common threads linking all these principal areas of study which assist in unifying certain macroeconomic theories, and also provide a better cohesion between micro- and macroeconomics.

2 Intervening Variables

The term 'intervening variable' was coined by Tolman (1936), although he may not have intended it to be employed precisely in the sense in which it is now used in psychology (Bolles, 1975), where it generally denotes some mental or physical intervention between a stimulus and the ensuing response to that stimulus. While the sequence of stimulus → intervening variable → response, denotes the normal order of events, it may sometimes be the case that the causal links in the chain are not unidirectional, in so far as the stimulus may not be wholly independent of the response. This is frequently the case in economics, where there are feedback effects, as with the impact of wage increases on prices, and prices on wage increases. There may nevertheless still be one or more intervening variables which do influence the response of a dependent variable to the change in an independent variable with which it is associated. These intervening variables must therefore be of prime interest to anyone wishing to explain the workings of society, and the economic developments taking place within that society.

Since our main concern in the present study will be with motivation as an intervening variable, we begin this section with a brief outline of some of the main theories of motivation and their historical development, relating them where possible to the progress of economic ideas. It is not, however, the intention here to provide anything like a comprehensive résumé of motivation theory; for that the reader may turn to works by such writers as Petri (1981), Bolles (1975), Steers and Porter (1987), from which the present section draws heavily, and numerous other writers.

Motivation is applicable to such a wide range of circumstances that it is necessary to be selective. Only certain aspects of motivation – and indeed only certain intervening variables – may be relevant in any given context, and we shall therefore concentrate on those which seem most relevant to our purposes. We shall be looking at motivation in particular as it relates to consumer behaviour, individual decisions about participation in the labour force and wage behaviour.

2.1 MOTIVATION

2.1.1 Early motivation theories and their place in economics

The subject of motivation has generally received scant treatment in economics. One would be hard put to find any economic textbooks which devote much space to this topic; yet it is central to economic theory. Even in psychology use of the term 'motivation' has only entered common parlance relatively recently, around the beginning of the present century. Nevertheless, the notion that individuals are motivated in their behaviour does have a long pedigree. For many centuries, one of the dominant philosophies was *rationalism*, which maintained that human beings choose what is best for them in the circumstances laid down for them by Nature. As Shackle (1972) has noted very eloquently, rationalism claimed to confer upon men the freedom to choose, yet was able to predict precisely what they would choose. All actions were available, but all except one were forbidden: forbidden by reasoning self-interest. The right choice, if known, would automatically be made. Within such a scheme of reasoning, motivation was superfluous.

The notion of human behaviour conforming to a pattern which achieves an optimum outcome is also to be found in the work of Adam Smith. Motivation as such does not feature in the *Wealth of Nations*, but Smith regarded that work as only one part of his integrated body of thought, and in his *Theory of Moral Sentiments* we are told which motives govern the activities of man, including, it would appear, the economic activities. According to Roll (1973), Smith envisaged human activity being naturally activated by six motives: self-love (or in more modern terminology, 'self-interest'), sympathy, the desire to be free, a sense of propriety, a habit of labour, and the propensity to truck, barter and exchange one thing for another. Guided by these motives, Smith believed that each man was the best judge of what was in his own interests, and should be left to pursue his goals as he saw fit. Untrammelled individualism need not, of course, produce an outcome beneficial to the common good, but Smith felt the motives underlying behaviour to be so carefully balanced that conflict between the individual and society would be avoided. What was best for the individual would also prove to be best for society. In pursuing his own advantage the individual would be led by the 'invisible hand' to promote the common good.

Smith's view of individual motivation, and the manner in which it was harnessed to the good of society, called for the minimum of state interference, since state activity could only serve to reduce the welfare of society. We have an interesting example, in effect, of the case for a particular economic model being based not on what might be regarded as primarily economic arguments, but rather on a view of what determines individual behaviour, and on the supposed nature of the forces governing the universe. Adam Smith's work provides us with an early example of the importance of motivation in economics.

A narrower philosophical approach, which contrasts strongly with Smith's idealistic view of the world, and which also has an underlying basis of motivation, even if a very mechanistic one, is *hedonism*: the belief that all human behaviour can be explained by the desires to seek pleasure and to avoid pain. Georgescu-Roegen (1968) traces these ideas as far back as the Greeks. Plato in his *Dialogues* argued that life was a juxtaposition of pleasure and pain, which alone formed the object of man's choice. Another staunch advocate of the hedonistic view of life was Hobbes, who held that it was the underlying cause of all behaviour, no matter what reasons the individuals themselves might advance. Bentham and Jevons were prominent amongst those economists who were influenced by the hedonistic approach. In one of the fullest statements of the importance of pleasure and pain, Bentham (1789, 1982) in defining utility wrote:

> By utility is meant that property in any object, whereby it tends to produce benefit, advantage, pleasure, good, or happiness (all this, in the present case, comes to the same thing), or (what comes again to the same thing), to prevent the happening of mischief, pain, evil, or unhappiness to the party whose interest is considered.

Bentham went on to examine the different kinds of pleasure and pain at some length. The simple pleasures to which human nature was susceptible he categorized as the pleasures of: sense, wealth, skill, amity, a good name, power, piety, benevolence, malevolence, memory, imagination, expectation, association, relief. A similarly long list of pains included the pains of privation, desire, regret, disappointment and the pains of the senses (hunger, thirst, taste, smell and sight, and those from exessive heat or cold, disease or exertion).

Hedonism was therefore associated with early versions of utility theory, but it had to be adapted to suit the new ideas which were emerging. Bentham advocated 'the greatest happiness for the greatest number' as the goal towards which society should strive; but since hedonism preached that each individual sought his own happiness, and would not therefore necessarily, as in the world of Adam Smith, promote the happiness of the community in general, utilitarianism added to hedonism the ethical doctrine that human conduct *should* be directed towards maximizing the happiness of the greatest number of people (Ekelund and Hebert, 1975).

Bentham's treatment of pleasure and pain placed the principle of maximization, both at the level of the individual and in respect of the community as a whole, right at the heart of economics. The combination of hedonism and utilitarianism established a powerful motivating force, in the form of a clearly set maximization *goal*; and the postulate of individual rational choice – the assumption that a rational individual would pursue the appropriate means for achieving desired goals – further assured that the goal would be attained. It was left to Jevons (1879, 1970), however, to show precisely *how* an individual with a given stock of resources would have to distribute it between alternative uses in order to achieve the maximum utility. His equimarginal condition was expressed in the form:

$$\partial u_1/\partial x = \partial u_2/\partial y$$

showing that the resources had to be distributed in such a way that the final inputs of resources to any two uses (i.e. x and y in the example) yielded equal amounts of utility (u_1 and u_2). This formulation was later developed into the more familiar general equimarginal principle (which does not appear in Jevons) allowing for price differences between goods.

Later attempts to overcome the problems posed by cardinal measurement of utility, by developing models relying only on ordinal measurement, still left the maximization goal intact, but the principle of hedonism was abandoned once its weaknesses came to be more fully appreciated. These weaknesses have been summed up well by Vroom (1964):

> There was in the doctrine no clear-cut specification of the type of events which were pleasurable or painful, or even how these events could be determined for a particular individual; nor did it make clear how persons acquired their conceptions of ways of attaining pleasure and pain, or how the source of pleasure and pain might be modified by experience. In short the hedonistic assumption has no empirical content and was untestable. Any form of behaviour could be explained, after the fact, by postulating particular sources of pleasure or pain, but no form of behaviour could be predicted in advance.

The way was now open for the development of a general equilibrium economic model, but it left unanswered one major question: if hedonism was not the basis of utility, what precisely was the basis? Here Jevons (1879, 1970) pointed the way. While lending support to Bentham's expression of the meaning of utility, as defined in terms of pleasure and pain, he carried it a stage further:

> Economics must be founded upon a full and accurate investigation of the conditions of utility; and to understand this element we must necessarily examine the wants and desires of man.

Others, such as Menger and Marshall, followed suit in highlighting the important role of wants, and needs, but, as we shall see in the following section, most economists were happier confining their analysis to utility *per se*, without enquiring too closely into what precisely it was in a good that gave rise to utility. That, many felt, was more properly the realm of those social scientists concerned with the subjective nature of things.

2.1.2 Instinct theories

Following the development of utility-maximization as the goal for individual behaviour, the interest of economists in motivation seems to have waned. The general feeling appears to have been that there was no need to probe further. Interest now focused on the most efficient means of allocating goods, rather than on goods as satisfiers of human needs, or on the underlying motives for acquiring goods. Motivation nevertheless continued to attract the attention of many psychologists, and it is of interest to our later analysis to examine, even if only briefly, the nature of this work.

The development of so-called 'instinct' theories in the later 1890s represented a further important stage in the progression of ideas about motivation. The idea of hedonism was not entirely rejected, but many argued that a more comprehensive explanation of behaviour was needed. James (1890) believed that instincts were similar to reflexes, and were excited by sensory stimuli. Such behaviour occurred blindly on the first occasion, without any knowledge of the end, or goal, towards which the behaviour led, but on subsequent occasions behaviour was influenced by previous experience. In other words, a learning process was at work. McDougall (1908) went further than James in attributing *all* behaviour to inherited instincts, and, unlike James, saw instinct as purposive and goal-directed. Both writers were on common ground, however, in believing that instincts could be modified by learning, although neither was able to spell out the precise nature of the relationship between the two.

The best-known advocate of instinct theories was Freud (1915), with his views on unconscious motivation. Freud claimed that an instinct possessed four characteristics: *source, pressure, aim* and *object*. The *pressure*, or impetus, took the form of *psychic energy*, which built up in an individual when some need (the *source*) such as the need for water, existed. The stronger the need the stronger the motive to satisfy it, leading the individual to regard satisfaction of the instinct as an *aim*. The *object* of the instinct was the means by which the aim could be satisfied – in our example, by drinking water, although drinking other fluids containing water, such as coffee and tea, could also satisfy the need, thereby posing difficulties when it came to predicting precisely how an individual would behave in the circumstances.

Freud's psychoanalytic theory has been criticized on a number of counts. Bolles (1975) makes much of the fact that the model needs to be refined in order to establish an unambiguous set of principles and hypotheses which could be used to provide firmer empirical foundations, beyond the customary clinical evidence. Bolles also notes that the theory lends itself to different interpretations of the same phenomena. Moreover, the 'explanations' of behaviour do not always make it possible to predict future actions. Other critics have noted that the list of instincts claimed is long, and appears somewhat arbitrary. Psychoanalysis none the less presents a powerful challenge to rationalistic interpretations of behaviour, and does seem to help in understanding what motivates people. Two aspects of his theories which are of special interest to us, since we shall be returning to them at greater length at a later stage, are: first, the part played in motivation by needs; and, second, the aims, or goals, associated with the needs.

2.1.3 Drive theories

During the 1920s, instinct theories were largely superseded by the concept of *drives*. The term 'drive' describes the energy that impels an organism to behave in a certain manner. The concept assumed that motivation depended upon some physiological need, such as hunger or thirst. When a state of need existed, the organism was motivated to reduce the need in some way or other.

Similarities with the instinct theories will be apparent. Both incorporated the notions of needs and goals; but as Bolles (1975) notes, the drive approach was thought to have certain theoretical advantages. In particular, the physiological basis of drives was felt to be more tangible and to lend itself more readily to empirical investigation – the physiological basis of instincts lay in the complex genetic make-up of individuals. Experiments with animals indicated that an animal's drives were sometimes directed towards very specific goals: a particular type of food, for example, rather than food in general (a desire for salt if kept for some time on a salt-free diet). Other experiments were undertaken to demonstrate, and to try and measure, the *strengths* of animal drives – not entirely successfully.

As in the case of earlier theories, drive theory eventually fell out of favour, partly because a great deal of research showed that it could by no means explain all behaviour. It was found, for example, that a generalized drive – of which the sex drive might be taken as an example – did not always activate behaviour. One of the most useful conclusions, however, is probably that advanced by Petri (1981):

> Drive theory was perhaps also useful in making apparent to most researchers that a single theory could not hope to explain all motivated behaviour. Increasingly it appears that motivation is multiply determined; some behaviours are programmed into the organism, while others are learned or depend upon social interactions or environmental conditions.

This comment could equally well be applied, it seems, to current economic orthodoxy, which, as we noted earlier, attempts to explain all economic behaviour on the basis of a very limited conception of human motivation.

2.1.4 Cognitive theories

One noticeable feature of the theories of motivation which we have discussed so far is that they generally do not assume the presence of a thinking being. Many of the theories, as we saw, are fairly mechanistic in their assumptions. Cognitive theories, however, are concerned with the manner in which thinking processes can motivate human beings. Once again, the subject area is a large one, and we are obliged to be somewhat selective. Two major strands in the cognitive approach are of special interest to us, and we concentrate principally on these: first, the emphasis placed on the future, and expectations about the future, rather than the past; second, the importance attached to social influences on human behaviour.

Among the cognitive approaches to motivation, one of the most popular is usually referred to as the 'expectancy-valence theory' (or sometimes the 'expectancy-value theory'), which we shall examine at greater length in a later section. Early work in this field was carried out in the 1930s, and is associated mainly with the names of Tolman (1932) and Lewin (1938). Once again, the basic idea is that an individual's needs lead to the setting of goals, which, if achieved, serve to satisfy the needs. The valence denotes the value placed by an individual on the possible outcomes of alternative courses of action. The effort made to achieve an outcome was held to be the product of the value placed on that outcome and the expectation of achieving it, i.e. effort = expectancy × value. The expectancy component, if weak, would generate only half-hearted action, or perhaps no action at all, even if a high value were placed on the outcome. Petri (1981) cites the need for achievement as one practical example which lends itself to the expectancy-valence approach.

Another cognitive theory we wish to examine (which could also, it seems, be regarded as part of what is sometimes referred to as the 'humanistic approach' to psychology) is concerned with the human desire for competence in coping with the environment, and for some control over it. This desire has a dynamic aspect to it, in that once an individual has become proficient at a particular task, he or she, so it is held, looks for the challenge of new tasks to perform. Carl Rogers, one of the leading theorists in the field, described this motive state as the desire to grow and attain fulfilment – the process apparent in young children continues, it seems, into adulthood. The main criticism of Rogers' work is that it is incompletely specified, and therefore difficult to test empirically. Kelly's work on personal construct theory, which deals with the ways individuals attempt to cope with a complex and uncertain world (see Kelly, 1955, 1963), also seems relevant in this context.

Another writer in this field, whose work has attracted considerable attention, is Abraham Maslow (1970), who described the developmental process as one of 'self-actualization'. Maslow's theory is based on an analysis of human needs, which he investigated in considerable detail.

Self-actualization is treated as one of the 'higher-order' needs, which come into play when lower-order needs, such as those for food and shelter, have been met (although not necessarily met in full). We shall be examining Maslow's hierarchy of needs at greater length in a subsequent section, but it is worth dwelling briefly on the self-actualizing aspect at this juncture.

In Maslow's work we find the individual being motivated to strive towards certain goals (goals did not feature specifically in the work of Rogers) with the meeting of needs yet again providing the underlying impetus. The attempt to satisfy needs will frequently be a conscious process, especially perhaps where basic needs for such things as food and shelter have to be met, but Maslow also stressed that the striving to meet other needs should not always be taken at its face value. Even the individual himself might not be fully aware of what he was striving for, and might not therefore be able to articulate his goals. The motivation might operate in part at an unconscious level, rather as Freud had maintained.

Maslow's picture of the self-actualized person is very positive, and therefore very attractive. The person who has reached this stage of development has overcome the threat of deprivation posed by other needs, and is now able to concentrate on developing his or her potential to the full. This picture of life doubtless has an intuitive appeal for many people, including probably many academics, some of whom may like to think of themselves in the role of cerebral mountaineers, motivated to scale ever more difficult intellectual peaks. On the debit side, critics of Maslow's theory have claimed that it is elitist, and that growth motivation is not universally applicable, or even widespread. There are, too, undoubtedly difficulties in testing any theory like Maslow's although several tests of it have been carried out. It seems fair to say that a number of the studies, such as those by Shostrom (1964) and Rizzo and Vinacke (1975) do provide important support for Maslow's ideas, although, as is so often the case in the social sciences, considerable scope still exists for further research.

With Maslow's work on self-actualizing behaviour we conclude our references to what might be called the general psychological models of motivation. As we noted earlier, these models have to be modified somewhat when applied to individuals in particular situations, as at work, where people are acting under constraints they may not have to observe in their private lives; or their behaviour may be dictated in part by those who have some control over them. In recent years, an important body of work has accumulated which is concerned specifically with the role of motivation in organisations. This work draws, of course, on the general psychological models we have examined, but it is of particular interest to us, in that we are concerned, among other things, with wage behaviour, which must be seen within some form of organisational setting. Work on motivation in organizations is also of interest to us in that it lays even greater stress on a number of aspects of psychological motivation to which we have repeatedly drawn attention, namely, the important roles of needs and goals.

2.1.5 Motivation in organisations

An examination of recent publications on behaviour in organizations (see, for example Warr, 1976; Gordon, 1983; Gibson et al., 1985; Landy, 1985; Miner, 1985; Steers and Porter, 1987) suggests that any reasonably comprehensive classification of theories of work motivation would give a prominent place to the following: needs theories; equity theories; goal-setting theories; expectancy-valence (values) theory. This classification is interesting, in that it highlights two aspects which have cropped up repeatedly in our discussion of the evolution of the general psychological theories of motivation. At several stages during our discussion of these theories we noted how some at least of the theories relied upon needs as a basis for motivation, and that drive theory and some of the cognitive theories attributed central roles to needs and goals. The only category of motivation we have not yet touched upon is that concerned with equity. We hope to show, however, that all four categories of motivation which we have singled out (needs, equity, goals and expectancy) complement each other, and can make a significant contribution to economic theory.

First, however, we must examine the four individual categories of motivation at greater length, in order to obtain a better understanding of the concepts with which we are dealing. We shall then be better placed to apply them to the specific areas of economics which are our principal concern: consumer behaviour, the supply of labour and wage behaviour.

2.2 ASPECTS OF MOTIVATION – NEEDS, WANTS AND SATISFIERS

Although needs play an important part in our subsequent analysis, the bulk of the work on wants pre-dates that on needs, and it is therefore convenient to begin with an examination of wants. Moreover, the ground covered in the discussion of wants will be more familiar to many economists, even if much of the material has tended to be ignored in recent years.

2.2.1 Wants

In his excellent survey of utility theory, Georgescu-Roegen (1968) noted that much of the early analysis of consumer behaviour was in terms of needs or wants, and, indeed, 'it was the early theorizing about wants that constituted the major source of inspiration for those who laid the foundation of utility theory in economics.' The early economists, however, frequently defined utility in terms of pleasure and pain, influenced perhaps by the scholars of ancient times, such as Plato, who saw the juxtaposition of pleasure and pain as a central feature of life. We saw earlier that Bentham and Jevons were among those influenced by the hedonistic approach. In his *Table of the Springs of Action* (1815), Bentham went on to link wants, which he regarded as synonymous with needs, to pleasure and pain:

> Wants bears a common reference to pleasure and to pain; satisfied it produces pleasure; unsatisfied, pain; though capable of being overbalanced by the pleasure of *hope*, i.e. of *expectation*.

Later writers tended to switch the emphasis to 'wants', rather than pleasure and pain. Jevons (1879, 1970) for example, while lending support to Bentham's expression of the meaning of utility, as defined in terms of pleasure and pain, carried it a stage further: 'Economics must be founded upon a full and accurate investigation of the conditions of utility; and to understand this element we must necessarily examine the wants and desires of man.' Later he comments that, 'Many French economists also have observed that human wants are the ultimate subject matter of economics.' One such source he quotes, Bastiat, wrote, 'Wants, Efforts, Satisfaction – this is the circle of Political Economy.'

Another notable French economist to refer to the role of wants was Walras, (1926, 1977) who went so far as to use the heading 'Utility Curves or Want Curves' for one of the sections in his *Elements*. He also noted that a want had more than one dimension, depending not only upon the number of people feeling it, but also the strength, or intensity, with which each person felt it. He might also have added a third dimension: the magnitude of the want felt by each individual, determined it would seem by the extent of the gap between a person's desired situation and his actual situation.

The reasons for Jevons' switch in emphasis towards wants are not made explicit, but he probably found wants a more satisfactory foundation on which to build his individualistic and subjective theory of value. The hedonistic implications of utility analysis founded on pleasures and pain were not to everyone's liking. One economist who illustrates the trend away from pleasure and pain is Marshall. Hutchison (1953) makes the interesting observation that Marshall in his earlier years appears to have read a great deal of hedonism into the marginal utility theory of value, but had become markedly cautious about this by about 1895 (the year of the third edition of his *Principles*). He quotes Guillebaud (1942) to the effect that:

> Particularly in his First Edition, Marshall used very freely the contrasting words 'pleasure' and 'pain' ... By the Third Edition (1895), however, Marshall was becoming sensitive to contemporary criticisms of utilitarian phraseology, and he went through the various pages in which he had used the words 'pleasure' and 'pain' and substituting in most (though not in all) cases, for 'pleasure' the word 'satisfaction' or 'benefit' or 'gratification'.

Marshall's work contains one of the most extensive discussions of wants. His treatment of wants was extended considerably between the first edition of the *Principles* in 1890 and the second edition in 1891, the main reason being, it seems, that he was anxious to stress the connection between man's activities and the wants to which they gave rise. In the second edition, a lengthy footnote appeared in Book III giving a list of those economists who had contributed to the development of the concept of wants. Among those listed, in addition to the writers already cited above, were Hermann, Banfield, Senior, Menger (who, as we shall see, dealt in fact with needs rather than wants) von Thünen and the Australian Hearn, from whom Marshall appears to have drawn heavily in his own analysis of wants. In his footnote Marshall also makes the interesting comment that, 'some analysis of wants and desires is to be found in the great majority of French and other Continental treatises on economics even of the last generation; but the rigid boundary which English writers have ascribed to their science has excluded such discussions.' This self-imposed limitation has continued right up to the present day.

Marshall's own work on wants is worthy of note. He wrote, in general terms:

> Human wants and desires are countless in number and very various in kinds. The uncivilised man indeed has not many more than the brute animal; but every step in his progress upwards increases the variety of his needs together with the variety in his methods of satisfying them. He desires not merely larger *quantities* of the things he has been accustomed to consume, but better qualities of those things; he desires a greater choice of things, and things that will satisfy new wants growing up in him.[1]

He did not consider it necessary for his purposes to draw up a formal classification of wants, but the outlines of one can be discerned. Haines (1982) from an analysis of Marshall's work, has classified his hierarchy of wants (we shall return later to the subject of hierarchy of wants) as: biological needs (mainly food, clothing and shelter); health, education and security; friendship, affection, belonging, conformity with social customs; distinction; activities and excellence; morality.

The graduation from lower-order to higher-order wants is quite clear. The uncivilized man's wants are little more than the requirements of the brute animal: food, clothing and shelter. Neither cares much for variety. As man's mental activities develop, however, his wants become more subtle and various, and 'in the minor details of life he begins to desire change for the sake of change'. The art of making a fire opens up the possibility of greater variety in cooking and the types of food eaten. Since the amount which can be eaten is limited by the size of the human stomach, eating also fulfils an important social function, 'gratifying the desires of hospitality and display'.

Marshall moves on from the biological wants to note how important it is to human beings to enjoy some feeling of distinction. He quotes with approval the remark of Senior that, 'Strong as is the desire for variety, it is weak compared with the desire for distinction: a feeling which if we consider its universality and its constancy, that it affects all men and at all times, that it comes with us from the cradle and never leaves us till we go into the grave, may be pronounced to be the most powerful of human passions.' However, it is worth noting in Marshall's comments that while the individual's choice of dress was often related to his desire for distinction, society itself frequently dictated by custom and social decree what a person should wear: 'In Scotland, for instance, in Adam Smith's time many persons were allowed by custom to go abroad without shoes and stockings who may not do so now.' We shall in our analysis be making much of these and other social influences on a person's consumption decisions.

Increasing one's house room was also seen by Marshall as a means of greater social distinction, but it fulfilled the further important function of enabling persons to pursue a greater range of possible 'activities', many again of a social nature. Marshall was thinking here not only of the pursuit of science, literature and art, but the growing desire for amusements such as games and travel which increased leisure made possible. The development of these new activities was important in that they gave rise to new wants – a pattern which seems very familar to us today, and which was already very apparent in Marshall's time. Activities – wants – demand for goods and services: that was the pattern Marshall saw in the higher stages of man's development. Crucially, however, he also saw the pattern unfolding over time and within a broad societal context: 'Tomorrow's wants depend on whether and how today's wants are satisfied. They depend further on all the influences – physiological, psychological, social, religious, political, environmental – that impinge on the personality and development potential of the unique individual.'

Despite Marshall's eloquent pleading, the influence of wants on personal consumption decisions has remained largely unheeded in mainstream economics since his time. As Haines (1982) has noted, wants do not merit a mention in most economics textbooks nowadays, and even texts on the history of economic thought tend to treat them only briefly, if at all. The shift from cardinal or ordinal utility, and the use of the indifference curve approach in the analysis of consumer behaviour has moved the emphasis away from utility *per se*, and there seems little inclination to examine the foundations on which indifference curve analysis itself stands. The revealed preference approach has also satisfied those who would like, so far as possible, to keep economics objective and easily quantifiable, even if thereby curtailing its scope.

2.2.2 Needs

Unlike wants, research into needs has been very largely the preserve of psychologists, and much of the work is of relatively recent vintage. Within psychology, needs are regarded by some psychologists as being of such fundamental importance that a school of thought largely based on needs (sometimes referred to as 'humanistic psychology') has developed. One difficulty encountered with this approach is that there is still no generally accepted definition of what is meant by 'need' – indeed, the problem may be insoluble, certainly at the present stage of development of the social sciences. The difficulty of defining key terms precisely is not, of course, an unusual problem in the social sciences. Economics is no exception. We have only to consider the problems encountered in trying to define such a basic variable as the money supply. Fortunately, our inability to define a concept precisely in practice need not prevent its use, even if it does thereby limit our understanding and qualify the conclusions we are able to draw from any analysis.

Despite the difficulties of defining need, it is worth our while dwelling on the subject for a time, since a clearer idea about the meaning of 'needs' will help us to appreciate better their relationship to wants. The relationship between needs and wants we will maintain is a crucial one for economics, and one to which economists have paid for too little attention.

One of the most extensive discussions of needs, and one which helps throw light on the link with wants, is contained in Lederer (1980). Lederer distinguishes two main schools of thought: one postulating the universal – and thus to a considerable extent objective – character of needs; the other their historical and subjective nature. She notes, however, that the two approaches need not be exclusive, and that the differences might ultimately only be terminological. To assist us in drawing our own conclusions, it is helpful to start with the case of an individual. Human beings differ both physically and mentally. Their metabolism varies, for example, and therefore the intake of food required to keep the body functioning normally varies. Some individuals also seem to have a greater need to socialize with their fellows, while others are perfectly happy as 'loners' in society. Many of these differences could, it seems, be susceptible to objective assessment.

Among the adherents of the 'objective' approach are Mallman and Marcus (1980) who define a need as an 'objective requirement to avoid a state of illness. Therefore needs are objective and universal because the states of illness are.' In an effort to provide logical clarification in the study of needs, these writers make a threefold distinction between needs, 'desires' (which seem to be synonymous with economists' 'wants') and 'satisfiers'. Further, they write:

> Desires and satisfiers are spatially, temporally and personally determined. Theoretically, each individual has specific desires, and these are explicitly correlated with given satisfiers. Some of these desires correspond to needs; some of them do not.

In order to clarify the links between the different concepts, Mallman and Marcus (the former a physicist by initial training and the latter a mathematician) constructed an interesting mathematical model, using set theory. In essence, the emphasis is on demonstrating the manner in which social structures influence the desires/wants of social groups.

Those taking a more 'subjective' line would tend to argue that, while organic needs, for example that for food, have to be satisfied if the body is to function effectively, the expression of these needs is influenced by social and cultural factors. Klineberg (1980), an exponent of this view, gives an example of how the biological need for food is satisfied in a variety of ways, with the number of meals per day, the kind of food eaten, the manner in which it is eaten, the company in which it is eaten (and probably also the quantity eaten) all being socially determined. He also observes that 'there is probably no community in the world that does not consistently refrain from eating certain available foods.' A good example is provided in Britain, where a wide variety of fish is available around its coasts, yet relatively few species are demanded by local consumers – other varieties often being caught by foreign fishermen for their customers.

Upon closer examination, it seems that Klineberg's 'expression of organic need' is in fact what those adopting the objective approach treat as desires or wants. The question of the possible influence of environmental factors (space, time and culture) on needs is, however, one which only empirical research can settle. It is the case, for example, that the average daily intake of calories varies widely from country to country, no doubt in part due to climate differences; and in hot countries we might also expect the intake of liquids to be higher than in moderate climes. Custom and practice also undoubtedly play a part in determining such differences, but it may even be the case that after a considerable time custom and practice themselves affect the biological needs of the individual. To take another example, does the life of a monk in one of the secluded orders reduce the need for social contact with fellow human beings, or is it simply the case that those who join these orders have little need for such contact – or perhaps a bit of both? Such questions are likely to be very difficult, perhaps even impossible, to resolve satisfactorily, but there seems little doubt that environmental factors do exert some influence on needs.

The above discussion helps bring out the crucial distinction between needs and wants. Needs originate in individuals (between whom there are organic differences) and through the influence of environmental factors (the influences of space, time and culture) are translated into wants. The wants, in other words, derive from needs. An important caveat, however, is that, although deriving from needs, wants may very well, and indeed frequently do, exceed the original needs. Obvious examples are the need for food, which may be taken to excess through gluttony, and the desire for new or different clothes, which may well extend far beyond the need for basic clothing, and even other needs, such as status. From the point of view of consumer behaviour, it is clearly the wants which are of most direct importance, but equally clearly, most – some might even claim all – wants cannot be divorced from the needs from which they derive. We cannot explain or understand most wants without reference to needs. Both are important to the economist studying consumer behaviour. It may be that the closer wants are to needs the more strongly are they felt, but observation suggests that wants are still a powerful force to be reckoned with, even when they clearly exceed needs by a considerable margin.

2.2.3 Classifications of Needs

In order to understand needs better, efforts have been made to classify them. Prominent in this field has been the work of Maslow (1970). His theory of motivation, first presented in 1942, was, in his own words, 'an effort to integrate into a single theoretical structure the partial truths I saw in Freud, Adler, Jung, D. M. Levy, Froman, Horney and Goldstein'. The formative influences on Maslow's work were therefore strongly psychological, and apparently independent of those influences which shaped the views of economists on the nature of wants – we should not, of course, rule out possible common influences, such as the thinkers of earlier times, like Plato and Aristotle. Despite these very different traditions, however, there are strong similarities, as we shall see, between the classifications of needs and wants which have been propounded. The explanation undoubtedly is that needs and wants are closely interlinked, as we saw earlier, but by no means identical.

It is quite helpful to think of Maslow's approach in terms of means and ends. If we examine carefully the desires which we experience in our daily lives, we find that they generally have one characteristic: they are generally means to an end rather than ends in themselves. When a conscious desire is analysed, we find that underlying it are other, more fundamental, aims of the individual. Money, for example, may in the case of the miser celebrated in many storybooks be desired for its own sake, but for most people it is desired as the means of purchasing goods and services. A good, for example a car, is desired because it in turn provides mobility, a pleasurable sensation of speed, and perhaps also status. An item of clothing may provide warmth, and perhaps also enable one to be in fashion. If we probe more deeply, in other words, we find that our desires are ultimately determined by certain needs which we have as human beings. Attempts to satisfy these needs are ends in themselves beyond which we cannot go (Maslow, 1970) – it is interesting to note here the growing concern among consumer behaviour researchers with the relationship between means and ends, and the desire to enquire more deeply into consumer values and preferences, using, for example, the ideas of Kelly's (1955) personal construct theory and useful research techniques such as repertory and implication grids (for examples of this work see Reynolds and Gutman, 1984; Earl, 1986).

The first category of needs identified by Maslow was man's physiological needs for food and water. Since these may vary from one individual to another, and become very numerous when one attempts to break them down into specific kinds of food, Maslow did not consider it worthwhile attempting to draw up a list of fundamental physiological needs. He mentioned nevertheless that the meeting of physiological needs was our dominant need, so long as it was not met. Only when it was met, or met to a substantial degree, was the individual able to consider his other needs.

Safety needs constitute Maslow's second major category. These include the needs felt for security, stability, protection, law and order, etc. Whilst very obvious in the case of children, such needs are also felt strongly by adults – and may become stronger still as adults grow older. Symptomatic of safety needs is the common preference for a tenured job with pension scheme attached, the desire to save (there may also be other motives at work here too, of course) and the widespread use of insurance schemes as a protection against such calamities as serious illness, disability and unemployment. Still further examples might be a preference for familiar rather than unfamiliar things, when a choice has to be made between the two, and the interest in religions and philosophies which attempt to give some coherence to the apparent chaos of much of everyday life.

Maslow's third category comprises the needs for 'belongingness' and love, which emerge after the first two categories are gratified, in some degree at least. Family, friends, loved ones, and even broader groupings such as neighbourhood and nation can help satisfy these needs. The thwarting of such needs is a common cause of maladjustment in individuals – for example, when children are constantly uprooted by parents on the move, and unable to form binding relationships. In the case of love, the need entails giving as well as receiving. Belonging, too, may not simply be a passive state, but may involve making a positive contribution of some sort to another party, or parties.

The need for esteem forms a further broad grouping, subdivided into the need for self-respect, or self-esteem, and for the esteem of others. These needs may be classified, according to Maslow, into two subsidiary sets. First, the desire for achievement, mastery, competence, and for independence and freedom; second, the need for reputation or prestige, status, recognition, attention, importance and appreciation. Satisfying one's self-esteem leads to feelings of worth, self-confidence, adequacy, of being useful and necessary in the world. Thwarting of these needs produces feelings of inferiority and helplessness, and may cause discouragement, or even neurotic tendencies.

Finally, Maslow listed the need for 'self-actualization', i.e. the desire for self-fulfilment, to become everything that one is capable of becoming. Such needs must vary greatly, it seems, from person to person. One individual may have an urge to be a writer, another to drive a train, teach, and so forth. At this level of needs, individual differences are greatest, according to

Maslow. Such needs also tend to emerge most clearly when the other categories of needs have been satisfied in some degree.

A number of points about Maslow's categorization of needs seem worth noting. He does not intend to imply that the categories are rigid. Their order may even differ on occasions, with perhaps esteem, or self-actualization, being more important for some people than love. In others, the level of aspiration may be very low, blunted perhaps by such life experiences as unemployment. Some people, too, may be very single-minded, motivated by one goal to the exclusion of all others.

A further important question, which we have touched on already, is the extent to which needs are culturally determined. In Maslow's view, what appear at first sight to be startling differences in needs turn out on closer examination to be superficial rather than basic. Differences in hairstyles, clothes, tastes in food, etc., do not represent differences in need. On the other hand, Maslow does not go so far as to claim that his classification is universal for all cultures, only that it is 'relatively *more* ultimate, *more* universal, *more* basic than the superficial conscious desires, and makes a close approach to common human characteristics' (Maslow, 1970).

Lastly, it should be understood that Maslow is not claiming that all behaviour is determined by basic needs. He remarks, 'We might even say that not all behaviour is motivated' – a statement which could be interpreted as questioning any notion of the maximizing behaviour of individuals. Amongst the determinants of behaviour other than motives he cites the 'external field', by which he seems to mean the external environment, and 'expressive behaviour', which reflects a person's personality (part of the organic differences we noted earlier)[2] – in Maslow's words, 'a stupid man behaves stupidly, not because he wants to, or tries to, but simply because he is what he is.' To those, on the other hand, who ask whether we can explain all behaviour as a reflection of character structure, his response is a firm negative.

Maslow's theory has a simplicity and logic about it which doubtless helps explain its continued popularity. It appears to accord well with the personal experiences of many people. Yet, as he himself was ready to admit, it is still not fully supported by laboratory and other experimental work. In general, it seems that there are probably only two or three main categories of needs, with the lower-order needs, such as security and safety, and the higher-order needs, such as love, esteem and self-actualization clustering independently. Moreover, instead of one need predominating at any given time, several needs are usually present, although in differing degrees.

Maslow's work has given rise to a great deal of associated theorizing and research. A summary of some of his work, with the main emphasis on the theories of McLelland, Alderfer and Herzberg and their associates, can be found in J. R. Gordon (1983). Briefly, although they differ somewhat in the needs identified, the general pattern which emerges shows a strong affinity with that of Maslow. McLelland's analysis (1961), which concentrates on the higher-order needs, identifies the needs for affiliation, achievement and power. The last mentioned is, it seems, a strong motivator among some businessmen, with managers who expressed a need for power tending to run more productive departments than those with needs for affiliation.

Alderfer (1972) reduces Maslow's hierarchy to three sets of needs: existence (covering Maslow's biological and safety needs); relatedness (Maslow's love and belongingness); and growth (including self-esteem and self-actualization). Individuals' needs differ according to their experiences and stage of development, but a broad pattern of needs is usual. Herzberg's (1959) twofold classification into hygiene needs and motivators again parallels Maslow's classification, with motivators being roughly the equivalent of Maslow's self-esteem and self-actualizing needs.

As we saw earlier, in discussing utility economists have tended to talk in terms of wants rather than needs, but they have also on occasions used both terms in tandem, usually without distinguishing between the two. Menger was an important exception to the rule. In the introduction to a translated edition of Menger's *Principles of Economics*, Frank Knight notes that Menger always spoke of 'need', not of want, desire or craving. The choice of term therefore appears to be deliberate, but the precise significance of the choice is not explained. Menger does say, however, that:

> Needs arise from our desires and the desires are imbedded in our nature. An imperfect satisfaction of needs leads to the stunting of our nature. Failure to satisfy them brings about our destruction. But to satisfy our needs is to live and prosper. Thus the attempt to provide for the satisfaction of our needs is synonymous with the attempt to provide for our lives and well-being. It is the most important of all human endeavours, since it is the prerequisite and foundation of all others.

Menger was also quite clear in his own mind about the relationship between utility and needs: 'Utility is the capacity of a thing to serve for the satisfaction of human needs.' A good having the capacity to satisfy a need he described as having 'goods character'. Menger also stressed the importance of time and uncertainty to the meeting of needs. Proper preparation was required in order to meet needs 'in good time', and such preparation he regarded as the hallmark of civilised countries. At the individual level:

> The quantities of consumption goods a person must have to satisfy his needs may be termed his requirements. . . . The concern of men for the satisfaction of their needs thus becomes an attempt to *provide in advance* for meeting their requirements in the future, and we shall therefore call a person's requirements those quantities of goods that are necessary to satisfy his needs within the time period covered by his plans.

In respect of long-term plans, it does not seem unreasonable to regard this as an early statement of the lifecycle of needs (of which we shall say a good deal more later on) since adequate plans would obviously take account, to some degree at least, of a person's likely needs over the remainder of his or her lifetime. However, Menger introduced the important caveat: 'Even with needs that we know in advance will be experienced in the time period for which we plan, we may be uncertain about the quantities involved.' The effect of this uncertainty on the individual's consumption is not, however, spelled out.

Another interesting reference to needs is to be found in Keynes' *Essays in Persuasion* (1972). In his essay on the 'Economic Possibilities for our Grandchildren' he classifies needs into two kinds: 'those which are absolute in the sense that we feel them whatever the situation of our fellow human beings may be, and those which are relative in the sense that we feel them only if their satisfaction lifts us above, makes us feel superior to, our fellows.' Needs of the second class he felt might indeed be insatiable, in that the higher the general level of affluence, the higher still would tend to be these needs. In the case of absolute needs, however, he was more hopeful. The point at which they might be satisfied could arrive sooner than we all expected – a tribute to the power of compound growth and accumulation. Keynes's emphasis on the relative nature of some needs is an aspect on which we shall later dwell at some length, since it appears to be of central importance to economics, and indeed has much wider implications.

2.2.4 Some further characteristics of needs and wants

Earlier discussion hinted at certain features of needs and wants which merited further examination. There is, first, the idea that some needs and wants are more pressing than others, and have to be satisfied, in part at least, before lesser needs assume importance. In other words, there may be hierarchies of needs and wants. Some writers have tried to argue, often for policy reasons, that there are certain basic needs, the satisfying of which should have priority. Some of these needs and wants may be irreducible below a certain point if an individual is to survive. Implicit, too, in the idea of a hierarchy of needs/wants is the view that many needs/wants can be fully satisfied. This so-called 'satiety of needs/wants' underlies the notion of diminishing marginal utility, and is therefore worth dwelling upon. Finally, not all needs and wants are fixed. Some, such as the need for food and drink, may alter little, but wants, especially, change over time. This dynamic aspect is an especially important feature of consumer behaviour. We shall look in turn at these important characteristics of needs and wants.

First, the aspect of hierarchy. Any study which examines needs and wants in depth cannot fail to be struck by the fact that some needs, and therefore wants, are likely to be more pressing and immediate than others, and that some will probably have to be met, in substantial part at least, before others. This idea of hierarchy is of long-standing – Georgescu-Roegen (1968) claims that it goes back as far as Plato's *Republic* – and, in terms of broad categories at least, there is probably fairly general agreement about the form of the hierarchy. One aspect which may tend to be overlooked, however, is that the hierarchy need not be strictly linear, as is often supposed. It might be more in the nature of a tree structure, as suggested by Strotz (1957, 1959).

There is probably greatest agreement about what are sometimes referred to as 'lower-order' needs. These are usually taken to include such biological needs as food, drink and shelter, and perhaps also security. These needs are fairly obvious, although, as we shall see later, there may still be arguments about the extent to which we can talk about 'basic needs' for food, drink, etc. Clearly, too, when we talk about a corresponding hierarchy of wants, the wants may include an element of, say, food, which exceeds any conceivable definition of food *needs*. In such a case, the want for food should perhaps distinguish between what we might call a lower-order want for food and a higher order want for food, with the latter probably ranking lower in the wants hierarchy than the former. The same distinction could be applied to other lower-order needs. Certain drinking, both from the point of view of quantity and quality, might better be linked to higher-order wants – excessive consumption of alcohol and expensive brands of whisky and wine would be examples – than to lower-order needs and wants. The homes we live in are also frequently a reflection of highly developed wants rather than the simple need for adequate shelter.

When it comes to trying to identify the relative importance of 'higher-order' needs, such as status and self-esteem, there is much more diversity of view. This is probably a question which can only be resolved by further empirical investigation. Once again, however, there ought almost certainly to be a distinction between the hierarchy of needs and the hierarchy of wants. People do not always want what they need, or what is good for them. Environmental factors, such as social customs, may also play an important part in determining orders of priority, certainly of wants. Religion, for example, may on occasions be a factor suppressing needs, such as self-actualization, causing the associated wants to rate less highly than otherwise would be the case. Social and political systems, too, may encourage the subjugation of self to the paramountcy of the group, community or the state. There may therefore be considerable differences between the hierarchies of needs and wants.

The idea of a hierarchy of needs and wants subsumes a number of principles, or, more accurately, subsidiary hypotheses. There is, first, what is often referred to as the 'irreducibility of wants'. Our analysis suggests that this term could most appropriately be applied to the needs of food, drink, shelter and anything else essential to mere survival – in the long term as well as the short term. In the case of this irreducible minimum, needs and wants would exactly coincide.

Closely associated with the idea of the irreducibility of needs and wants is the popular notion of 'basic needs'. There has been a failure to agree on which particular needs should be included in such a term, but it features widely in work on development economics, where it would obviously be helpful if minimum criteria could be agreed upon as a basis for policy decisions on levels of aid required, planning targets, etc. Stewart (1985) distinguishes two main interpretations of the meaning of basic need. The first is that there are certain goods and services which every human being ought to be able to enjoy in order to 'live a decent life'. This is the more conservative interpretation of the two noted by Stewart, yet it still suffers from the difficulties of justifying particular bundles of goods as being 'basic'. Since societies, even those at an early stage of development, differ greatly in climate, social customs, etc., there is little hope of agreeing a universally applicable bundle of goods and services. It is also very difficult for those not actually living in a society – and most of those in authority will tend not be typical representatives of the society – to judge exactly what is basic to requirements. Nevertheless, at this level there is the prospect of being able to reach a measure of agreement on society–specific targets which allow plans to be drawn up and costs assessed, even if the targets may contain a – probably relatively small – margin of error.

The second interpretation of 'basic' is described by Stewart as the 'full-life objective'. A minimal definition of this term would probably include reasonable standards of health and education. A more extensive definition would also comprise provision of social, cultural and recreational activities. The more extensive the interpretation of 'basic', the more difficult it is likely to be to agree on an appropriate package of goods and services, since more items will be included and the wider will be the potential range of quality offered. The differences between countries and areas will again further complicate matters.

Faced by such problems, there seems little prospect of agreement on a universal bundle of basic needs; nor is there much hope of objective measurement. Only if 'basic' were to be so basic as to be no more than adequate for human existence might measurement be more readily undertaken; but even such a definition would entail area and country differences, and it is doubtful if such a restricted definition would be of great practical value – at such a level, too, the irreducibility of needs and wants and basic needs would amount to the same thing, and these needs/wants would form the first level in the needs/wants hierarchies. 'Basic', therefore, will probably continue to be defined as what seems reasonable in the circumstances to those in authority at any given time.

In addition to irreducibility, a second principle underlying the hierarchies of needs and wants is the idea of the saturation of needs and wants, first expounded by Gossen (1854, 1927): 'The amount of one and the same enjoyment diminishes continuously as we proceed with that enjoyment without interruption, until satiety is reached.' This basis for the 'law' of diminishing marginal utility can perhaps best be illustrated by the consumption of food and drink, where needs, and indeed also our wants, can be satisfied with relatively small quantities of each in relation to what is generally available – at least in the prosperous industrial countries. The principle of saturation, however, seems to apply more closely to needs, as we have defined them, than to wants. Such 'basic' needs as shelter can be met fairly easily, but the corresponding wants may be satisfied much less readily. In Western countries, a growing number of people are now accumulating more than one home, although it does seem that even those with large financial resources eventually run out of a desire to accumulate still more. We can, however, point to other wants, accumulation of which may proceed to great lengths before satiety is reached – for example, the accumulation of clothes and land. We ought, therefore, it seems, to distinguish the satiety of needs from the satiety of wants, since the two will not necessarily march in step.

A further hypothesis linked to the idea of hierarchy is that of the subordination of wants. Jevons (1879, 1970) expressed the hypothesis in the following manner: 'the satisfaction of a lower want ... permits the higher want to manifest itself.' Once again, this principle is most easily illustrated at a basic level, and it seems more appropriate to needs than wants. A starving and thirsty individual can think of little else until these needs are satisfied, not necessarily fully, but to a degree sufficient to make them less pressing. At a somewhat more elevated level, poor households have to concern themselves predominantly with those needs essential to the 'decent life', on which we touched earlier. Only when these needs have been largely satisfied are individuals and groups likely to concern themselves much with the needs encompassed by the 'full-time objective', such as regular recreational activities.

The principle of the subordination of wants appears to have some value, but it would undoubtedly be a mistake to assert it in too rigid a form. There seems no reason why a more pressing need must be satisfied in full before satisfaction of a higher-order need assumes some importance. When, too, we move into the realm of higher-order, and generally less pressing, needs, a 'full-life' almost certainly consists of partial satisfaction of a variety of needs, rather than full satisfaction of certain needs in strict order of precedence. The hierarchy of needs, in other words, is certainly not rigid or inflexible. Nor is it likely to be unchanging.

Finally, with respect to wants, a number of writers have expressed the belief that satisfaction of wants leads to the development of additional wants – in this context wants seem more appropriate than needs, although to the extent that environment influences needs, it is also possible to conceive of needs developing over time. One of the most extensive and interesting analyses of this phenomenon is contained in Marshall's *Principles*. Talcott Parsons (1931–32) has even gone so far as to maintain that Marshall's theory of the progressive development of human character and activities in relation to economic wants and want satisfaction is one of the two major strains of thought in his economic work. Certainly, Marshall's discussion of wants repeatedly refers to the manner in which wants develop over time. Speaking of dress, for example, he noted that, 'There is a constant increase both in that variety and expensiveness which custom requires as a minimum, and that which it tolerates as a maximum.' Observation of the improvement in the quantity, quality and range of attire of the general public over time would almost certainly bear out this claim. Clothes for every season are now commonplace in Britain, for example, whereas at one time the changing seasons were for most people marked more by the shedding or wearing of additional clothes rather than their variety.

As we noted earlier in our discussion of wants, Marshall (1961) laid great stress upon the manner in which the activities undertaken by people influenced their wants, certainly in the more advanced stages of economic development:

> Speaking broadly therefore, although it is man's wants in the earliest stages of his development that give rise to his activities, yet afterwards each new step upwards is to be regarded as the development of new activities giving rise to new wants, rather than of wants giving rise to new activities.

Later, Marshall quotes with approval from McCulloch, who, when discussing 'the progressive nature of man', wrote:

> The gratification of a want or a desire is largely a step to some new pursuit. In every stage of his progress he is destined to contrive and invent, to engage in new undertakings; and when these are accomplished to enter with fresh energy upon others.

Who in our own time can have failed to notice the revolution which greater leisure is having upon the wants of individuals? Participation in a whole range of leisure activities, from skiing in winter to surfing in the summer, and from the active pursuit of travel to the more passive occupation of reading, have greatly increased and broadened the scope of wants associated with leisure. Such wants are evolving all the time, and there is no reason to doubt that this pattern will continue for the future. It is part of the nature of men and women to evolve and progress, and the general environment in which they live is also changing. The present toolkit of economics does not enable us to cope adequately, certainly on the consumer side, with these dynamic influences in society. The reluctance to recognize needs and wants means that economists are forced simply to react to changes in consumer preferences, without being able to understand, explain or predict changes in them. It is high time that this self-imposed intellectual straightjacket was removed.

Finally, we must note that for the most part we have been discussing the needs and wants of the individual, whereas in a group or a community, individual needs and wants might be different, and also their relative importance in the hierarchy. Even at the level of mere survival, for example, the needs of separate individuals, as for safety, may be rather greater than the combined safety needs of a group. For a group too, the order of priority in the hierarchy may be different. One of the main reasons for joining a group is the added security it affords, therefore security needs for the group may rate rather lower than those for the individual. To the extent that there are economies of scale in cooking, food requirements to satisfy needs for a group might also be less per head than the sum of individual food requirements. Many individual social needs are also met by participation in group activities – the important need for belonging, for example, and perhaps also for self-esteem, or status – so that those already living in close-knit groups or communities have less reasons to seek such satisfaction outside the group. We cannot, in other words, simply sum the individual needs and wants of certain individuals and equate them with the needs and wants of the same number of individuals living in a close community – as standard consumer theory generally assumes we can do.

2.2.5 Satisfiers

Discussion of needs and wants does not take us very far unless we also consider the means of satisfying these needs and wants, often referred to as 'satisfiers'. One's view of satisfiers must be coloured, of course, by one's view of the nature of needs and wants. Mallman and Marcus (1980), for example, consistent with their definition of needs as an objective requirement to avoid a state of illness, defined a satisfier as 'an element whose use or consumption human beings require in order not to become ill.' In our case, however, we treat a satisfier as a means of meeting a want, leaving open the question of precisely how the need from which it derives is defined. Each want, therefore, will tend to have one or more corresponding satisfiers.

The notion of satisfiers linked to wants appears to correspond well with Lancaster's (1966) view that goods have characteristics which yield utility. Many goods have more than one characteristic, and may therefore be able to satisfy more than one want. Certain fruits, for example oranges, have more than one characteristic. Oranges are generally juicy, sweet and fibrous, and may therefore satisfy, to some degree at least, the wants associated with hunger and thirst. Similarly a vacation may help satisfy the wants associated with the needs of the body for rest and recuperation. Goods may therefore contain more than one satisfier, but each satisfier will be specific to an individual want. On the other hand, one want may be satisfied by various, alternative goods. To pursue our earlier example, thirst may be satisfied by drinking water or the juices of a variety of fruits.

We can now bring the various strands of our analysis together. In Figure 2.1 we start with the individual, who, because of organic variations, differs in some degree from every other individual. We also show certain environmental influences acting on persons – no man (or woman) is an island – which help explain, why, for example, eskimos need more animal fat in their diet, and more warm clothing, than those living in milder climes. Not only do needs differ between individuals, however, they also translate into different wants, even for those same basic needs, such as food. Once again, environmental factors, which include such influences as social customs, play an important role in the transformation. Wants, or desires, in turn, tend to be linked to specific satisfiers, giving rise to utility, or satisfaction, for each person. We have come full circle.

2.2.6 Conclusions

Our examination of needs shows that they are difficult to define precisely. Only at the most basic level of mere survival does it seem that objective measures might be possible. There is an irreducible minimum set of needs which individuals must

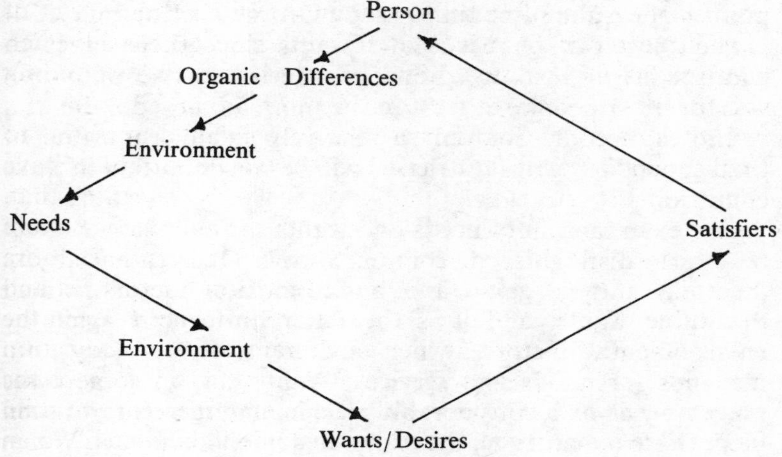

Figure 2.1 The link between needs, wants and satisfiers

have in order to survive, although this will vary according to the person, geographic location, etc. Attempts at an objective definition of basic need seem doomed to failure since the term 'basic needs' is generally taken to include more than is necessary for mere survival, and is therefore open to personal interpretation. This need not, of course, prevent a consensus emerging about what might reasonably be regarded as 'basic'.

The mere fact that some goods, such as food and drink, are more basic to survival than others, necessarily means that there is a hierarchy of needs. We saw that there is no evidence to suggest that this hierarchy can be classified neatly, or in any great detail, but needs do appear to fall into at least two broad categories: lower-order needs, such as food, drink and shelter; and higher-order needs, concerned with the desire of individuals to develop their human potential more fully. The irreducibility of needs, and therefore also of wants, and the hierarchy of needs and wants, must of course, limit the applicability of the standard utility and indifference curve analysis, in that consumers may not be prepared to swap certain goods for others, or only to swap them within limits – a point made quite some time ago by Georgescu-Roegen (1954) – and the work on needs and wants since then serves to confirm his view. Since, however, the irreducible minimum will for most people, at least in the more advanced industrial countries, account for only a relatively small proportion of total expenditure, this restriction will be less important in these countries.

Our examination of needs and wants shows that they must be clearly distinguished from each other. It is the needs, as determined by organic and environmental factors, which determine wants; and it is the latter, influenced again by environmental factors, which are translated directly into demands for goods and services. Wants may in some cases exceed needs by a considerable margin, and it might not even be possible to satisfy all the wants of some individuals. Wants also develop over time. Most wants appear to be satiable, however, and it is probably the case that not all wants have to be fully satisfied in order to make people happy.

The early economists recognized that needs and wants were among the most powerful motivators of human actions, and that consumers derived satisfaction, or utility, from purchases which helped meet these needs and wants. However, the largely subjective nature of needs and wants, and the inability to devise an acceptable cardinal measure of utility, persuaded many economists to look for alternative ways of explaining consumer behaviour. The problem was simplified by reducing needs and wants to the common denominator of utility, and concentrating on the analysis of utility *per se*, rather than on the basic foundations upon which utility itself rested. This still left the apparently insurmountable problem of how to devise an acceptable cardinal measure of utility. The development of indifference curve analysis provided what at first sight seemed a way round the problem. It enabled analysis to proceed on the basis of ordinal measurement of utility, even if it did suffer from the weakness that it required a great deal of information from consumers about their preferences, which might in practice be very difficult to obtain.

Although in some respects an improvement on marginal utility theory, indifference curve analysis suffers from the same overwhelming deficiency: both theories assume that consumers make their spending decisions in complete isolation from each other. The consumer is cocooned in a world of its own, impervious to all societal influences. Yet one inescapable conclusion which emerges from the study of needs and wants is that many of them, such as the needs for protection, belonging and self-esteem, only make sense within, and can only be fully satisfied within, a social environment. Moreover, such needs as status and self-esteem entail social comparisons covering many aspects of people's lives. Individuals will inevitably exert influence on each other's behaviour, including consumer behaviour, and therefore the utility derived from purchases of goods and services. Consumer preferences must therefore necessarily be interdependent, with the utility obtained by consumers from their spending deriving in part from the spending of others. Traditional utility theory is implicitly based on the special case of the individual acting in isolation, with wholly independent preferences, a case of such limited applicability in practice as to be of only very minor importance, and certainly not one which can serve as a general theory of consumer behaviour.

By resorting to the expedient of adopting utility as a convenient cut-off point beyond which they are not inclined to stray, since it takes them into the realms of subjective variables which are generally felt to lie more within the preserve of psychologists, economists have been led into the error of misinterpreting the fundamental nature of utility and how it is derived. It may be, of course, that some regard utility as being founded on a basis other than that of needs and wants. If so, it should be made explicit, so that we may evaluate it.

The development of revealed preference theory, while it circumvented the measurement problem and the subjective nature of utility, does not really take us much further along the path of explaining consumer behaviour. We still cannot explain why certain goods might be more important to the consumer than others, nor provide an adequate explanation of changes in consumer preferences. The needs-based approach, we shall argue, is potentially very fruitful in this respect.

The more recent work on consumer behaviour of writers such as Lancaster and Becker is certainly valuable in providing us with fresh insights, but it suffers from being grafted onto a basic theoretical structure which is itself unsatisfactory. A good deal of this work could, however, be incorporated to good effect in the needs-based approach – Lancaster (1971), for one, has himself effectively recognized this point, even if only in a passing reference.

2.3 ASPECTS OF MOTIVATION – EQUITY

Considerations of equity arise almost inevitably whenever individuals interact with each other, most obviously when they enter into transactions with one another, for example as employer and employee, or as buyer and seller. Since it clearly is relevant to economic transactions, equity is a subject with which economists seem increasingly willing to grapple, but it has still to be accorded the important place in economic theory which it merits. Discussion to date has tended to be at a fairly aggregated and abstract level, concerned more with aspects of 'distributive justice' than with the more immediate concerns of those in the workplace. The present study does recognize the importance of the broad principles which govern, or ought to govern, the distribution of rewards in society as a whole, but in this section on equity we look first at an important body of work which is directly relevant to wage behaviour, yet is largely ignored by most economists.

A useful starting point for the analysis of equity theory at the micro-level is the work of Leon Festinger (1954, 1957). One approach to motivation maintains that an individual's behaviour is influenced by his attempt to maintain an internal balance of psychological tension – hence the term 'balance theory' which is sometimes applied to this approach. Festinger's theory of 'cognitive dissonance' is a version of balance theory which rests on the proposition that individuals attempt to maintain consistency between their beliefs, attitudes and opinions on the one hand, and their overt behaviour on the other. So long as consistency is maintained, no motivational force arises. Cognitions about ourselves in relation to our environment may take three forms: consonant, irrelevant or dissonant. Only in the last case, where there is discord, does the individual feel it necessary to take action in order to reduce the state of dissonance.

2.3.1 Inequity in social exchange

Using the language of Festinger's theory of cognitive dissonance, Patchen (1961) postulated that when making wage comparisons, workers employed a cognitive relationship of the form:

$$\frac{\text{My Pay}}{\text{His (their) pay}} \quad \text{compared to} \quad \frac{\text{My position on dimensions related to pay}}{\text{His (their) position on dimensions related to pay}}$$

Patchen's view was that a worker, in comparing his pay with that of someone else, would also take account of the relative 'dimensions' related to pay, i.e. of the relative levels of such attributes as skill, education and seniority. If the two proportions matched, a situation of consonance existed. If, on the other hand, the worker were to find that the left-hand ratio were smaller than the right, i.e. that his pay compared unfavourably with that of the other worker, given their relative dimensions or merits, then cognitive dissonance would be experienced. The worker would be dissatisfied, and would wish to do something to rectify the situation.

Homans (1961) and Sayles (1958) also expressed their views on equity in ratio form. Homans was concerned with people in an exchange relationship with each other, either directly or indirectly through the medium of an employer who was rewarding both, and was therefore expected to maintain an equitable relationship between the two. In Homans' terms, 'distributive justice', as he called it, required that in an exchange relationship between two people, say A and B, the profits of each should be proportional to their investments, i.e.

$$\frac{\text{A's profits (rewards less costs)}}{\text{A's investments}} = \frac{\text{B's profits (rewards less costs)}}{\text{B's investments}}$$

Profits here are not defined solely in economic terms, since the rewards include not only pay, but also the variety and interest, and degree of autonomy, in the work performed. Similarly, the costs comprise the degree of responsibility undertaken, and such factors as the dullness and dirtiness of the work, or any risk entailed. Investments include a person's 'background characteristics', such as skill, effort, abilities, seniority, age and sex, some of which increase in value with the passage of time. Profits could therefore be seen in terms of a return on investments, and equity could be said to exist when the returns were equal.

Some of the variables which enter the calculation of equity and inequity may lend themselves to objective measurement, but others, such as the mental effort expended on work, or the degree of dullness of a job, are more subjective in nature, and not amenable to precise measurement. Differences of opinion may also arise over what should or should not count as rewards, costs and investments. When we deal with equity in the work situation we are therefore dealing with people's perceptions of equity, and these may not agree with the facts of the situation (to the extent that these can be measured) or with the perceptions of others. The scope for differences in perception is undoubtedly one of the principal factors which make it so difficult to deal with equity in practical terms.

The equity theories which we have examined so far are useful, especially in stressing the importance of proportionality between a person's job input and the output, or 'outcome', received in return. The theories do not tell us sufficient, however, about the *processes* by which behaviour is energized and sustained. We need a more dynamic framework which helps explain, for example, the consequences of feelings of inequality, and the actions which persons experiencing inequity are likely to take. The theory which seems most useful in this respect is that of Adams (1963, 1965). Adams' theory combines aspects of the theory of distributive justice, along the lines touched upon above, with the concept of *relative deprivation*. After looking at Adams' theory of equity in exchange we shall return to the subject of relative deprivation.

2.3.2 Adams' theory of equity in exchange

The studies of distributive justice which we have examined specify some of the conditions which cause feelings of inequity (or, conversely, feelings of being equitably treated) but they still do not tell us what the consequences of such perceptions will be other than dissatisfaction. Adams' theory attempts to take us a stage further. It examines in some detail both the conditions which give rise to feelings of inequity and the actions likely to be taken to remove such feelings. This theory draws heavily on some of the earlier work which we examined – a debt which Adams readily acknowledged.

Adams' theory is presented primarily in terms of the exchange relationship between employer and employee, but he is at pains to stress that it is of general application to any social situation in which an exchange takes place, explicitly or implicitly. The analysis is also expressed primarily in terms of the individual, but it is made clear that it is also applicable to groups of people, since inequity may just as easily arise between groups as between persons on their own.

A person engaged in a social exchange makes a contribution to the exchange – what Adams called an 'input' – for which he expects to receive something in return – an 'outcome'. Adams' 'inputs' are defined in the same manner as Homans' 'investments', and therefore include such contributions as intelligence, experience, education and skill. On the outcome side, pay will be one of the most important rewards, but job satisfaction, fringe benefits, status, etc. will also form important constituents of calculations about equity. As in the case of earlier writers, the importance of perceptions is stressed. Differences of view between the parties to an exchange may arise if there is a failure to agree on *recognition* and the *relevance* of inputs and outcomes. If a person is working hard, but his employer fails to recognize this, then the value of that person's input may be underrated by his employer.

Similarly, an employee may fail to recognize adequately the value to him of all the perquisites – free sports facilities, say – provided by his employer. In the case of relevance, a common cause of differences of view is the importance to be attached to seniority. To an employer, the time spent in his service may be irrelevant, but an employee may feel that it ought to count for something in the tally of inputs. On the outcome side, an employee concerned primarily with financial reward may feel that his rate of pay is more or less all that counts.

Expressed in Adams' terms equity exists when

$$\Sigma O_{ip} / \Sigma I_{ip} = \Sigma O_{ia} / \Sigma I_{ia}$$

where ΣO_i and ΣI_i are the weighted sums of outcomes and inputs (weighted because an individual is unlikely to attach the same importance to the separate inputs and outcomes) and 'p' and '*a*' are subscripts denoting Person (the individual for whom equity or inequity exists) and Other (any individual with whom Person is in an exchange relationship or with whom Person compares himself when both he and Other are in an exchange relationship with a third party, such as an employer, or with third parties who are considered by Person to be comparable, such as employers in a particular industry or geographic location). Both Person and Other, as we noted earlier, may be groups rather than single persons. We should note, too, that, as in the case of relative deprivation, a Person may compare his current position with himself in an earlier situation, in which case the latter adopts the role of Other.

Inequality is experienced when either

$$\Sigma O_{ip}/\Sigma I_{ip} < \Sigma O_{ia}/\Sigma I_{ia} \text{ or } \Sigma O_{ip}/\Sigma I_{ip} > \Sigma O_{ia}/\Sigma I_{ia}$$

In the former case, in which Person finds himself treated inequitably, feelings of dissatisfaction and tension will be created, and Person will be motivated to try to rectify the situation, either by increasing ΣO_p, reducing ΣI_p, or a combination of the two (Adams cites empirical evidence in support of both reactions). The strength of the motivation, Adams maintains, will vary in direct proportion to the magnitude of the inequity experienced. In the opposite situation, in which the inequity favours Person, the empirical evidence cited by Adams also suggests that Person will be motivated to try and remedy the situation, although there may be a threshold which has to be reached before action ensues.

One further aspect of Adams' theory which should be emphasized, since it is of special interest to our study, is the underlying social comparison process inherent in equity theory. The normative expectations of what constitute 'fair' relationships between inputs and outcomes are not simply plucked out of the air. They have been formed in the process of socialization at home, school, work or any other social environment within which Person circulates. These social influences are strongest when they emanate from a reference person, or group – others with whom Person is in the habit of comparing himself. We shall have more to say about reference groups in a later section: for the present it is sufficient to note that notions of equity dovetail closely with the social comparisons process, which may also be regarded as an intervening variable. Both, as we shall see, are helpful in understanding certain features of wage behaviour.

Adams' theory of equity has not been without its critics, but generally these critics have been constructive, attempting to improve aspects of the theory rather than replace it. Walster *et al.* (1973) have suggested reintroducing Homans' notion of negative outcomes, or 'costs', since these seem likely to arise quite frequently in the process of exchange. Conflict between the parties involved is one obvious negative outcome. Similarly, Walster *et al.* point out that there may also be negative inputs, such as unsocial behaviour or disruptive activities. Clearly, these negative elements pose problems when trying to assess what is equitable, since the notion of equity, for practical purposes, rests on personal perceptions, and the perceptions of the parties to the exchange may differ appreciably in such cases. Nevertheless, it is personal perceptions which motivate behaviour, not any objective calculus of the relative inputs and outcomes, and we cannot therefore afford to ignore perceptions or play down their importance.

A number of commentators have found it difficult to accept that a person being over-rewarded would necessarily experience feelings of distress or tension, and feel obliged to try to remove the disparity between inputs and outcomes. Weick (1966) maintained that such behaviour was not consistent with the model of Economic Man. Only adequate empirical evidence can still these doubts, and it is interesting, as we shall see below, that the available evidence does tend to support Adams' thesis.

A further frustrating feature of equity theory to many commentators is that it does not always yield precise hypotheses and predictions. The theory is unable to predict, for example, whether a person suffering inequity will reduce his input, try to increase his outcome, or use a combination of the two. There is little in the theory, too, which permits a prediction to be made about which reference person or group will be selected for the purposes of comparison when a free choice is available from a range of alternatives. Pritchard (1969) has even suggested that Person, instead of comparing himself with Other, may use an 'internal standard' by which to make judgements about equity. He cites as an example a person receiving an exceptionally low rate of pay, arguing that in such a situation no reference person would be necessary in order to know that it was inequitable. This, however, may be an example, not so much of an internal standard, but of a more general notion of equity to which we shall return below. No person living in a society can be entirely free of influence from the mores or standards of that society. An 'internal standard' would therefore be likely, in some degree at least, to reflect the 'external' standards of society. Equity, in other words, is in essence a comparative concept.

One final point about the analysis of equity in exchange relationships is of crucial importance to economics. Equity in exchange is sometimes discussed under the general heading of 'distributive justice', but the problem of how the *total* resources of the community should be distributed is not treated in the literature. It could well be the case, therefore, that if we summed up the outcomes we would find that they exceeded the total resources of the community, even if all the outcomes were judged equitable. It may be that this point has been disguised by the fact that there are both monetary and non-monetary outcomes.

Among the outcomes, pay is likely to be the largest financial cost, but fringe benefits and even status and job satisfaction may have financial costs attached to them. On the other hand, status and job satisfaction may also have something to do with the way a firm is run, for example, and therefore constitute a non-pecuniary element in the outcomes. We can therefore demonstrate our point by dividing outcomes into a pecuniary element O_x and a non-pecuniary element O_y, which together make up the sum of outcomes O.

$$O_x + O_y = O$$

If we then denote the financial resources available to our two-person community of Person and Other as O_x *max*, and financial outcomes as $\acute{O}_p$ and $\acute{O}_a$, all will be well so long as either:

$$(\acute{O}_p + \acute{O}_a) < O_x\ max \text{ or } (\acute{O}_p + \acute{O}_a) = O_x\ max$$

When, however, $(\acute{O}_p + \acute{O}_a) > O_x\ max$, the difference can only be made up either by the existing money stock circulating more rapidly, or through an increase in the money stock itself. With some increase in the latter likely, we would be in the all too familiar inflationary situation in which the money supply was being increased in order to finance excessive claims on resources. If unduly rapid, the situation might prove untenable.

If therefore equity in exchange is to avoid the problem of inflation we have to add the condition that the sum of pecuniary outcomes must not exceed the financial resources available $O_x\ max$. We would then have a form of distributive justice in the work situation. Whether it would be possible *in practice* to devise such a distribution of resources which is both *perceived* to be equitable by all and at the same time within the limits of the financial resources available is a question to which as yet we have no answer. We can see here, however, the possible seeds of disequilibrium in the economic system.

2.3.3 Relative deprivation

We saw earlier that Adams treated the concept of relative deprivation as part of his model of equity in exchange. He stated his intention that relative deprivation and Homans' notion of distributive justice would be 'integrated into a theory of inequity from which it will be possible to specify the antecedents and consequences of injustice in human exchanges'. He went on to describe relative deprivation as 'a condition occurring naturalistically', which elicited feelings of injustice, and he seemed to see it as complementing Homans' approach, under which the conditions for equity, if not satisfied, could also give rise to feelings of injustice, and therefore of dissatisfaction. The two together were, however, still said to be lacking in one vital respect: 'Relative deprivation and distributive justice, as theoretical concepts, specify some of the conditions that arouse perceptions of injustice and, complementarily, the conditions that lead me to feel that their relations with others are just. But they fail to specify theoretically what are the consequences of felt injustice, other than dissatisfaction.' It was in this respect that Adams felt his theory represented an important advance on earlier work, and he makes no further reference to relative deprivation.

Later writers have nevertheless continued to use both the concepts of relative deprivation and Adams' theory of equity in exchange, although generally not at the same time. Both are still found useful, but some writers have questioned whether there is in fact a need for both, since they can find no essential difference between them. Wheeler and Zuckerman (1977) conclude, for example: 'Are relative deprivation and inequity different constructs? We think not. . . . Our own position is that relative deprivation is a state experienced by the victim of inequity.'

In order to enable us to form our own conclusions, we turn now to examine the concept of relative deprivation at greater length – we shall also have more to say about the concept when we come to discuss the question of social comparisons, which are often closely associated with feelings of relative deprivation.

Developments in the theory and analysis of relative deprivation Although the term 'relative deprivation' first appeared in a study *The American Soldier* by Stouffer *et al.* (1949), no comprehensive statement of the concept was attempted in that work. Merton and Kitt (1950) tried to formalize the idea, basing themselves on its use in *The American Soldier*. Davis (1959) extended the analysis, highlighting the importance of the comparison process, and distinguishing between 'in-group comparisons' (between people in the same social sub-category) and 'out-group comparisons' (between people in different social categories). Careful analysis of the concept was also undertaken by Runciman (1966) in his study of attitudes to inequality in twentieth-century England. Runciman defined relative deprivation as follows:

> A is relatively deprived of X when (1) he does not have X, (2) he sees some other person or persons, which may include himself at some previous or expected time, as having X (whether or not this is or will be in fact the case) (3) he wants X, and (4) he sees it as feasible that he should have X.

Relative deprivation is a subjective sense of feeling deprived because of the lack of X, which may be anything ranging from material goods to non-material desires, such as promotion to a particular post, in line with one's qualifications and other inputs. Runciman's definition also stresses the importance of reference others, which he formalizes in terms of reference groups (about which we shall have more to say in our section dealing with social comparisons). The reference other may include the person himself at some previous time – an example might be a person currently earning a certain salary making a comparison with a level of salary previously earned. Runciman's definition also recognizes the need to introduce the caveat of feasibility, in order to exclude unrealistic or fantasy wishes. It is important to appreciate, however, that feelings about relative deprivation are based upon personal perceptions, which may not accord with reality, or with the perceptions of others. The feelings of deprivation are, however, bounded, in so far as the individual must himself see the attainment of X as feasible.

Relative deprivation, as used by Runciman and others, applies not just to an individual but to groups. Runciman notes, first, that an individual may feel deprived in comparison with other members *in his group* (what he calls 'egoistic' relative deprivation), or he may feel that his group is deprived in relation to other *groups* ('fraternalistic' relative deprivation). He notes, further, that relative deprivation may vary in magnitude, frequency and degree. The magnitude of relative deprivation is defined as 'the extent of the difference between the desired situation and that of persons desiring it (as he sees it)'. The frequency of relative deprivation is the proportion of a group feeling it, and the degree of relative deprivation is the intensity with which it is felt. These distinctions help make clearer the subjective nature of the concept.

Runciman went on to relate the dimensions of relative deprivation to inequalities of class, status and power in society. This complicated the analysis (see Baxter, 1973) but enabled Runciman to draw some interesting conclusions with regard to the consequences of social inequalities in England during the period 1918–62. Using a sample survey drawn from electoral registers, and an extensive interview programme covering over

1400 subjects, Runciman was able to conclude that relative deprivation deriving from inequalities of class was low, both in magnitude and frequency, even among those at the bottom of the class hierarchy. With regard to inequalities of status, his conclusions were very different:

> In Britain since 1918, the relation between inequality and relative deprivation of status has been clear in outline and consistent in direction. As the manual stratum has advanced towards greater equality with the non-manual (without yet reaching it), relative deprivation of status among working-class people has increased in both magnitude and frequency.

The relationship between relative deprivation and inequalities of power differed yet again from those between relative deprivation and inequalities of class and status. Runciman's conclusion, briefly, was that while some reduction of inequalities of power certainly took place after 1918, there was no fundamental change in the hierarchy of power. The changes were, however, sufficient to induce a diminished feeling of relative deprivation amongst manual workers – more so than was warranted by the realities of the situation – helping to explain why there was no significant class militancy in the early 1960s.

Relative deprivation has also been used in a very different context by Gurr (1968a, b, 1970) and with different objectives in mind. Whereas Davis and Runciman were principally concerned with the antecedents of relative deprivation, Gurr's interest was in using relative deprivation to explain violent political events. He envisaged relative deprivation being caused by a divergence between people's expectations of the goods to which they felt entitled and the goods which they felt they were likely to be able to obtain. Using archive material from published sources, Gurr's statistical analysis indicated that it was possible to use measures of deprivation to predict the likelihood of civil strife.

The concept of relative deprivation has been further developed in a series of studies by Crosby (see, for example, 1976, 1982). In its initial form the model contained a number of similarities with that advanced by Runicman. Crosby summarized the model as follows:

Individuals feel relatively deprived of x when they: (1) want x; (2) see that another possesses x; (3) feel that they deserve x; (4) think it feasible to obtain x; and (5) do not blame themselves (i.e., they disclaim personal responsibility) for failure to possess x.

The basic emotion generated is one of resentment, which may be directed against either oneself or society, and which may be either constructive or destructive. The behavioural consequences may be: stress symptoms, self-improvement, violence against society or the constructive change of society.

The origins of the five psychological preconditions of relative deprivation are traced in Crosby's model to a variety of objective determinants having to do with: (a) a person's personality (which might, for example, encompass a need for achievement); (b) his personal past (the person might, for example, have possessed x in the past); (c) a person's immediate environment (e.g. the number of others possessing x); (d) the wider society in which the person lived (which would have customs and conventions, including perhaps attitudes towards possessions); and (e) biological needs which must be met if a person is to survive. Any one of these determinants might affect one or more of the preconditions for felt deprivation. A society's views about entitlement would, for example, have a bearing on all five preconditions.

Crosby later modified her model to incorporate a distinction between estimates of feasibility which had been made in the past (i.e. past or previous expectations held) and estimates of future feasibility (expectations about the future). The latter refer to person's *current* assessment of the prospect of 'attaining or retaining the object or opportunity'. Crosby went on to hypothesize that felt deprivation arose when there was a combination of high past expectations with low future expectations.

The empirical research on relative deprivation is extensive (for reviews of some of this work see Crosby and Gonzalez-Intal (1984) and Cook *et al.* (1984)). It seems fair to conclude that while the findings are generally supportive, devising satisfactory tests of theory make it difficult to provide conclusive evidence as to its validity. Wanting, comparison with others, feelings of entitlement and feasibility are variables which are difficult to identify or represent, and also difficult to manipulate or follow over a period of time. Too many of the studies are not sufficiently rigorous in setting out the theory and devising adequate tests. With few exceptions, too, the research has concentrated on egoistic deprivation rather than fraternal deprivation. The continued interest in using relative deprivation to help explain human behaviour in a variety of contexts suggests, however, that many researchers recognize the need for such a concept, and we can expect to see more work in this field. We shall also find the idea of relative deprivation useful in our later analysis of wage behaviour. Before leaving the subject, however, we turn to the question of the similarities, and differences, between relative deprivation and the theory of equity in exchange.

Relative deprivation and equity in exchange Relative deprivation and the theory of equity in exchange have a common core which comprises social comparisons, perceptions about the rewards, or outcomes, being received by others, and perceptions of the rewards to which an individual feels entitled. The two theories also agree that anyone not obtaining a perceived entitlement will be motivated to take action to remove the felt injustice. It is hardly surprising, therefore, that a number of commentators have draw attention to the similarities between the two theories. There are, however, also significant differences between the theories, as Crosby (1984b) has pointed out. First, the theories may apply to different levels of analysis. Equity in exchange is concerned with a relatively narrow context, in which the individual is being rewarded for his contribution to an exchange. It is therefore well suited to an analysis of the work situation. Relative deprivation, on the other hand, recognizes no such confines, and has been applied to a wide variety of situations, ranging from worker discontent to unrest among black people in the United States and studies of civil strife in different countries.

Furthermore, while the two theories agree that an attempt will be made to remove perceived inequity, relative deprivation is concerned only with under-reward, whereas equity in exchange embraces both under- and over-reward. As we saw earlier, empirical evidence relating to equity in exchange suggests that those who benefit from over-reward also tend to be motivated to remove this form of inequity, as well as any inequity arising from under-reward. This indicates symmetrical behaviour in relation to equity in exchange which is not part of the theory of relative deprivation – nor does relative deprivation theory have anything to say about the feelings or reactions of an over-rewarded individual whose excess reward is removed.

Perceptions about the feasibility of attaining a desired outcome – a form of expectation – enter into feelings of relative deprivation, as we noted earlier. Equity in exchange theory is devoid of expectations – certainly of future events – and would, it seems, benefit greatly if this more dynamic element were to be brought into consideration. It is difficult to envisage perceptions about inequality being formed in practice without some reference to the past or to the future. We are all in some degree creatures of past experiences. Evidence that past and future expectations are indeed important predictors of dissatisfaction and resentment is provided by Bernstein and Crosby (1980).

Finally, although social comparisons constitute an important means by which outcomes are judged in both theories, feelings of relative deprivation may also arise in other ways. Gurr (1970) makes the point as follows:

> It is more generally recognized ... that ... standards can have other sources. An individual's point of reference may be ... an abstract ideal, or the standards articulated by a leader as well as a 'reference group'.

It will be apparent from the above that although there are many similarities between the concepts of relative deprivation and equity in exchange, there are also important differences which make it worthwhile continuing to distinguish between the two.

2.3.4 Distributive justice

Until now we have been concerned principally with equity in exchange relationships, in which relative rates of pay are of central importance. In practice, these differentials and relativities may operate at various levels of aggregation, ranging from comparisons between two individuals to comparisons between groups in society at large. In discussing distributive justice we are moving on to the highest plane of all, searching for the principles which govern, or ought to govern, the distribution of goods and services in the community as a whole – which nowadays invariably means the nation-state, although some would even extend discussion beyond these bounds. We are no longer concerned solely with a comparison of inputs and outcomes. We must also consider the distribution of assets as well as income, and the problem becomes one not only of the fair distribution of goods and services between those living, but also between different generations. The concept of relative deprivation remains operative at this level of analysis.

There is, of course, a close association between equity in exchange and notions of distributive justice, although the two are often discussed separately. To the extent that it proves possible to reach a consensus about the principles governing the distribution of rewards in society, we may expect these principles to influence individuals' views about the appropriateness of income differentials, and therefore the equitable relationships between inputs and outcomes – there would, however, still be plenty of room for disagreement over perceptions about such matters as relative skills, the value of seniority, etc. Despite the manifold difficulties entailed in reaching some sort of consensus on the principles of distributive justice, it is therefore still worthwhile continuing to strive towards this end. The problem is not one which will go away.

The issues raised by distributive justice have spawned a large literature, to which a number of economists, such as Arrow, Sen and Atkinson, have made valuable contributions. It is not the intention here to survey these contributions in depth, but rather to try to give some indication of the nature of the debate, and to highlight those promising developments which are relevant to our main purposes. We are concerned especially with the motivational aspects of distributive justice. While individuals may be motivated primarily by those aspects of equity concerned with exchange relationships, equity, or the lack of it, at the societal level also impinges on people's daily lives, and many are highly conscious of this fact. The environment within which a person lives is dictated not just by the outcome of exchange relationships, but by the structure of society and the distribution of rewards, and obligations, within it. The tax system and the social benefits system have direct and significant roles in determining the rewards and obligations, and are examples of some of the more obvious links with incentives and motivation.

When allocating the resources available, the presumption in neo-classical economics, upon which social welfare theory is based, is that account must be taken of individual preference scales relating to the alternative courses of action available. It is assumed that each individual has some means of ranking social actions (which will affect not just the individual but others as well) according to his preference for each. The nub of the problem, however, is that where numerous individuals are involved, each with his own opinions about the desirability of the various courses of action, some way must be found of combining the different preferences in order to arrive at social decisions affecting the whole community. Classical utilitarianism as pioneered by Bentham (1789), argued that one man's utility was as good as another's, and therefore the sum of satisfaction obtained by adding individual utilities ought to determine the preferred course of action. In mathematical terms, if we denote the utility of the n individuals in a society by $U_1, \ldots, U_n$, then the course of action selected ought to be that for which the sum of $U_1 + U_2 + \ldots + U_n$ was greatest.

Bentham and the other followers of classical utilitarianism had no doubts that utility could be measured cardinally, and that where social decisions might entail losses for some but gains for others, a net total utility for each course of action could still be calculated. There was no difficulty, in other words, in making interpersonal comparisons of utility, and the aim was simply to maximize the sum of that utility. Such a principle, it has been pointed out, could be interpreted in a strongly inegalitarian fashion, although Arrow (1985) has maintained that the individual preference orderings which formed the basis of the utilitarian calculus expressed desires not only about individuals' own consumption, but also about their social attitudes and their views on justice in distribution, and the benefits to others of collective decisions. Even if cardinal measurement were to be ruled out, Arrow takes the view that it could at least be said that implicit in classical utilitarianism was a second level of evaluation at which the judgements of individuals were themselves evaluated. It remains true, nevertheless, that, as presented, classical utilitarianism did not concern itself with ethical questions of distribution.

That other pillar of traditional welfare economics, the Pareto optimum, is likewise of little avail in the search for principles of distributive justice. Indeed, the concept was devised expressly to overcome the need for judgements about distribution. Using Sen's (1973) apt example of the distribution of a cake, if we assume that everyone prefers more cake to less, then every possible distribution will be Pareto optimal, because any change that makes someone better off will also make someone else worse off. The implications for the poor are obvious, and disheartening. When it comes to questions of distribution, the Pareto optimum, in Sen's words, 'has no cutting edge'.

The whole approach to welfare judgements based on individual preference orderings has suffered a severe blow from Arrow (1951, 1967). Laying down what seem to be reasonable conditions required of any 'constitution', or rule, for selecting a preferred course of action from a range of alternatives, he has shown that there is no process of selection which will always satisfy these conditions. The four conditions imposed he summarizes (Arrow, 1985) as: (i) collective rationality – that is, the social choice system has the same structure as that assumed for individual value systems; (ii) a Pareto principle – if alternative x is preferred to alternative y by every single individual according to his ordering, then the social ordering also ranks x above y; (iii) independence of irrelevant alternatives – the social choice made from any environment depends only on the ordering of individuals with respect to the alternatives in that environment; (iv) non-dictatorship – that is, there is no individual whose preferences are automatically society's preferences independent of the preferences of all other individuals.

Arrow has shown that every set of individual preference orderings will violate one of these conditions. He illustrates the point by reference to the system of majority voting, a popular method of social choice. This voting system satisfies conditions (ii), (iii) and (iv) above, but it may not lead to an ordering since instability is possible. To demonstrate the point, if there are three alternatives, x, y and z, between which a choice has to be made, and we assume one third of the voters rank the alternatives in the order x, y and z, one third in the order y, z and x, and one third z, x and y. Then as Arrow points out, a majority prefer z to x.

The conditions imposed by Arrow effectively rule out interpersonal comparisons of utility, and it is interesting that many of those working in this field have now concluded that further progress is only possible if interpersonal comparisons are permitted. This brings us full circle, however, because we are then immediately faced once more with the associated problem of cardinal measurement. It will be interesting to see how far this newfound freedom enables economists to progress in devising principles of distribution. The omens, it must be said, are not promising. Hammond (1985) sums up the situation well in an otherwise optimistic survey of the current state of welfare economics:

> ethical disagreements are very often matters of personal opinion that are hard to resolve. All that welfare economics can do is to help each individual ethical observer form his personal opinions concerning economic policy; if different individuals hold different opinions because of different ethical value judgements – including, perhaps, different interpersonal comparisons of utility – welfare economics alone cannot be expected to reconcile them.

Given the state of economic theory, some economists have been prepared to look beyond the normal bounds of economics for inspiration. One writer in particular who has caught their attention has been the philosopher John Rawls. In his *Theory of Justice* (1971), Rawls attempts to devise a general concept of justice which not only takes account of other principles of justice – in particular those based on rights, needs and deserts – but is also a forthright attack on what he considers to be the main competing general theory of justice, namely, utilitarianism. Whilst not able to accept his theory of justice, including its implications for distributive justice, in all respects, a number of economists, such as Arrow, have found themselves in agreement with the broad thrust of his arguments. In order to do Rawls himself justice, we are obliged at this point to give a brief outline of his theoretical structure, in so far as it relates to the subject matter of our study.

Rawls summed up his objective as being 'to present a conception of justice which generalizes and carries to a higher level of abstraction the familar theory of the social contract as found, say, in Locke, Rousseau, and Kant.' But whereas Rawls views his work as being in the tradition of contract theory, his version of the contract does not take the form of an agreement to enter a particular society or to set up particular institutions. Instead, we are asked to assume that individuals decide at the very outset, in one joint act, the principles which will assign basic rights and duties and decide the division of social benefits. The principles, in other words, govern all further agreements. This way of regarding the principles of justice Rawls calls 'justice as fairness'.

Rawls' discussion of justice as fairness falls into two main parts. The first of these is further subdivided into: an interpretation of the initial situation in which decisions on principles are taken; and a formulation of the various principles available for choice. The second main part is concerned with the argument about which of the principles would in fact be adopted.

Rawls begins by discussing the principles available for choice and states, in a provisional form, the two principles which he believes would be chosen in the original position.

(1) 'Each person is to have an equal right to the most extensive basic liberty compatible with a similar liberty for others.'

(2) 'Social and economic inequalities are to be arranged so that they are both (a) reasonably expected to be to everyone's advantage, and (b) attached to positions and offices open to all.'

The above have been subjected to a good deal of criticism. It was pointed out, for example, that the phrases 'to everyone's advantage' and '(equally) open to all' were ambiguous. Much of Rawls' book, *A Theory of Justice*, is taken up with his attempt to meet these criticisms and to reformulate his principles. (For the final statement of his principles, which may be compared with the initial statement above, see Rawls (1971), pp. 302–3.)

Rawls' view of the original position – a purely hypothetical position, it must be stressed – in which individuals select the principles of justice they most prefer, is central to his model. He goes into considerable detail, making numerous assumptions concerning the state of the parties involved. It is assumed, for example, that the parties have roughly similar needs and interests so that mutually advantageous cooperation is possible. The parties are also assumed to be ignorant of 'particular facts', such as their place in society, class position, social status, etc. in order that they will not be tempted to take a selfish viewpoint about justice. Rawls notes that the closest express statement known to him of this idea of what he calls the 'veil of ignorance' is to be found in Harsanyi (1953, 1955). Arrow (1973) has pointed out, however, that Vickrey (1945, 1960) also adopted an original position assumption. Rawls' veil of ignorance has the added virtue of enabling the parties to arrive at a unanimous decision in selecting from the alternative principles of justice.

In contrast to the assumed ignorance of 'particular facts', in so far at least as these pertain to their position in society, those in the original position are assumed to know whatever 'general facts' might affect their choice of principles – an assumption of perfect knowledge to which economists are no strangers. Finally, it is assumed throughout that the persons in the original position are rational, with a coherent set of preferences between the options open to them.

Rawls' model is basically egalitarian. His general attitude is expressed in the folllowing terms:

> All social values – liberty and opportunity, income and wealth, and the bases of self-respect – are to be distributed equally unless an unequal distribution of any, or all, of these values is to everyone's advantage.

This attitude to distribution is spelled out using what Rawls refers to as the 'difference principle' (or, for reasons which will become clear, as the 'maximin rule'). This principle is applied

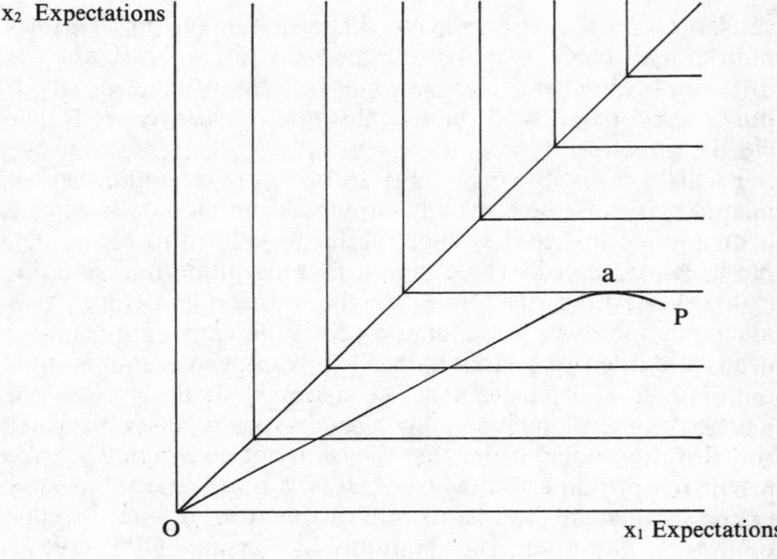

Figure 2.2: The maximin

only to 'primary goods', excluding liberty, which is accorded the highest priority in Rawls' lexicographic ordering of 'goods', and is not therefore tradeable for an improvement in economic well-being – at least not once a certain level of wealth has been attained.

The operation of the maximin rule is illustrated by Rawls in the following manner. If we assume indifference curves which represent distributions of goods which are judged equally just, then in the simplest two-person case in which x_1 is the most favoured representative person and x_2 is the least advantaged person, the indifference curves could take the form depicted in Figure 2.2. No matter how much each gains, the indifference principle is not upheld unless the other also gains. Curve OP shows how the relative expectations of benefits (taken over the lifetime of each individual) might change as they moved away from point O at the origin, which represents the stage of equal distribution. The OP curve is always below the 45° line, since x_1 is always better off. The difference principle is perfectly satisfied only at point *a*, where x_2 attains the highest possible indifference curve – at points to the left of *a* on OP, the difference principle is also satisfied, since both x_1, and x_2 gain, but x_2's expectations are not maximized. Point *a*, in other words, represents the maximin (the maximum expectations of the least advantaged). Beyond point *a*, only x_2 benefits as inequality is increased.

One might claim to detect in the difference principle shades of the 'trickle-down' theory, but Rawls does not go so far as to claim that additional benefits for the more advantaged will *always* benefit the least advantaged as well. The difference principle is satisfied only if this *does* happen. This issue does serve, however, to draw attention to what may be a significant flaw in Rawls' analysis. The maximin criterion could be used to justify the most extreme disparities in income and wealth, provided only that the expectations of the least fortunate were raised in some slight degree thereby, with gains of a billion pounds for the better off being justified perhaps by a gain of only a few pence for the least advantaged. Rawls' answer is that his two basic principles are tied together as one conception of justice, and that the principles of equal liberty and open positions would prevent situations of the sort outlined ever happening. There would in a just society, he believes, be a persistent tendency for inequalities to be levelled down by the increasing availability of educated talent and ever-widening opportunities. He is forced to admit, however, that under his system of justice, 'nothing guarantees that inequalities will not be significant'.

One of the principal themes of our present study is that it is not just the absolute level of rewards which matters to an individual, but the size of the reward relative to those obtained by others in society – relative income, as we saw earlier, has a crucial bearing on the ability to satisfy needs and wants. This aspect of *relative* rewards must, it seems, lie at the heart of any theory of distributive justice. Rawls attempts to cope with it by helping the least advantaged – which has the benefit, as Rawls points out, of not requiring a cardinal measure of rewards obtained – but it seems possible to argue even so that a small increase in the absolute level of benefits to the least advantaged could leave them *feeling* worse off, if the differential between the least well off and others in society were at the same time widened. This would seem especially likely if the least well off were already able to afford more than just the basic necessities of life. One possible way of overcoming this problem in Rawls' model might be to redefine the expected benefits an individual received to encompass his *relative* position in the scale of rewards within society.

Arrow (1973) has raised a number of other problems with respect to Rawls' theory. Although the theory only requires a rank ordering of the benefits pertaining to different individuals, there is no underlying numerical magnitude to use for this purpose, and the question still remains, what is the operational meaning of the interpersonal comparison? Furthermore, Arrow also notes that, so long as there is more than one primary good, there is an index-number problem in commensurating the different goods. He also queries the implications of the maximin rule for allocative justice in the distribution of savings and wealth over generations, and he takes issue with the idea that people can argue themselves back into an original position with common information. The thrust of his argument with regard to the latter question could, it seems, also be directed against a number of economic theories.

What, then, may we conclude from Rawls' theory about the requirements of distributive justice? Although one may take issue with particular aspects of his theoretical structure, he assembles a formidable body of argument in support of the view that we ought to accord the highest priority to helping the least advantaged members of society, and that we ought to depart from a broadly egalitarian distribution of benefits only if we can be shown to be helping those least advantaged. On the grounds of justice, then, the distribution of rewards *does* matter.

Another conclusion which has been drawn from Rawls' work is of direct relevance to our study. Runciman (1966) has argued that, in the initial position postulated by Rawls' model, comparisons between individuals, or between groups, would not be restricted in any way. In deciding the distribution of rewards in society, those in the original position, who do not know their place in society, would be concerned to ensure that all occupations, for example, would be open to comparison in order that they might be justly rewarded.

At a practical level, this would mean that governments should not try to prevent individuals, or groups of employees, comparing themselves with other groups when arguing their case for pay claims. Yet some governments in the United Kingdom have adopted precisely this policy. To take a case close to home, academics used at one time to compare their rates of pay with those in certain grades of the civil service, but having fallen so far behind these grades, some governments have no longer accepted such comparisons as valid. Yet the gist of Rawls' model would seem to be that, on the grounds of justice, no such comparisons should be barred. What seems at first sight an innocuous conclusion is nevertheless one which, if implemented, could in practice have far-reaching implications, and probably also repercussions.

A rather different approach to distributive justice has been adopted by Atkinson (1972), another prominent writer in the field, whose principal concern has been the distribution of wealth, acquired either through accumulation out of income, or through inheritance or gift. In contrast to Rawls, his starting point is the situation as it exists in society, but like Rawls there is a strong egalitarian streak in his work. The case *for* greater equality, he argues, is one for what he calls 'social justice', and rests on:

(1) the acceptance of the basic principle that the distribution should be equal unless departures from equality can be justified according to what are considered relevant criteria;
(2) the demonstration that the existing extremes of inequality cannot be justified by appeal to such criteria.

The case *against* measures to bring about greater equality must rest, Atkinson maintains, on arguments that existing inequalities can be justified according to certain relevant criteria which are likely to include: (1) merit or deserts; (2) need; (3) social benefit.

With regard to the first of these, it is noted that in respect of income, merit or deserts would take account of skills, knowledge, type of work, etc. – in effect, the 'inputs' of Adams and the other writers on equity in exchange. Applying this approach to the distribution of wealth, Atkinson believes that it can be used to justify a situation in which a person who has saved out of past income has more wealth than someone who has failed to save – abstinence, or the postponement of consumption, deserves its reward. Akinson does not go so far as to say that *all* accumulated wealth can be justified according to deserts, since some of this wealth may in turn be used to generate large additional wealth, through property speculation, for example. Where the line should be drawn is left unanswered; and while it may not matter greatly in most cases, in some it may, since the additional accumulations may be sizeable.

Inherited wealth, Atkinson believes, is in an entirely different category from accumulated wealth. Since it cannot, in his view, be justified by reference to deserts, any arguments in its favour must be based on need. One argument commonly used is that married persons ought to be able to provide for the needs of their children, should the parents die or become incapacitated (in such circumstances, it could also be argued, it would not be unjust if the remaining parent(s) had wealth to fall back on in order to meet their own needs, quite apart from those of the children). It might even be argued that ensuring the survival of the family line is a 'basic' human need, although it is not one which featured in any of the classifications of needs reported earlier. Kotlikoff and Summers (1981) in a recent study produced evidence which they claimed showed that most saving was done to provide for bequests rather than for consumption when old.

Making adequate provision for children's needs is certainly a strong argument in favour of wealth, although there is plenty of room for dispute over what constitutes 'adequate', and whether a better alternative – the one preferred by Atkinson – would be an improved system of social security benefits, so that all children in such circumstances could benefit, not just those whose parents were wealthy. Alternatively, if it were felt that restrictions on bequests to children – or perhaps even other relatives – interfered with the rights of individuals, it might be considered preferable to tax the transfer of wealth, as some countries now do. Whatever the policies, their distributional effects, Atkinson stresses, should be judged by their effects on the total inherited wealth received by a person *over his lifetime*, thereby avoiding the problems which arise from different inheritors being at different stages of the lifecycle.

Finally, Atkinson looks at the 'social benefit' arguments against greater equality, many of which are of prime concern to economists. He looks first at the possible effects on personal savings of greater equality of wealth, and concludes that, while a reduction in personal savings would, if it occurred, have implications for the level of aggregate demand, for the rate of investment and for the balance of payments, sufficient evidence is not in fact available to enable us to reach any definite conclusions about the effects of the greater equality of wealth on savings. Similarly, Atkinson finds that when it comes to assessing the effects of greater equality of inherited wealth on work incentives, 'there is no presumption that the effect of redistribution would necessarily be adverse'. The possibly detrimental effects on enterprise, risk-taking, managerial performance and the 'quality of life' are also quickly dismissed – perhaps too quickly for some – as unlikely to be important. Only over the administrative costs of a wealth redistribution is there much hesitation.

2.3.5 Conclusions

In the work situation, Adams' theory of equity in exchange seems to give us useful and practical insights into the factors which weigh most heavily with employees when they are making judgements about the equity, or inequity, of their position in relation to that of others. A number of aspects of these judgements about equity seem particularly worth stressing. First, they are based on comparisons with relevant others, and will be influenced by the social environment, including family, work and play environments, within which Person finds himself. In our study we need to examine the whole question of social comparisons in greater depth, and we do so in a later section.

Second, judgements about equity are based on personal *perceptions*, and as we noted earlier, these need not accord with reality or the perceptions of others. While there may be stable elements in these perceptions, in that much the same variables will probably continue to be taken into account in making equity judgements, some of these variables may alter in value quite quickly. In particular, pay awards to Others, or lack of them to Person, could quickly alter perceptions of equity. Even such variables as educational qualifications, or certified levels of skill, to the extent that these are not quickly rewarded, could alter perceptions. Judgements about equity may therefore be very volatile, and this possible source of short-term instability should not be overlooked in economics.

One of the most important conclusions to be drawn from our consideration of equity in exchange is that, based as it is upon *perceptions* about equity, what are considered to be equitable outcomes may, in the case of financial outcomes, exceed in sum the financial resources available for distribution. To keep financial outcomes within the resources available would then require adjustments to outcomes which might make it impossible to reconcile them with perceptions of equity. If so, we could have here a continuing source of conflict causing disequilibrium in the economic system. The only solution then might be improved economic education and attempts to arrive at a consensus about the appropriate distribution of rewards.

The concept of relative deprivation, as we saw, has many similarities with the the theory of equity in exchange, but there are sufficiently important differences between the two to justify our distinguishing between them. Both have features which are helpful in the analysis of wage behaviour, and we shall make use of both when we come to try and explain wage behaviour.

Perceptions also colour personal views about what we have termed 'distributive justice'. On the whole, it seems reasonable to expect such perceptions to be more stable than in exchange relationships of the sort examined by Adams and other writers, but that certainly does not mean that we can afford to ignore them. Changes in government policy affect outcomes, or deserts, through, for example, the tax system, and may therefore motivate people's actions in particular directions. On the grounds of needs, fairly strong arguments can be advanced for bequests of wealth, accumulated or inherited, to close relatives, but it is difficult to define with any degree of precision how large such bequests might reasonably be. A great deal more empirical research is required in the whole area of needs and deserts: for the moment the links between distributive justice and motivation remain rather obscure.

One important conclusion we do draw from the discussion of distributive justice, however, is that it requires that social comparisons should not be artificially restricted. Equity demands that people should be able to compare their rewards with those of others. Such comparisons will in any case continue to be made, and attempts to limit them, for example by governments, are only likely to lead to feelings of being inequitably treated and a build-up of resentment. The evidence available suggests that, ultimately, those feeling aggrieved are likely to resort to actions to try and correct the inequity.

Many people do care about the *relative* share-out of rewards in society. Our earlier analysis of needs helps explain why this should be so. It is not just the absolute level of rewards, but also relative rewards, which determine personal feelings of satisfaction, or otherwise. It is not enough to claim that measures are justified because they will benefit the least advantaged if, at the same time, these same measures will result in even greater proportionate gains to the better endowed. Distributive justice would seem to require that the *relative* position of the least advantaged is improved, or, at the worst, does not deteriorate.

2.4 ASPECTS OF MOTIVATION – GOALS

While some writers have thought in terms of needs giving rise to actions to satisfy these needs, and of the desire for equity likewise leading to actions to achieve equitable treatment, other investigators have argued that goal-setting is the immediate, or proximate, instigator of motivated activity. These different approaches appear to be complementary rather than contradictory. Many of the writers on goal-setting, including Lewin (1935, 1938), who played a leading role in developing this area of research, have introduced needs into their explanations of the process by which goals come to be set. Needs, in effect, are seen as the basis for the goals. In recent years, goal-setting has been researched mainly within an organizational setting, deriving from the early work on what has come to be known as Management by Objectives. Before turning to this work, and eventually to the treatment of goals in economics, we shall look first at the manner in which needs, in particular, may fit into the process of goal-setting. The most useful work for this purpose seems to be that of Ryan (1970), who was concerned with what he called 'intentional behaviour', a term which embraces goal-setting – as does the 'level of aspiration', another term much used in this field.

2.4.1 Goal-Setting: The Causal Chain

Ryan's emphasis on *intention* is indicative of the fact that he sees goal-setting as a conscious, cognitive process. Writers in the organization field, such as Locke (1968, 1970) also hold to this viewpoint. This does not mean that unconscious goals are ruled out, but in the opinion of Locke (1969) at least, 'At the nonconscious level the concept of goal-directed is a descriptive term referring to the fact that the actions are survival orientated.' This would seem to rule out any objective of satisfying 'higher-order' needs, such as a need for achievement, or for self-actualization, and may therefore be too extreme a view for some to swallow. Whatever one's views, it remains the case that most writers on goal-setting have treated it as a conscious, cognitive process.

Ryan finds it useful to treat intentions as part of a causal chain comprising four 'levels' of explanation, which are admitted to be somewhat arbitrary, and therefore not rigidly fixed. Running in parallel, or interacting with, this causal chain are stimuli, both internal and external, and physiological conditions – the latter possibly also affecting behaviour directly. At the first, and most immediate, level of explanation, intention causes the individual to behave in a certain manner. Ryan, however, interposes what he calls a 'determining tendency' between intention and behaviour, to denote that behaviour, or activity, may be separated in time from the actual formation of an intention.

Level 2 in Ryan's causal chain is concerned with an individual's perception of his environment, not solely with respect to the past and the present, but also with respect to an individual's expectations about the future. These perceptions of the world, together with an individual's perceptions of himself, are referred to as the 'phenomenal field'. The second level of explanation deals with the interrelations between this phenomenal field and the formation of intention.

At the third level of explanation, questions are asked about why the individual perceives the situation as he does, and why he wishes to undertake a particular activity. The explanation offered by Ryan is that each individual has a set of ready-made reactions to stimulation – what he calls 'stored products'. Some of these 'products' are specific, such as likes and dislikes, others are more in the nature of general systems of products. Among the latter he includes general rules, priorities and needs.

Finally, at level 4 Ryan allows for influences arising from an individual's past experiences and historical development. These influence the nature of the stored products. Needs, therefore, are not seen as fixed, or purely determined by biological factors. They will change over time.

Ryan reviewed at length the theories and evidence having a bearing on the links between the four levels of explanation, and concluded that there was sufficient supporting evidence to validate these links. He did, however, express reservations about the nature and role of motives (under which heading he included needs, drives and instincts). Motives he found to be the only general conceptions which might be expected to contribute to explaining the properties of the phenomenal field, although he did not go so far as to claim that motives must exert their effect only through the phenomenal field. Indeed he conceded that, 'Undoubtedly we shall eventually find that intention and behaviour cannot be completely accounted for by the phenomenal field.' What did cause him disquiet, however, was that the analysis of motives as explanatory concepts was still in an unsatisfactory state. Whereas such motives as hunger, thirst, sex and fear of pain were obvious, accepted by all theories, and clearly affected the phenomenal field, other motives were less clearly defined, and the supporting empirical evidence unsatisfactory.

The answer to some of these difficulties may well lie, it seems, in our earlier discussion of needs, wants and satisfiers in section 2.2. Economists, as we saw, have largely ignored the role of needs, and latterly have also lost interest in the analysis of wants, preferring instead to concentrate on expressed wants, or preferences, as indicated by consumer purchases. Psychologists, on the other hand, have confined their attention to needs (and the related concept of attitudes) whereas it is the wants deriving from these needs which are likely to give rise to goals, and therefore to individual behaviour – with people concerned to obtain the satisfiers appropriate to their wants. Categories of needs may well continue to be rather vague and ill-defined, if only because they may be associated with a variety of different wants and satisfiers – even the simpler biological needs, such as hunger and thirst, but especially the so-called 'higher-order' needs. An appropriate area of analysis for psychologists would therefore appear to be the factors determining the transformation of needs into wants – we concluded earlier that environmental factors, such as geographical location, or religion, would play an important part in this transformation, although it may be that organic differences also come into play at this stage. The wants and satisfiers might then be treated as part of a causal chain explaining behaviour which also included goals – an example might be an individual saving up to buy a consumer-durable good which he was unable to afford for the time being; or some wants might be regarded simply as immediate determinants of behaviour – impulse buying, for example.

2.4.2 Goal-setting in organizations

We turn now to goal-setting within organizations. One of the principal researchers in this field has been Edwin Locke, a one-time pupil of Ryan, on whose work he draws heavily – a debt readily acknowledged. Locke did not regard his work on goal-setting as a formal theory of motivation: 'Goal-setting is more appropriately viewed as a motivational technique rather than as a formal theory of motivation' (Locke, 1975). Nevertheless, his work contains a theoretical element, backed up by considerable empirical research. A helpful summary of this work, and of other recent work in the field of goal-setting, is given in Locke *et al.* (1981).

Locke *et al.* (1981) define a goal as follows:

> A goal is what an individual is trying to accomplish; it is the object or aim of an action. The concept is similar in meaning to the concepts of purpose and intent.

They go on to say:

> The basic assumption of goal-setting research is that goals are immediate regulators of human action. However, no one-to-one correspondence between goals and action is assumed because people may make errors, lack the ability to attain their objectives (Locke, 1968) or have subconscious conflicts or premises that subvert their conscious goals. The precise degree of association between goals and actions is an empirical question . . .

Since much of the work on goal-setting in organizations is concerned with task performance, it is of limited value for our purposes, but it seems useful nevertheless to summarize some of the main conclusions drawn by Locke *et al.* (1981) from their survey. They note, first, that there are at least four mechanisms by which goals affect task performance: by directing attention and action; by mobilizing the expenditure of energy or effort; by prolonging effort over time; and by motivating the individual to develop strategies for goal attainment.

Goals are most likely to affect performance under the conditions listed below.

1. Individuals with specific, hard or challenging goals generally out-perform those with easy, general or no assigned goals.
2. Goals seem to regulate performance most predictably when they are expressed in specific quantitative terms, rather than when set as vague exhortations or in subjective form. Intermediate goals, or sub-goals, may be an aid to the attainment of long-term goals – although more research was required, it was felt, before definite conclusions could be reached on this aspect.
3. Individuals must have the ability to attain, or at least approach, their goals. Where tasks are difficult or complex, individuals often redefine the task in a way which facilitates goal attainment.
4. Knowledge of performance in relation to a goal, i.e. feedback, appears to be necessary if goals are to improve performance.

5. Money may be an effective method of improving performance in relation to a goal, but the amounts involved must be large rather than small.
6. There is no consistent evidence that participation by individuals in the setting of their goals leads to greater commitment on their part, or to improved performance.
7. There is no evidence that personality differences, other than ability, help explain relative success in achieving goals.
8. Finally, Locke *et al.* (1981) note that: 'The beneficial effect of goal-setting on task performance is one of the most robust and replicable findings in the psychological literature.'

It will be apparent from the above that work on goal-setting in organizations has progressed sufficiently for it to hold an important place in the literature on motivation. There are, nevertheless, still certain weaknesses. One of the principal of these, to which Miner (1985) draws attention, is that the theory does not really provide us with an understanding of how goals are created and developed, and how goal acceptance occurs. He continues: 'Simply to move this problem back from individual goals to personal values is not sufficient. It then becomes important to specify the origins of the values in order to predict them and the goal-based behaviour they generate.' We seem to need, in other words, an explanation of why specific goals are important to an individual, and why he is prepared to accept them. One obvious explanation, which inevitably emerges from our earlier analysis, is that goals, even in an organizational setting, are a means to help satisfy the needs of individuals. Goal achievement may bring with it monetary reward, enabling many needs to be satisfied; but in an organizational setting goal-attainment may also directly satisfy many needs, such as the needs for achievement, esteem, and perhaps also for self-actualization. One might argue, therefore, that work on goal-setting in organizations would benefit from being linked more closely with the ultimate motivating forces, which, as we saw earlier, formed part of Ryan's causal chain – his historical influences and 'stored products'.

2.4.3 Goal-setting in economics

In standard economic theory it is assumed that consumers are motivated by the goal of maximizing their utility from consumption, and that entrepreneurs are motivated by the desire to maximize their profits. It is upon these two crucial assumptions about human behaviour that much of the edifice of neo-classical economic theory is constructed. The arguments advanced in support of these assumptions boil down to the view that men and women are 'rational' beings, i.e. they have a stable and consistent system of preferences which will lead them to select the course of action yielding them the greatest possible satisfaction. Criticisms of this view of rationality have led to its being re-presented in more sophisticated forms, but the maximizing assumptions remain, as they must do if the system of general equilibrium is to be sustained. We now need to examine these key assumptions about goals in the light of the criticisms to which they have given rise, and of our earlier analysis.

Simon's view of rational decision-taking Of the many criticisms of the optimizing behaviour predicated by economic theory, the work of Herbert Simon has been among the most sustained and fruitful, and instrumental in the development of an alternative body of theoretical and empirical analysis which has established itself as a rather uncomfortable neighbour alongside the standard theory. Simon's basic argument falls into two parts: first, the decision-making organism (i.e. the consumer or the entrepreneur) has certain characteristics which place limits on the decisions it may take; second, the environment within which the organism functions has features which enable the decision-making process of the organism to be simplified.

With regard to the first part of the argument, Simon (1955, 1983) notes the extensive requirements of the economists' customary models of rational behaviour. These include: a clear set of alternatives from which a choice may be made; knowledge of the likely future outcomes resulting from particular choices; values or utilities attached to each of the outcomes available to the organism; information about which outcomes will actually occur; and information about the probability that a particular outcome will ensue if a certain alternative is chosen. These are very testing requirements, and, as Simon also notes, there is insufficient evidence to support the view that individuals are either able to, or do in practice, perform such complex computations.

Simon goes on to argue that, whereas the entrepreneur of economic theory has little in the way of limitations placed upon his ability to tackle the complex problems facing him, in the real world his abilities are confined by the limits of 'bounded rationality', which Simon (1957) defines as follows:

> The capacity of the human mind for formulating and solving complex problems is very small compared with the size of the problems whose solution is required for objectively rational behaviour in the real world – or even for a reasonable approximation to such objective rationality.

Among the reasons advanced by Simon (1976) for thinking that human rationality falls far short of that demanded of Economic Man are, first, that there are physical and other biological limitations on the ability of human beings to respond, especially within a limited timescale, to problems. Skills may be improved, minds broadened, reflexes sharpened up, bad habits discarded, but ultimately there are limits in the case of each individual. Even if such limitations are offset in part by the assistance of modern aids, such as computers, the demands of economic rationality in most decision-making still far exceed the capacity of human beings.

In addition to physical limitations, there are limitations of knowledge. Simon argued that, in reality, individuals seldom have more than a fragmentary knowledge of all that they would need to know if they were to make the 'right', or rational, decisions, as foreseen by economic theory. We might illustrate the point by the purchase of an item of clothing. The individual can never be sure that he or she is getting the best value for money. Feel, texture, thickness, etc. give some indication, but only the wearing of the article will provide the necessary evidence of its longevity. How often, in one's own experience, has one come to regret a purchase? In the writer's case, selecting new shoes poses problems which he has not yet been able to overcome. At the macroeconomic level, decision-taking is even more problematic, since the final repercussions of policy decisions are quite likely to be several removes from the initial act. Purchases on the stock market represent yet another good example of the decisions being taken without the availability of full information.

Finally, Simon noted that rationality might be limited by an individual's failure to identify himself correctly with the goals of the organization for which he worked. An individual might, for example, have his own sub-goals – an undue emphasis on quantity, perhaps, rather than a more reasonable balance between quality and quantity – thereby making it impossible for an organization to attain its own principal goals, including profit-maximization.

When to the above limitations on rational decision-taking we add the uncertainties attaching to any decisions requiring judgement about the probability of *future* events, then bounded rationality, Simon believes, will prevent individuals from making rational decisions of the sort envisaged in economics. Faced by overwhelming complexity, individuals will construct a simplified model of the real situation, and 'satisfice' rather than maximize, i.e. look for a course of action which is satisfactory, or at least acceptable. Examples might include: setting a goal of an adequate level of profits, or of a minimum level of sales; replacing abstract or global goals by tangible sub-goals whose achievement could be observed and measured (Simon, 1979); dividing up the decision-making task between many specialists, operating within an organizational structure. Closely associated with this view of satisficing is the concept of *search*: if the alternatives for choice are not given initially to the decision-maker, then he must search for them (Simon, 1979).

Recent work by Kahneman, Tversky and Slovic (1974, 1979, 1982) has also shown how the introduction of risk into decision-taking may cause the utility-maximizing model to break down. They maintain that, in taking decisions relating to complex, multi-dimensional problems, individuals commonly adopt a heuristic approach in assessing probabilities and predicting the values of outcomes. These heuristics may result in severe and systematic errors in the decisions reached. Three common heuristics they cite are 'representativeness', 'availability' and 'anchoring'. The first of these concerns the way in which individuals, when confronted with the problems of the form: what is the probability that object A belongs to class B, or that process B will generate event A, commonly evaluate the probabilities by the extent to which A is thought to be representative of, or resembles, B – ignoring other factors which should also affect judgements of probability.

The availability heuristic relates to those cases in which individuals assess the probability of an event according to the ease with which similar instances or occurrences can be brought to mind. Assessment of the risk of heart attacks for persons of a particular age might, for example, be made by recalling the frequency of such occurrences among people of one's own acquaintance. Finally, anchoring concerns those frequent situations in which individuals are required to make a series of estimates, perhaps over a period of time. Starting off from an initial value, subsequent estimates may require adjustment of that value, but full adjustment tends not to be made – new information, for example, may not be fully taken into account. The result is a bias towards the initial value or values.

Turning our attention now away from the decision-making organism (the consumer or the entrepreneur) to the environment within which the organism makes its choice, Simon (1956) maintained that the environment had a certain structure which facilitated the process of satisficing. The environment, he said, 'will depend upon the "needs", "drives", or "goals" of the organism, and upon its perceptual apparatus.' The precise nature of the links between needs, drives, goals and perceptions is not spelled out, but we are back once again, it seems, with something akin to Ryan's causal chain, which embraces these variables. Simon's argument is that while the desire to satisfy such needs as hunger and thirst may lead to multiple goals, each need will have a threshold which, when reached, will give that need a priority. A person may, for example, be both hungry and thirsty, but if he is especially thirsty and passes the said threshold, the satisfaction of thirst will have first priority, and therefore the problem of choice is simplified. We end up, in effect, with a limited hierarchy of needs, and associated wants and satisfiers. This does not, of course, wholly obviate the need for choice, since there may be a number of needs for which thresholds have been reached, but if such a process were operative, it could at least serve to reduce the number of alternatives from which a choice had to be made. We get a clearer picture from such an example of the way in which satisficing might work in practice.

Goals in theories of the firm Simon's work on bounded rationality and satisficing, while only one of numerous critiques of the standard theory of the firm, has played an important role in encouraging the growth of alternative models of entrepreneurial behaviour which reject the assumption of profit-maximizing, and attempt to work out the economic implications of non-maximizing behaviour. Since this area of research has already been extensively developed, and reported upon elsewhere (see, for example, Sawyer, 1979), it has not been felt necessary to include it as part of our study, but it is pertinent to examine the nature of the assumptions made about managerial goals in these theories, and to see how they relate to our own analysis. We turn now, therefore, to look briefly at this aspect of the principal behavioural and managerial theories of the firm.

A point to note at the outset is that only individuals, not firms *per se*, have motives, and therefore goals – a point made forceably by Leibenstein (1976). Any goal claimed for a firm, including that of profit-maximization, must therefore be explicable in terms of the personal motivation of those who in any way control the activities of that firm. No such explanation is offered of the profit-maximizing assumption in conventional theory. It is simply assumed to be the sole overriding motive. One of the merits of the theories of the firm which we will examine here is that they attempt to face up to this problem.

One major model of the firm to draw heavily on the work of Simon is that of Cyert and March (1963), who explore the decision-making process within large corporations. They begin by noting that an organization is a coalition of individuals (including, in the case of a joint stock company, shareholders), and that these individuals may have substantially different preference orderings, i.e. goals, one from another. There is therefore a potential for internal goal conflict inherent in organizations which must somehow be resolved. In standard economic theory this problem is not recognized. It is simply assumed that the goals of the entrepreneur are also the goals of his staff. Another way of tackling the problem would be to assume that the participants in an organization reach a consensus on the goal, or goals, to be pursued. Both approaches represent an attempt to define a joint preference ordering for the coalition, an attempt which Cyert and March feel is misdirected, and is as likely as not to lead to the development of highly ambiguous goals. This, in turn, may result in disagreement and uncertainty about sub-goals within the organization, so that conflicting objectives may even be pursued. Finally, it is maintained that the goals of most organizations are in the nature of aspiration levels – aspiration levels, moreoever, which change over time – rather than an imperative to 'maximize' or 'minimize'.

Cyert and March see an organization's goals emerging from a process of bargaining between the interested parties (from which the largely passive stockholders are excluded) over 'side payments', which include not just money but also such matters as the treatment of personnel and policy commitments. This bargaining process goes on more or less continuously, but is given stability by the fact that it operates within certain constraints, among which are the organization's budget, limits to the discretion accorded to individuals within the organization and organizational precedents. There is, however, provision in the model for the changing of goals with time as the demands of individual members of the organization alter. An interesting feature of the model is the link it makes between aspiration levels, goals and goal achievement. The argument – backed up by empirical evidence – is that aspiration levels frequently exceed attainment, but may then be revised according to how far the goals have been reached.

The above process, Cyert and March argue, leads to the adoption of five major goals within firms, relating to production, inventories, sales, market share and profit. Because of the form of the goals, and the way they are established, conflict between them is never fully resolved, and there is a degree of *organizational slack* – a difference between the organization's total resources and the total payments necessary. Such an organization cannot be a profit-maximizer, since the slack in effect represents profits forgone.

Two other theories of the firm which attempt to take account of personal goals in arriving at overall goals for the firm are those of Williamson (1964) and Marris (1964). They place rather less emphasis, however, on the relationships within the firm than did Cyert and March. Williamson cites evidence to the effect that there is a substantial consensus among organization theorists, and among economists who have studied the operations of business firms, about the 'immediate determinants' of behaviour. These main determinants he lists as: salary, security, status, power, prestige, professional excellence and social service. The last-mentioned he eliminates on the grounds that the scope for behaviour of this nature is probably not great in the business firm – although charitable donations, for example, may sometimes be substantial, and would be difficult to justify in every case on purely commercial grounds.

Williamson goes on to compare the various determinants of behaviour with Maslow's hierarchy of needs, noting that security might be said to overlap Maslow's safety and love needs, that dominance (under which heading he groups status, power and prestige) would accord with the need for esteem, and that professional excellence could be a form of self-actualization. Only salary did not fit neatly into the hierarchy. Salary may, however, be regarded as a general means for the satisfaction of a variety of needs requiring a financial outlay. Williamson also notes that his list of motives may not be complete – one obvious omission in the light of our earlier analysis would be a desire for equitable treatment.

Having identified the principal motives in operation, Williamson then introduced the notion of *expense preference* to provide a bridge between the motives and actual economic behaviour. Whereas conventional economic theory treats all expenses equally, expense preference takes account of the fact that individuals within firms are likely to have preferences for certain types of expenses. This approach also enables Williamson to express his model entirely in monetary units.

Williamson identified three main types of expense relevant

to the notion of expense preference. First, that of staff. Managers exhibit a special preference for more staff, it was argued, because it helps satisfy some of the needs itemized above, such as that for esteem. The second expense identified was that of emoluments (defined as discretionary additions to salary and to corporate personal consumption) which we might also categorize as helping to meet the need for esteem, and perhaps also security. Finally, Williamson identified what he called 'discretionary profit' – the difference between net (after-tax) profit and the minimum profit felt necessary by management. This profit provided an incentive to management, since, as the term suggests, they had greater discretion over its use, and it therefore also helped satisfy their needs – perhaps those of esteem and self-actualization. Bringing together these personal motives of managers and the profit requirements of the firm, Williamson hypothesized that the goal of the firm would be to maximize a utility function of the form:

$$U = u\,(S, M, \Pi_r - \Pi_o - T)$$

subject to $\Pi_r \geqq \Pi_o + T$, where S represents staff expenses, M managerial emoluments, Π_r actual profits, Π_o minimum (after-tax) profits demanded and T taxes.

In formulating his model of the firm, Marris (1964) at the outset also faces up to the question of motives. His theory is explicitly managerial, largely ignoring the motives of manual workers and how these may influence a firm's goals. It therefore contrasts strongly with the approach of Cyert and March, who attempt to arrive at a corporate goal, taking account of inputs from all the interested parties. Marris's theory is also concerned essentially with the long run, and a firm's choice of a sustainable growth path.

In his analysis of motivation Marris distinguishes three main approaches: the psychological, the sociological and the economic. While this distinction helps segment discussion, the three, as we shall see, have a large measure in common, and they lead to much the same conclusion. Under the heading of 'psychological motives' Marris lists the drive for achievement among managers and the tendency for their aspiration levels to rise as their objectives are achieved. He also refers to Katona's (1951) contention that executives do not see the firm as a mere apparatus for satisfying personal wants, but rather do they see the prosperity and success of the firm as an actual proxy for their wants. In effect, work in the firm is envisaged as satisfying much more than the need for pecuniary gain. On the sociological side, the evidence cited points to the business executive being 'many sided and multi-motivated'. Marris concludes, however, that two aspects of motivation seem particularly worth pursuing: first, the determinants of 'narrow' economic rewards, or pecuniary gain; second, the implications of growth of the firm as an objective.

The discussion of the 'economic' motives is one of the most extensive in the literature, and is especially interesting in the way Marris is able to bring out the motivational aspects of economic topics not usually treated in this light. Drawing mainly on the work of R. A. Gordon (1961), Marris concludes that business executives desire not just 'narrow' economic rewards, but also power, status, the opportunity for creative satisfaction, and for group-belonging and security. The list is in fact one which could be fitted into a categorization of needs, and could therefore equally well have been brought in under the umbrellas of psychological and sociological motives.

The 'narrow' economic rewards to managers take three main forms: bonuses, stock options and basic compensation. Marris's analysis leads him to conclude that it is the growth of the firm which plays the dominant role in determining the extent of these financial rewards. Likewise, growth is important in helping satisfy most of the other objectives listed – non-economic as well as economic – such as the desires for achievement, power and status. There is also, however, a desire on the part of management, as we noted, for security. Managers will generally wish to avoid a take-over of their firm, since it may well lead to the loss of their jobs. Managers are therefore constrained to maintain the valuation ratio of their firms (defined as the ratio of the market value of the firm to its book value). All these considerations lead managers to set as their goal the maximization of the rate of growth of their firms, subject to the constraint imposed by the security motive.

Although primarily concerned with managerial motives, it is interesting that Marris also included a chapter on consumer demand for the products of firms, in which great stress was placed on the role of personal needs (including previously latent needs) in consumer behaviour. Following Duesenberry (1949), he also emphasized the process of interpersonal stimulation in want-creation. These are matters to which we shall return in our later section on consumer behaviour.

In attempting to provide a firmer theoretical basis for the existence of X-inefficiency, Leibenstein (1976) was also led to inquire into human motivation. Once again, there are differences between Leibenstein's approach and those of the other theories we have examined, but the analysis nevertheless contains elements common to these other theories. At the outset, Leibenstein stresses what should be obvious, but is all too frequently overlooked, namely that 'only individuals make decisions, and not the socially or legally constituted entities we call firms and households, although individuals may make some decisions in the name of such entities.' Furthermore, 'Only individual members of firms have motives, and the meaningfulness and nature of firm motives depend on the study of individual motives.' For clues to the behaviour of firms, we therefore have to examine the behaviour of the individuals and groups who constitute the firm. There are echoes here of Cyert and March's emphasis on the need to take account of the coalitions of interests operating within firms, and of the stress placed on the importance of individual motivation by Williamson and Marris.

Leibenstein's concern is to show why firms may fall short of the profit-maximizing goal of conventional economic theory, resting on the assumption of 'rational' behaviour by the individual. The implication is that individuals will 'use their capabilities' or capacities to the greatest degree possible in order to obtain from the context the largest economic gain.' But a perfectly rational individual, Leibenstein argues, may be motivated to take actions which cause firms to fall well short of the maximization goal. Individuals pursue their own goals as well as the interests of the firm.

Leibenstein's case for the existence of what he calls 'selective rationality', as opposed to 'economic rationality', rests on the belief that individuals pursue their goals as best they can, and to differing degrees. Any economic situation imposes certain constraints on a person – in the case of a consumer, an example would be the need to pay bills, in the case of an employee, perhaps the necessity of arriving at work on time, or to meet an output quota. Individuals try to some extent (not 100 per cent) to work within these constraints, thereby expressing a measure of what Leibenstein refers to as 'constraint concern'. The degree of concern varies from person to person, depending upon personality traits. These will affect the extent an individual is prepared, for example, to persevere in the pursuit of an objective, or to be calculating when choosing between alternatives – a consumer on a spending spree would probably be an example of 'loose calculation'. While the person may not feel he wishes to work fully within the constraints of a particular situation, there are pressures ('felt pressures') tending to impose conformity. The outcome is a constraint concern – pressure trade-off compromise with which the individual feels comfortable.

One might ask how it is that employees are able to exercise such a large measure of discretion in their working lives. Leibenstein's answer is that work *effort* is variable – there would seem to be a link here with the expectancy-valence approach to motivation which we examine in section 2.5. Employees work under contractual arrangements with their employers which are incomplete, in the sense that they do not, and cannot, cover every possible aspect of a person's behaviour while employed. Moreover, labour inputs, even if purchased as man-hours of work, do not represent purchases of specific inputs to the production process. Generally speaking, too, the difficulties of obtaining the maximum possible effort are compounded when individuals are required to work together. The problem of management boils down to improving the monitoring capability of the organization and trying to influence the motivational relations between individuals in a way which benefits the organization. In Leibenstein's theory we do not end up, therefore, with a modified goal for the firm as an alternative to profit-maximization, but rather with an explanation of why the latter goal is unlikely ever to be attained.

The emphasis on personal motivation and its effects in preventing the attainment of the conventional goal of profit-maximization give a certain cohesion to the above theories. Acknowledgement should also be made, however, of the contributions of numerous other writers who have also stressed, explicitly or implicitly, the importance of personal motivation, such as Katona (1951), Baumol (1967), Scitovsky (1976) and Galbraith (1969). Together these writers represent a formidable challenge to the neo-classical theory, and they are backed up by a good deal of evidence to suggest that they give us a better understanding of how organizations and individuals function in practice. It will be apparent from the motivational aspects of the four theories outlined that our present study has much in common with these works, drawing essentially from many of the same sources.

2.4.4 Conclusions

Psychological work on goal-setting by Ryan, Locke and others indicates that it is a complex process, with a variety of causal links. Simply to assume, as conventional economics does, that consumers and entrepreneurs adopt very specific goals – goals, moreover, which lie at one extreme of a range of possibilities – without examining the motivational process giving rise to these goals, must raise serious doubts about the goals' validity and usefulness. At best, their use for the purposes of analyses represents an investigation of one special situation which is far removed from reality. One must question, too, the assumption that the goals set remain unchanged for all time, and are not subject to reassessment in the light of the degree of success achieved. The evidence available indicates that goal-setting is a dynamic, continuing process, not a rigid unchanging one. Nor is it clear from economic discussions whether goal-setting is seen as a conscious operation, in which the individual participates – in which case periodic reassessment would seem most likely – or as an unconscious decision – in which case the cerebral process leading to the adoption of the said goals ought still to be spelled out.

Ryan's work is persuasive in the way it stresses the variety of influences, including environmental influences and motivation, which enter the process of goal-setting. In subsequent sections of the present study we shall be maintaining, on the basis of our earlier analysis, that needs (and the associated wants) and equity are two of the principal motivating forces underlying goals. No study of goals would be complete without them, it seems, although their relative importance will inevitably vary according to the specific context in which they are used.

While the treatment of goals is generally inadequate in economics, there are encouraging exceptions to the rule. The most thorough analysis of goals has been undertaken in pursuit of alternative theories of the firm, building in particular on the path-breaking work of Simon. The theories differ somewhat in emphasis, but each has a contribution to make, and new developments in this field are still taking place – Earl (1986), for example, in a recent work, links managers' aspirations and attitudes and the ways in which they change, or fail to change, in response to firms' attainments. The basic building-block used in the principal theories is individual motivation, which must surely be the right approach. It is then possible to go on to examine how the need to relate to, and work within, groups of individuals, as in firms, may cause the individuals to modify their goals and behaviour. The final step is to work out the economic implications of these modified goals.

The principal theories of the firm we examined go a long way towards meeting these requirements, and while they may vary somewhat in their emphasis and approach, the underlying foundations are similar: individual motivation, based largely on a recognition of the importance of people's needs, the meeting of which requires not just financial reward, but the satisfaction deriving from a sense of achievement, status, power, etc. These common foundations, we hope to show, can be extended into other important areas of economics, and provide a unity at present sadly lacking.

2.5 ASPECTS OF MOTIVATION – EXPECTANCY-VALENCE MODELS

The so-called 'expectancy-valence' model of motivation is

classed as a cognitive theory, since it rests on the view that individuals have cognitive expectancies, or expectations, concerning the likely outcomes of their actions. They also have preferences among possible outcomes. The theory is therefore of interest in that it places emphasis on conscious choice, which in turn is based on expectations about the probability of certain occurrences, and their relative valence to a person. The theory is also interesting in so far as it incorporates most of the aspects of motivation which we have already examined, demonstrating yet again the complementary nature of the work on motivation. Furthermore, the theory provides a link with our later analysis of wage behaviour through the roles it attributes to need fulfilment and satisfaction with rewards, or outcomes, including pay. Certain aspects of the theory have been criticized, as we shall see, but it nevertheless introduces valuable, additional features of motivation. In particular, its emphasis on expectations and uncertainty would be especially relevant to a more dynamic treatment of motivation.

Early development of the theory was associated with the names of Tolman (1932) and Lewin (1938), the former working mainly with animals, the latter with humans. The basic approach of these early writers rested on the view that motivated behaviour resulted from a combination of individual needs and the goals associated with these needs. An important additional element, however, was the belief that the likelihood of action on the part of the individual also depended upon the *valence* attached to the goal by the individual and the *expectancy* of attaining that goal.

2.5.1 Vroom's VIE model

Vroom's (1964) work marked a further major stage in the development of the expectancy-valence approach, although Vroom readily acknowledged his debt to earlier writers, including Tolman and Lewin. Vroom's theory appears in a number of guises, being referred to as an 'instrumentality theory', or as a VIE (valence-instrumentality-expectancy) theory. In the case of the valence component, Vroom assumed that at any given point in time a person had a set of preferences relating to the range of possible outcomes available. In his own words, 'For any pair of outcomes, x and y, a person prefers x to y, prefers y to x, or is indifferent to whether he receives x or y.' He also noted that psychologists had used a number of terms to refer to preferences in addition to 'valence', including 'incentive', 'attitude', and even expected 'utility'. The concept of *needs* he regarded as being rather broader in nature, embracing large classes of outcomes.

In Vroom's terminology, an outcome was said to have a positive valence when a person preferred attaining it to not attaining it (i.e. when he preferred x to y), to have a valence of zero when a person was indifferent to attaining or not attaining it (i.e. when a person was indifferent to x or not x), and to have a negative valence when he preferred not attaining it to attaining it (i.e. when not x was preferred to x). Valence is distinguished from value. At any given time there may be a substantial discrepancy between the *anticipated* satisfaction from an outcome (its valence) and the *actual* satisfaction that it provides (its value).

Furthermore, Vroom noted that there were many outcomes which were not in themselves anticipated to be satisfying or otherwise, i.e. 'The strength of a person's desire or aversion for them [outcomes] is based not on their intrinsic properties but on the anticipated satisfaction or dissatisfaction associated with other outcomes to which they are expected to lead.' This latter point is made clearer in Vroom's statement of his first proposition:

Proposition 1. The valence of an outcome to a person is a monotonically increasing function of the algebraic sum of the products of the valences of all outcomes and his conceptions of its instrumentality for the attainment of these other outcomes.

In equation form he expresses the proposition as follows:

$$V_j = f_j \left[\sum_{k=1}^{n} (V_k I_{jk}) \right] (j = 1 \ldots n)$$

$$f_j' > O; \; iI_{jj} = O$$

where V_j = the valence of outcome j

I_{jk} = the cognised instrumentality
($-1 \leq I_{jk} \leq 1$) of outcome
j for the attainment of outcome k

In effect, Vroom is maintaining that the valence attached to some outcomes is dependent upon their 'instrumentality' in attaining other outcomes. There are, in other words, two levels of outcomes (a point made by Galbraith and Cummings (1967) and incorporated explicitly in their own development of Vroom's model). The first outcome is essentially a means which acquires valence because of its expected relationship to desired ends (other outcomes) which also have a valence. A first-level outcome with a large valence would tend to be one that was instrumental in obtaining a large number of second-level outcomes which it was anticipated would yield appreciable satisfaction. A practical example of the operation of Proposition 1 would be a pay increase (a first-level outcome) which was instrumental in obtaining second-level outcomes such as food, drink, shelter, and perhaps enhanced status.

Vroom's idea of *expectancy* brings in the element of uncertainty attaching to choices of outcomes. Wherever outcomes are uncertain, behaviour is said to be affected not only by preferences but also by the degree to which a person believes the different outcomes to be probable. Vroom defines expectancy as 'a monetary belief concerning the likelihood that a particular act will be followed by a particular outcome.

Expectancy, it is stressed, is an action–outcome association, taking a value ranging from zero (no subjective probability that an act will be followed by an outcome) to 1 (complete certainty). Instrumentality, on the other hand, is an outcome–outcome association, taking values ranging from –1 (indicating that attainment of the second level outcome is thought certain without the first level outcome) to +1 (indicating that the first outcome is believed to be necessary and sufficient for the attainment of the second outcome).

Vroom went on to combine expectancy and valence to yield what he called a 'force'. The precise relationship between the variables was set out formally in his second proposition:

Proposition 2. The force on a person to perform an act is a monotonically increasing function of the algebraic sum of the products of the valences of all outcomes and the strength of his expectancies that the act will be followed by the attainment of these outcomes.

This proposition was expressed in the following form:

$$Fi = f_i \left[\sum_{j=1}^{n} (E_{ij} V_j) \right] \quad (i = n + 1 \ldots m)$$

$$f\acute{\imath} > O; \; i \cap j = \Phi, \; \Phi \text{ is the null set}$$

where Fi = the force to perform act i
Eij = the strength of the expectancy ($O \leq Eij \leq 1$) that act i will be followed by outcome j
Vj = the valence of outcome j

The proposition assumes that people act rationally, i.e. they choose from among alternative acts the one corresponding to the strongest positive (or weakest negative) force. This assumption, Vroom notes, is similar to the assumption that people choose in such a way as to maximize subjective expected utility.

2.5.2 The Porter-Lawler model

Later models using the expectancy-valence approach have introduced a number of improvements. One model which has attracted a good deal of attention is that of Porter and Lawler (1968). In some respects, this model has a broader compass than we wish to embrace, but it also has a number of interesting features which link it with other aspects of our analysis. The diagrammatic representation of the model used by Porter and Lawler is reproduced in Figure 2.3. It is helpful to remember that the model was constructed mainly with the work situation in mind, and it is therefore likely to be most relevant in our analysis of wage behaviour.

It is worth saying a brief word of explanation about the different variables in the model before commenting on some of its key features. Boxes (1)–(3) on the left-hand side of the figure draw heavily on the work of Vroom (1964) to which we

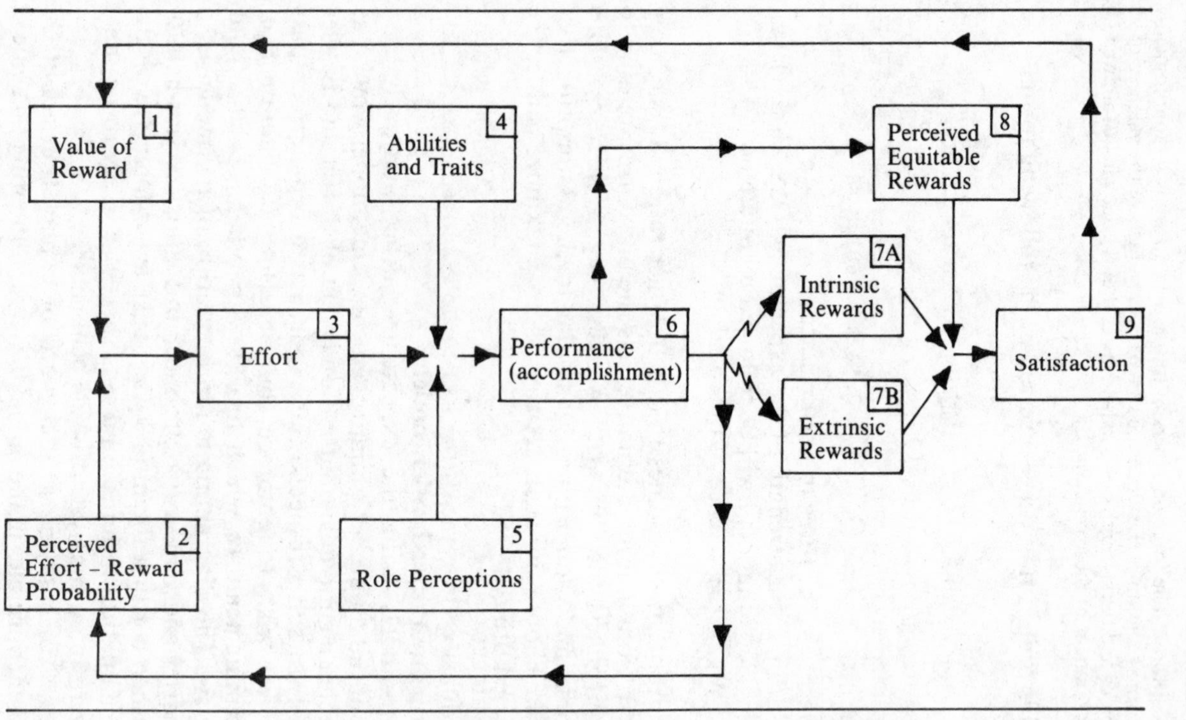

Figure 2.3: The Porter-Lawler model of work motivation
Source: Porter, L.W. and Lawler, E.E. (1968).

referred earlier. The *value of reward* [1] gives the *valence* attached to an outcome, depending upon the individual's outcome preferences.

The perceived effort-reward probability [2] is the subjective assessment by the individual of the likelihood of reward if greater effort is expended. Porter and Lawler point out that this assessment comprised two elements: first, the estimate of the probability that improved performance would lead to greater reward – the *expectancy* component, sometimes represented in the form (P → R); second, the estimate of the probability that greater effort would lead to improved performance – the *instrumentality* component (E → P).

Effort [3] is distinguished from *performance* [6]. The former signifies how hard a person works in performing a task, the latter how effectively the task is accomplished.

The relationship between effort and performance is explained, first, by certain personal characteristics – described as *abilities and traits* [4] – which include such attributes as intelligence and innate skills, and may obviously differ considerably from one person to another. Moderate effort in one case might yield high performance, while in another great effort might have little to show for itself. Also relevant to performance are *role perceptions* [5], i.e. the manner in which individuals believe the effort has to be deployed in order to perform a particular job effectively.

We now pass to the question of rewards for performance. Some of the rewards from performing a task are *intrinsic* [7A], i.e. subjective, arising from the nature of the job itself; others are extrinsic [7B], deriving from external agents, such as a job supervisor, or perhaps from the approval of colleagues, or recognition (financial or otherwise) from an employer. The irregular nature of the lines linking performance and rewards signifies, in the case of [7A], that a direct relationship exists only when a worker feels challenged, and in the case of [7B], that the link between performance and reward is irregular.

The rewards for performing a job yield *satisfaction* [9], or perhaps dissatisfaction. The degree of satisfaction or dissatisfaction felt is determined not just by the intrinsic and extrinsic rewards, but by the extent to which these rewards are *perceived to be equitable* [8] in relation to performance.

The Porter-Lawler model represents an advance on Vroom's model in a number of respects. There is, first, an attempt to spell out the expectational relationships in rather greater detail. Effort, the motivated force, is now shown to depend upon two expectancies: the (E → P) expectancy and the (P → O) expectancy. To each was attached a probability ranging in value from 0 to 1, so that if either probability were zero, the perceived effort-reward probability would also be zero. To take an example, a worker on a production line might think that there was only a 50:50 chance of increased effort on his part resulting in a greater rate of output of the product, perhaps because some of his fellow workers might be tempted to slacken their efforts. Nevertheless, he might consider the extra effort worthwhile; but if, despite the greater effort, he expected that there was no chance of receiving higher pay, or any other form of reward for his extra effort, then his perceived effort-reward probability would be zero. He would not consider it worthwhile making any additional effort.

If the same worker were now to take a rather more optimistic view of the situation, so that at the end of the day he did expect to receive more pay for his additional effort, then this might be expected to increase his sense of satisfaction, especially if the additional pay received was regarded as a desirable outcome. The likelihood of an outcome which had a high valence would, according to the model, feed back into the effort box, making it even likelier that the individual would be motivated to work harder. The role of expectations in the model, and the feedback loops to take account of secondary effects, make the Porter-Lawler model a very dynamic representation of the operation of motivational variables.

In a later work, Lawler (1973) attempted to spell out the determinants of the (E → P) and (P → O) expectations. With regard to the former, he envisaged four main influences. First, the objective, or actual, situation. Although not explained, this appears to be in the nature of a catch-all variable, which might include, for example, the situation in the workplace and relationships with workmates and other workers. Linked with the actual situation is 'communications from others', a form of information variable which helps the person understand his situation better. A third influence on expectations is the person's past experience of similar situations. This is in the nature of a learning process. Expectations about the future, in other words, are influenced by experience in the past, a view familiar to economists. Finally, personality factors are also brought into play. Psychologists concerned with the anlysis of personality have emphasized that individuals have a self-image. This image may not always accord with reality, but the individual does tend to form an image of what he can or cannot do. Beliefs are therefore formed about performance capabilities, and about the individual's value and effectiveness. These beliefs lie at the core of what is often referred to as *self-esteem*.

In the case of (P → O) expectations, Lawler (1973) cites evidence that the actual situation, past experience in similar situations, and communication from others (often workmates) also play a part in influencing these types of expectations. Raiffa (1968), for example, has shown that people's subjective probabilities are generally related to actual mathematical probabilities although the subjective probabilities tend to be greater than actual at low values and smaller than actual at high values. Personality once again plays a part too. Some individuals, it seems, believe they can influence events, while others are prone to believe that things are beyond their control. The perceived attractiveness of outcomes is a further factor. Studies suggest that most people believe positive outcomes are more likely than negative ones. Finally, the (E → P) probabilities appear to have a bearing on certain (P → O) probabilities. Lawler quotes research findings to the effect that when the (E → P) probability is around 0.5, the achievement motive is aroused, and that, consequently, (P → O) expectancies linked with achievement-type outcomes are affected.

Another weakness of Vroom's model was that no adequate explanation was offered of the underlying basis for the valence attached to a particular outcome. The Porter-Lawler model copes with this question more satisfactorily. The degree of satisfaction with rewards, or outcomes, is said to depend upon an individual's perceptions about the equity of the rewards – based upon Adams's model of equity in exchange (Lawler, 1971).

The valence of an outcome also depends upon its ability to satisfy needs. Intrinsic rewards, or outcomes, such as job satisfaction, may help satisfy a need, perhaps for achievement. Extrinsic rewards, including pay, could perform a similar function. The more an outcome is perceived to be capable of satisfying one or more needs, the greater, the model suggests, will be the valence of an outcome. Not only, therefore, is the Porter-Lawler model valuable in stressing the forward-looking features of motivation, it also performs a useful function in helping integrate many of the important aspects of motivation within a dynamic framework.

Note, finally, that, as with needs and equity, the expectancy-valence approach may be integrated with the theory of goal-setting. Menlo *et al.* (1980), for example, have suggested that expectancies and valences may play a part in goal-setting. The degree of goal difficulty, and therefore the expectation of achieving the goal, and the value attached to the goal appear to be interrelated, with feedback effects operating.

2.5.3 Conclusions

The expectancy-valence approach complements our earlier analysis of other aspects of motivation, incorporating a number of the key concepts, such as need-fulfilment and equity in exchange. It also embraces other ideas of interest to economists, including the expression of individual preferences, expectations and uncertainty. It would therefore be relevant to a more dynamic treatment of motivation. It is as well to note, however, that as with most theories, there are critics of the expectancy-valence approach. Locke (1975), for example, in his critique of the theory has questioned what he calls the 'calculative, psychological *hedonism*', and the implicit assumption that all motivation is conscious. He doubts, too, that people are basically the same with respect to search habits and the ability to make the sorts of calculations demanded by the theory. He also notes that the multiplication of valences, expectancies and instrumentality in the basic theory assumes the existence of ratio scales, yet no known method of measuring values or valences on a ratio scale exists – although Schmidt (1973) thinks that this problem may not be insoluble.

The expectancy-valence approach has generated a great deal

of research work designed to test the theory's predictions. A useful summary of this work is contained in Miner (1985). Despite the various limitations of the theory, he is able to conclude that:

> ... research tests have now yielded sufficient theoretical support so that it seems safe to conclude that expectancy theories are on the right track. They certainly do not explain all motivated behaviour in all types of work organisations, but they do explain enough to be worth pursuing further.

2.6 SOCIAL COMPARISONS

We have already noted at several stages in our analysis that people have a habit of comparing themselves with others. It appears to be a strong and continuing feature of personal behaviour. People really do seem to feel a *need* to compare themselves with others. Judgements about status and self-esteem, and the process of self-actualization, generally entail in some degree social interaction and interpersonal comparisons. In making judgements about equity, people also compare their situation with that of others. These comparisons provide a yardstick by which judgement can be made. Goals may also be set and expectations formed by reference to others. Social comparisons therefore lie at the very heart of our analysis. Up to the present, we have noted the importance of such comparisons without trying to define their role more precisely. We have now reached a stage, however, where we need to set out more formally the manner in which the process of social comparisons appears to work. The theoretical literature on the subject is extensive, and it is supported by a good deal of empirical evidence. We shall once again be dealing only with general principles in the present section, leaving specific applications to later sections, where we shall examine, in particular, the importance of social comparisons in helping explain consumer behaviour, the supply of labour and wage behaviour.

2.6.1 Reference Groups

A useful concept in analysing social comparisons is that of the 'reference group', a term coined by Hyman (1942) in a study of status. Writers after Hyman have greatly refined and developed the idea. Sherif (1953) has suggested a definition of reference group which is now widely used: 'Those groups to which the individual relates himself as a part or to which he aspires to relate himself psychologically.' As Stafford and Cocanougher (1977) point out, this definition has the advantage of distinguishing between two major categories of reference groups: those to which an individual belongs, and those of which he is not a member but to which he aspires to relate himself in some manner – the latter category being especially important to an understanding of consumer behaviour. Finally, it should be understood that when we talk of reference groups, the term 'group' does not necessarily signify that these bodies are organized groups. They may be loose collectivities, or even broad and ill-defined categories, such as social classes – one individual may also, of course, use another individual for the purpose of comparison.

Reference groups have been the subject of study in a variety of fields within the social sciences – mainstream economics being a notable exception – all of which have found the concept useful. This is one of the strengths of the idea, but is probably also a source of the confusion which sometimes arises. Pollis (1968) has suggested that we ought to distinguish three levels at which reference group analysis takes place. First, the psychological level, where we are primarily concerned with the perception, judgement, motivation, personality, etc. of the individual. Second, the sociological level, where we are dealing with two or more individuals, and are interested in group, institutional and collective influences. Finally, there is the social psychological level, where we are concerned con-

Table 2.1: Membership and Reference Status of the Individual and the Other

Reference status	Membership Status Membership Other	 Non-membership Other
Reference other	1	2
Non-reference other	3	4

Source: Schmitt (1972).

currently with individual and social behaviour of all sorts. These categories cannot be sharply delineated, since they overlap and complement each other, but they do seem worth bearing in mind.

Most of the work on reference groups, it seems true to say, has been concerned with the relationship of the individual to these groups. Schmitt (1972) has broken down this relationship into its basic components in a manner which helps clarify discussion. This breakdown is reproduced in Table 2.1.

Cell 1 denotes a situation in which an individual is a member of the reference other, i.e. his reference group. In such cases reference groups are sometimes referred to as 'primary membership groups', examples of which are the family, peer group and work group. All have a strong influence on the individual.

Cell 2 represents a reference other of which the individual is not a member, but to which he may aspire to belong. His behaviour is certainly influenced by it. Examples of such groups are a sports club, a social club, or, at a more aggregated level, a social class. As the last example suggests, such reference groups need not be clearly delineated in practice, although the image they present may have identifiable characteristics.

The other cells are of no importance for our purposes. In cell 3 the individual is a member of a group, but it exerts no significant influence on him. The case in cell 4 is once again irrelevant. It is therefore those reference groups depicted in cells 1 and 2 which are our prime concern. From the examples we have given, it will be apparent that an individual is likely to be influenced by a number of reference groups, each of which may be important to one or more aspects of his life. It would obviously be helpful if we could further classify these reference groups in a systematic and empirically meaningful manner.

A variety of classifications has been suggested for reference groups. Hyman in his original (1942) study of these groups was interested in determining which were used by individuals when assessing their status in society. He found that individuals were accustomed to thinking in terms of certain 'dimensions of status', including social, intellectual, economic, cultural and other dimensions. Comparisons with others, generally groups with which those interviewed came into regular contact, such as friends, relatives and those at work – and sometimes also other 'reference individuals' i.e. single persons rather than groups – enabled the interviewees to form judgements about their own status. Hyman's work therefore provides us with an example of the use of what are usually referred to as *comparative* reference groups, since the individuals studied were using their reference groups for the purpose of self-evaluation – and also for the evaluation of others.

A further study, by Newcomb (1947), is frequently cited as an example of the other main form of reference group: the *normative* reference group. Newcomb followed the changes in attitudes of the entire student body at Bennington College over a four-year period. The college was physically isolated from the rest of the local community, and the students were fairly homogeneous, coming mainly from urban, economically privileged familes whose social attitudes were conservative. Most students during their four-year stay at the college underwent marked changes in their attitudes on public issues, starting out as conservative at entry (perhaps because of the influence of their parents) but ending as 'senior non-conservative' by the finish of the course. The approved attitude among the older students, it appears, was one of non-conservatism, and with most students using the membership group of the college as a reference group, they generally adopted the norms of the group.

In a much-quoted work, Kelley (1952) formalized the distinction between normative and comparative reference groups, and it has now been widely adopted, even if not everyone accepts it. Even those who accept the validity of the distinction, however, recognize that there may be some overlap. Hyman and Singer (1968) pointed out that the two types of reference group may not always be empirically distinct. Group *norms* may even lay down restrictions on *comparisons* with other groups if, for example, these other groups happen to be socially inferior or superior.

Kelley envisaged the two functions of reference groups as:

> special cases of more general theories about the *sources* and *nature* of standards which, in turn, should ultimately derive from fundamental

> theories of motivation and perception. The normative functions of reference groups may be expected to become part of a general theory of goal-setting and motivation.... The comparison functions of reference groups will be part of a general theory of perception and judgement such as is presently represented by the psychological theories of reference.

Kelley notes that comparison groups are only one of a number of comparison points that may be used within a framework of references. Others might be single individuals (as Hyman discovered in his study of status) or standards set by inanimate objects or units of measurement (such as a ruler for judging a person's height) or impersonal descriptions of desired behaviour (sets of rules, for example).

In the present study we shall be exploring the links between reference groups and motivation, including goal-setting, noted by Kelley. Normative reference groups may be an important means by which goals come to be adopted more widely; and these goals, as we saw earlier, are in turn likely to take account of needs and wants, and notions of equity. The use of comparative reference groups for the purpose of self-evaluation has a bearing on views on status and self-esteem, and is therefore also linked to the meeting of certain needs. Comparison groups are used, too, as we shall see, for the comparison of social rewards. Both types of reference group may therefore be regarded as relevant to our own study, and we should not make too much of the distinction between them, useful as it is for some purposes.

Although much of the discussion about reference groups is based on the normative-comparative distinction, it is worth saying a brief word about a third form of reference group used by Ofshe (1972) since it is likely to be of interest to economists. Ofshe identifies what he calls an 'informational reference' source, which may be an individual as well as a group. He gives as an example an individual who is attempting to solve a problem, and who may receive advice or information from an individual or a group, which he may (or may not) use in order to solve the problem. In the same manner, an individual may be helped to attain a *goal*, so we have a potential link here, too, with motivational variables, as in the case of the other forms of reference group. Ofshe refers to a wide range of empirical work which supports the existence of reference sources.

The availability of information is also important to the use of normative and comparative reference groups. An individual must have certain information about these groups before he can use them at all. He must first be aware of the groups' existence, and he must know something of group standards and norms. Information therefore plays a vital role in enabling the system of social comparisons to function effectively.

The selection of reference groups Can we predict with reasonable certainty which reference groups are likely to be selected by an individual, or a group, in any given circumstances? It would certainly be helpful if we could, since it would enable us to identify the groups on which we ought to concentrate our attention when trying to explain individual or group behaviour. One difficulty is that an individual may use a number of reference groups, and it is not easy to assess their relative importance. Moreover, the same group may even serve both the comparative and normative functions. Using the comparative-normative approach to reference group functions does, however, at least give us some pointers to the factors most likely to influence reference group choice.

The self-evaluation function of reference groups suggests that anyone wishing to select a group for this purpose would only select one which was *relevant* (Turner, 1955). There would be no point in choosing a group which was so dissimilar from an individual that he could draw no meaningful conclusions from comparisons with it. Associated with this requirement of relevance is the view that there is likely to be a *similarity* between an individual and a selected reference group. Festinger (1954), although not employing the concept of reference group, concluded from a review of the evidence that when comparing their abilities and opinions with those of others, individuals would tend to choose others whose abilities and opinions were reasonably close to their own. When groups were not available to permit such close comparisons, evaluations tended to be unstable.

Hyman (1942) in his study of status also concluded:

The rare occurrence of the total population as a reference group and the great frequency of more intimate reference groups are characteristic of the process of judging status. Individuals operate for the most part in small groups within the total society, and the total population may have little relevance for them.

Improvements in mass communication and the breakdown in social barriers may have made broader comparisons more meaningful today, but there is no doubt that the gist of what Hyman and Festinger had to say on the subject remains valid.

What we have said about selection so far mainly concerns comparative reference groups, but in selecting normative reference groups *relevance* also seems an important consideration. A further factor frequently mentioned, however, is *saliency*, which affects not just the choice of reference groups, but the relative importance attached to each. Stafford and Cocanougher (1977) state that:

The available theoretical and empirical work on salience indicates an individual may make decisions or resolve conflict in the direction of the references that are most prominent or salient for him at a particular point in time. This suggests that situational factors, such as psychological proximity or time sequency, may be of substantial importance in explaining the differential effects of various effects on an individual's behaviour.

Stafford and Cocanougher quote a number of examples of saliency. Charters and Newcomb (1952) found that a religious group had very little influence on attitudes unconnected with religion. Schachter (1960) demonstrated that the power of a group to influence its members was a function of the relevance of the group to the activity under consideration. Witt (1969), in a work on consumer behaviour, made a number of suggestions which seem especially relevant to our own study. First, he suggested that the selection of a reference group might be influenced by the perceived importance of the group to a particular goal of the individual. Second, the more important the activity was to the individual, the likelier it was that a wider range of references would be considered. Finally, the individual might compare his own hierarchy of needs with those of potential references, and base his selection on the groups whose hierarchies appeared to coincide most closely with his own.

Hartley (1960, 1968), in another study of a college community, found that a reference group was likely to be chosen if it was seen to be fulfilling personal needs, and if there was congruity between the individual's personal values and norms and those perceived to be held by the group. In some instances, it seems, individuals are looking for confirmation of their norms, rather than searching for new ones. Those desiring something radically different may well be a minority. College students may not, of course, be wholly representative of the population at large, but the findings seem consistent with the ones we have noted above, and the emphasis placed once more on the needs of individuals gives some grounds for thinking that the findings are not atypical.

The degree of influence exercised by reference groups An individual is not influenced to the same extent by all his reference groups, and even two people sharing the same reference group may be influenced differently. Why should this be so? Our discussion above of the reasons for selecting particular reference groups offers a partial explanation. The degree of relevance and saliency in the meeting of needs and goals will have a bearing not just on the choice of group, but also on the extent to which those groups selected exert an influence. A number of writers have distinguished other ways in which groups and individuals may make their influence felt. These ways of bringing influence to bear apply not only to reference groups, but they are certainly relevant to them.

French and Raven (1968), in a study of the bases of power, identified five bases which seemed especially common and important – but which were not claimed to constitute an exhaustive list – with the ability to influence and bring about psychological changes in a person, including changes in needs, goals, attitudes, opinions, etc. We look at each of these briefly.

REWARD POWER, as the term suggests, is based on the ability of a social agent (O) – which may be a person as well as a group – to reward a person (P). The strength of this power is said to increase with the *magnitude* of the rewards which P perceives that O can mediate for him. It is dependent also upon the *probability* that O can mediate the reward, as perceived by P. A common example of reward power, given by French and Raven, is the addition of a piece work rate in a factory as an incentive to increase production. The fulfilment of the promise of reward for improved performance will tend to enhance reward power by increasing the probability attached to future promises.

COERCIVE POWER is similar to reward power in that O once again is in a position to affect P, but this time there is a threat of punishment rather than the prospect of reward. There is an expectation on the part of P that he will be punished by O if he fails to submit to the attempt to influence him. The ability to dismiss a worker if his output falls below a set level could be taken as an example of coercive power. If the probability of receiving punishment when P did not conform were low, coercive power might be ineffective.

LEGITIMATE POWER is defined as the power stemming from values held by P which dictate that O has a legitimate right to influence P, and that P has an obligation to accept the influence. The notion of legitimacy entails a code or standard which is accepted by P, thereby enabling O to exert power over him. In some cultures age, caste or intelligence are a source of legitimate power. Holders of certain offices may also be accorded such power, for example elected representatives, trade union leaders (sometimes appointed rather than elected) or religious appointees.

REFERENT POWER is probably the most obviously applicable of the five to reference groups. It arises when P identifies with O, is attracted to O and wishes to be closely associated with O. If not already associated with O, there will be a desire to form an association. The source of the attraction may be the reference group's norms.

EXPERT POWER is based on P's perception of O's expertise, in relation to his own knowledge, or perhaps in relation to some absolute standard of measurement. The expertise must, of course, be one which is valued by P.

Stafford and Cocanougher (1977) draw attention to yet another two possible sources of reference group influence. First, group cohesion. Generally speaking, the greater the cohesiveness of a group, the greater will tend to be the ability of the group to exert an influence over its members. While the balance of the empirical evidence available appears to support this contention, not all the findings are supportive. Finally, there is the influence of group leadership. A number of empirical studies, many of them in the marketing field, have shown that group leadership helps explain the influence of groups on their members. The group leader is usually the member who is best able to initiate and maintain the expectations and interaction within the group. The ability of the leader to fulfil his functions effectively will, of course, in turn be determined in part by the organizational structure of the group.

Changes in reference groups The factors determining the selection of reference groups and the influence they wield suggest a reasonable degree of stability in reference group choice. The use of a multiplicity of reference groups also makes it less likely that the dropping of one or the addition of another will lead to abrupt changes in personal behaviour – one can, however, think of examples in one's own experience of people whose behaviour has changed abruptly. The choice of reference groups will nevertheless alter over time. One of the principal causes of changing reference groups will be the ageing process. We can think of it in terms of a lifecycle – a term about which we shall have a good deal more to say later in our study. In the early stages of life, family and friends are likely to be the dominant influence. Growing older, one becomes more aware of others outside these restricted circles. Popular music and clothes may assume growing importance, and therefore new reference groups among one's peers are likely to be adopted.

Leaving home for college may be another important step, as we saw earlier, in the selection of new reference groups. Starting work will be yet another. The changing of jobs, promotion and a rising standard of living are also likely to have reference group repercussions. Later in life, retirement will mark yet another major stage.

Closely linked with this lifecycle will be changing personal needs and wants. As people mature, they tend to develop new interests, and to seek out others with similar interests. With the changes in needs and wants new goals will also be adopted, and perhaps old ones modified. The use of reference groups, therefore, will certainly be a dynamic process, although in the aggregate it need not be an unstable one. It is nevertheless possible to envisage major changes in reference groups over time, even quite short spaces of time, especially in an era of mass communication. Unfortunately, there appears to be little longitudinal evidence bearing on such changes.

2.6.2 Reference groups and relative deprivation

The concept of relative deprivation, which we looked at earlier, was based upon a comparison of a person, or group, with other persons, or groups, to whom the former related themselves. Using our new terminology, an individual or group may compare themselves with a reference group and experience feelings of relative deprivation. The concept of relative deprivation dovetails closely with that of reference groups. One of the best examples of the complementary nature of this relationship is still the study of *The American Soldier* by Stouffer *et al.* (1949) in which the term 'relative deprivation' was first used. This study produced a number of findings which could not be explained in terms of conventional analysis. It was found, for example, that resentment about induction into the armed forces was highest among older men, and among those who were married. Contrary to what one might have expected, those enjoying the status of high school and college graduates were also less likely to be optimistic about their promotion in the army than non-graduates.

In explaining the first of these findings, the authors of the study suggested that a married man, when comparing himself with his unmarried associates in the army, could feel that induction required greater sacrifices from him. Comparisons appeared to be made not just with immediate associates, however: married soldiers also compared themselves with married civilian friends. Comparisons with both these selected reference groups engendered feelings of relative deprivation.

The explanation of the second finding was rather different, but the basic cause was the same. The better educated, it was suggested, had greater expectations and higher levels of aspirations then less well-educated colleagues. The better educated therefore had more to lose if they failed to achieve promotion, and with it, status. Hence the sense of frustration tended to be correspondingly greater. Feelings of relative deprivation, in other words, were higher.

Merton and Rossi (1968) carefully pulled together the various strands of the argument relating to relative deprivation which were used at different stages of *The American Soldier*, but not set out formally in the study. They found that the sentiments and attitudes of the soldiers – their attitudes toward induction, for example, or their appraisals of the chances of promotion – were typically treated as dependent variables. The findings that these attitudes differed among soldiers of varying status – with the older, married men exhibiting more resentment, and the better educated being less optimistic – pointed to the use of status attributes as the independent variables. Relative deprivation was then treated in effect as an intervening variable, providing an essential link between the dependent and independent variables which helped explain changes in the former.

Another writer who has successfully woven together reference groups and relative deprivation in explaining personal behaviour is Runciman (1966). In his extensive study of social and economic inequalities in twentieth-century England, the choice of reference groups proved to be indispensable in helping explain differences in feelings of relative deprivation among groups in society. Relative deprivation among manual workers, for example, was found to be low, despite their relatively low incomes. Non-manual workers on low rates of pay (in some cases as low as manual workers), on the other hand, experienced a high level of relative deprivation. The explanation, Runciman maintained, was that in comparing their income levels with that of others, manual workers mainly selected other, poorly paid, manual workers as their reference groups, and therefore did not feel deprived. In the case of low paid non-manual workers, however, their reference groups were not restricted to others with low pay: they tended to compare themselves with other non-manual, and generally better-paid, groups. In consequence, dissatisfaction among low-paid non-manual workers was more pronounced.

2.6.3 Social comparison processes

Until now our analysis of social comparisons has been based mainly on the use of reference groups. The early writers on reference groups drew inspiration from studies of social comparisons carried out in the early years of this century and the latter part of the last century. As frequently happens, these early works in turn led to the development of yet another avenue of fruitful investigation, the beginnings of which were marked by the publication of Festinger's (1954) study of social comparison processes. This work constituted a new departure, in so far as it attempted to set out a rigorous and fully-developed theory of self-evaluation, resting on the enunciation of a number of hypotheses which could be subjected to empirical study.

Festinger and other writers on social comparison processes have not made use of the reference group concept, but their work necessarily entails group comparisons, especially by individuals seeking information from groups, or wishing to evaluate themselves in relation to group members. The work on social comparison processes should therefore be looked at in conjunction with the study of reference groups.

One of the central tenets of Festinger's theory concerns the choice of others for the purpose of comparison. His Hypothesis III states: 'The tendency to compare oneself with some other specific person decreases as the difference between his opinion or ability and one's own increases.' Corollary IIIA further stipulates that, 'Given a range of possible persons for comparison, someone close to one's own ability or opinion will be chosen for comparison.' It is these claims in respect of the choice of comparison others which has attracted most attention in Festinger's work.

The inclusion in Corollary IIIA of references to ability and opinion are an indication of two of the principal reasons why Festinger thought people were in the habit of making comparisons. In attempting to evaluate one's ability, there would be little point, Festinger argued, in making discrepant comparisons, since that would provide only limited information. These comparisons would only tell a person that his abilities differed greatly from that of some others (perhaps minorities, since the best and worst will be only small proportions of the total in any normal distribution of abilities). Evaluation based on similar abilities gave a person a better guide to the potential for action on his part.

One can detect possible flaws in such an argument, and later writers were to point them out. Latané (1966), for example, suggested that a novice chess player might well want to compare his ability with the Grand Masters of the game, in order to see just what could be achieved, and how far short he fell of the best. It is doubtless a matter of personal disposition, and it is not perhaps surprising that research findings on this matter have differed.

With regard to the evaluation of one's opinions, Gordon (1966) tested the hypothesis that those who were uncertain of the correctness of their opinons would choose to compare themselves with those holding similar opinions, and found this in fact to be the case. Festinger believed that where difference of opinion did occur, the view of the person making the comparison would tend to be unstable and imprecise. There may therefore be pressures bringing together people of roughly similar viewpoints, and tending to impose some sort of consensus on them.

Although similar in many ways, the evaluation processes in respect of abilities were held to differ in certain important respects from those concerning opinions. Festinger (1954) maintained, first, that 'there is a unidirectional drive upward in the case of abilities which is largely absent in opinions'. That is, an individual always tends to compare himself with someone of greater ability when making comparisons, whereas no such yardstick is available to apply to opinions. Second, while individuals may change their opinions at will, improvements in ability may be limited by the psychological characteristics of the individual.

Wherever possible, Festinger cited empirical evidence in support of his hypotheses. It has been pointed out, however, that not all of this evidence is wholly unambiguous, and in some instances is open to alternative interpretations. Festinger's theories nevertheless retain a pivotal position in many studies concerned with self-evaluation, and he continues to inspire work in this field. A useful review of this work can be found in Suls and Miller (1977). For our purposes, Festinger's work and that deriving from it is important in providing further backing for the importance of social comparisons in determining personal behaviour.

2.6.4. Conclusions

It is hoped that enough has been said to demonstrate that there is already in being a formidable body of theory and empirical evidence to indicate that social comparisons play a central part in people's lives. We know this too from our own personal experience. Festinger's (1954) first hypothesis attempted to explain this phenomenon in terms of a human *drive*: 'Hypothesis I. There exists, in the human organism, a drive to evaluate his opinions and his abilities.' This, however, could only be part of the story. Festinger's concern was primarily with personal opinions and abilities, but social comparisons extend well beyond these. Moreover, as early writers pointed out, drives may themselves originate in needs.

There are certainly strong grounds for thinking that social comparisons are inherent in the meeting of many needs. A need for esteem, for example, might be satisfied in part by a comparison of oneself – perhaps one's attainments – with absolute standards, such as those provided by measures of distance, height, time, etc., but comparisons would be incomplete and inadequate without corresponding interpersonal comparisons. An athlete might be pleased with his improving performances, measured against the absolute standards available, but he would almost certainly also wish to know how these performances compared with the attainments of others – was he a world champion, simply an 'also-ran', or something in between? The acquiring of possessions is another long-standing source of esteem. Once again, mere acquisition may be a source of self-satisfaction, but comparison with others is necessary to give any sort of balanced perspective, and probably essential too if the self-esteem is to be given full validation.

Self-actualization, to the extent that it requires participation in cultural and artistic activities, education, work and numerous other human engagements, also generally implies a degree of social intercourse, with the prospect once more that social comparisons will be made. The need for belongingness (love and affection, or whatever other terms might be used) also ensures the communal life which makes it possible to meet the other needs of the sorts to which we have referred. Those who wish to live in isolation from their fellows are the exception, not the rule. By living together we make it possible to meet a whole range of needs (lower-order – the provision of food, heating and shelter, for example – as well as higher-order) and in so doing we also provide the social environment in which interpersonal comparisons are a fact of life.

Judgements about equity may likewise be made according to absolute standards, or laid-down rules, but the evidence once more is that social comparisons enter the process by which personal judgements are made. They are an indispensable part of the analysis of equity in exchange relationships, and fundamental to the advances made by writers such as Rawls in the field of distributive justice. Social comparisons are also inherent in the notion of relative deprivation, to which we shall have recourse in our discussion of wage behaviour. Furthermore, goals, which as we have seen are likely to take account of needs and considerations of equity, will frequently be set in relation to reference others, or reference groups. Likewise, expectations are not formed in a social vacuum. Those with whom we rub shoulders frequently in our daily lives inevitably influence our goals and expectations.

Social comparisons, we may conclude, are essential to an adequate explanation of social behaviour, and provide a common link between all the social sciences. Only in the case of economics, it seems, has there been a failure to incorporate this phenomenon in the main body of theory – a notable exception is the work of Frank (1985) who has shown how the quest for status by individuals entails a variety of social comparisons which have important economic consequences, e.g. for wage behaviour, to which we turn in a later section. We have already given some indication of the reasons for economists' neglect of social comparisons. We shall pursue the matter further in the following section on consumer behaviour, where we shall be able to trace the failure to its source.

3 Consumer Behaviour

Having examined what we consider to be a number of key intervening variables, we now go on to reassess conventional economic theory in the light of our conclusions about personal motivation. We shall be looking at both micro- and macroeconomic theory, although our approach tends to suggest that a marked distinction between the two is inappropriate, since the same motivating forces are at work throughout. The basis of our analysis will be individual needs and wants, and the means of satisfying them. Social comparisons will also have a very important role to play. Initially, it will not be necessary to question the validity of the utility-maximizing assumption underlying the neo-classical theory of consumer behaviour, since there is always a case for examining the implications of the assumptions at the extremes of any range of options, but we shall return at a later stage to the question of consumers' goals. The only intervening variable considered in section 2 which we omit from our discussion of consumer behaviour is equity. Its importance will become more apparent in the section on wage behaviour.

In the conventional theory of consumer behaviour, the consumer aims, as we have seen, to maximize the utility gained from the consumption of goods. We may represent his goal as being to maximize

$$U = u(x_1, x_2, \ldots\ldots, x_n) \qquad (3.1)$$

subject to the constraint that

$$\sum_{i=1}^{n} p_i x_i \leq M \qquad x_i \geq O$$

where, U represents the total utility gained from the consumption of goods, x is a vector of the goods consumed, p the corresponding vector of the prices of the goods, and M the consumer's budget.

We have already touched on a number of the assumptions underlying this view of the consumer's goal. The consumer is assumed to behave 'rationally' with regard to his clearly defined set of preferences for different goods, i.e. he is assumed to vary his expenditure between goods in such a way as to yield the maximum total utility from his income. The reason for assuming 'rationality' and maximization is, of course, that it greatly simplifies the analysis of consumer behaviour. A heavy price has to be paid, however, for this simplification. The consumer, far from having freedom of choice, is, as we saw earlier, constrained to exercise his choice in a specific manner. He is free only to choose one consistent course of action. There is no room for impulse buying, laziness, habit, sheer stupidity or any of the other traits which make human beings only human. The consumer, in effect, is no more than a 'desiccated calculating machine' – a phrase once used by one British politician in speaking of another (an economist by training, it so happened) but very apt in the present context, it seems.

If it had proved possible to devise a suitable cardinal measure of utility, things might have turned out very differently. Despite the conviction of many economists over the years, however, that such a measure was feasible, none has yet proved acceptable. The search for alternatives led, as we know, to the development of indifference curve analysis, culminating in the work of Hicks and Allen (1934); later expanded in Hicks (1939, 1946). While representing an advance in certain respects, in that it relied only on an ordinal measure of consumer satisfaction rather than a cardinal one, it probably also served to reinforce a trend which was already apparent at that time: the tendency for economists to become more concerned with the analysis of the common yardstick of utility *per se*, rather than with the basic foundations upon which utility theory itself rested, namely personal needs and wants. Concentrating analysis on the common denominator of utility is, however, of limited value in itself. As Georgescu-Roegen (1954) pointed out, 'it conceals the real problem'. If we wish to improve our understanding of consumer behaviour, we must get down to the basics of personal needs and wants. Georgescu-Roegen (1954) again put the point very well: 'The reality that determines the individual's behaviour is not formed by utility, or ophelimity, or any other single element, but by his wants, or his needs.'

Attributing consumer expenditure decisions to the utility or satisfaction gained does not help us understand *why* consumers' preferences for different goods yield different utilities, nor does it help us understand *why* these preferences may change over time, causing the consumer to alter his pattern of spending. The standard neo-classical analysis is forced to fall back on the limp catch-all explanation of changes in 'tastes' when changes in expenditure cannot be explained either by income or price effects. The same criticisms can be applied to the revealed preference approach, which, when stripped down to its essentials, may help explain what has happened, but is of only limited value in trying to explain *why* it has happened. It may be argued, of course, that all that matters is the predictive ability of a theory (Friedman, 1953). Such an argument might be tenable if standard theory did in practice enable consistently accurate predictions of consumer demand to be made, but few would deny that there is generally plenty of scope for improvement in accuracy, and frequent instances where predictions are woefully wrong. Further improvement in the accuracy of consumer-demand predictions would come from a better understanding of the basic forces at work.

The inability of the present theoretical structures to offer more than a partial analysis of consumer behaviour is weakness enough in itself, but using our earlier examination of intervening variables we will show that the neo-classical analysis is seriously flawed. The unwillingness to inquire into the nature of the foundations upon which utility and indifference analysis rest – namely, needs and wants – has resulted in economists being gravely misled about the true nature of consumer preferences and the way in which they are formed.

A number of economists, such as Lancaster and Becker, have in recent years attempted to make good some of the deficiencies in the conventional analysis of consumer behaviour. Much of this valuable work, however, has been grafted on to the unsatisfactory structure of the basic consumer model, and its contribution is thereby limited. A good deal of this work could be incorporated to good effect in the needs-based approach which we adopt in the present study. We turn now to look at some of the principal implications of intervening variables for the analysis of consumer behaviour.

3.1 RECASTING THE UTILITY FUNCTION

Our discussion of intervening variables in section 2 has important implications for the specification of the utility function (we draw heavily here on Baxter, 1987). The standard utility function, as we represented it in equation (3.1), relates utility gained to the quantities of commodities consumed. In making his choice between goods, the individual is assumed to do so independently of the rest of society. He makes his decisions effectively in a vacuum, with no account taken of the possible influence of other consumers on his spending decisions. Our analysis in section 2 indicates that this is a wholly unrealistic assumption, totally at odds with the way people behave in practice.

Looking first at needs and wants, we have seen that it is in satisfying wants that the consumer derives utility, or satisfaction. Yet many needs and wants, such as those for love and belonging, and for esteem, and in many instances, also, for self-actualization, imply a measure of social intercourse. Indeed the process of satisfying most needs and wants must surely be viewed within a social context, certainly so far as the great majority of people are concerned. We saw, too, in section 2 that social comparisons are a central feature of most people's lives and clearly influence personal behaviour. In allocating expenditure between goods, we would therefore expect a consumer to be influenced by what others were buying. The influence of fashion must be one of the clearest demonstrations of the way in which social comparisons have a bearing on spending decisions.

Taking expenditure on clothing as an example, a particular

style of new dress may yield a higher utility than previous purchases of dresses because it is in high fashion, and confers on the wearer a certain degree of prestige and status. Conversely, if in order to purchase the new dress the consumer had to forgo the purchase of a replacement fur hat, there might be little or no loss of utility if animal rights protesters had successfully persuaded the public that the wearing of fur hats was no longer desirable or fashionable. We have here an example of how the purchases of others may influence a consumer's own purchases, and the utility he derives from them. Duesenberry (1949), Boulding (1972), Leibenstein[1] (1976), Thurow (1983) and other economists have noted this important feature of consumer behaviour, yet it continues to be ignored in the standard consumer model. There is nevertheless considerable evidence, as we shall see, that consumer preferences are indeed *interdependent*. It therefore follows that the utility which a person derives from spending his income is a function not just of his absolute income but also of his *relative* income, since it is the latter which places a limit on the extent to which he is able to enjoy the same purchases as those with whom he compares himself.

Relative income is also relevant in another important respect. In comparing the gains and losses of utility from trading the purchase of one commodity against the loss of another, given a fixed income constraint, the traditional textbook examples generally employ simple, inexpensive goods. If we take bread and potatoes as examples of two relatively cheap staple products, these commodities yield pleasant but different tastes, they can be eaten in a variety of forms and they also quell the pangs of hunger. They therefore satisfy a variety of human needs. Since they are relatively cheap commodities, they can be purchased by virtually all consumers, who therefore have the choice of how much of each to buy within their fixed budgets.

Not all goods, however, are quite so cheap. Even if we stick to the basic essentials of food and clothing, choice is not so unrestricted as the standard consumer model implies. Better quality foodstuffs, such as the leaner cuts of meat, are beyond the purses of many people, as are quality clothes. Some poorer familes may not even have the option of meat every day. When we progress to the still more expensive items of consumption, such as yachts and foreign holidays, the proportion of the population able to afford such items diminishes even further. In effect, the budget constraint imposed by a person's absolute income limits not only the *quantities* which may be consumed of the different commodities, it also limits the *choice* of commodities available, and therefore the utility which may be attained.

Choice is especially restricted for those on low incomes, since they must first purchase the basic essentials of life, for which utility will be greatest. If they can only afford such items, they will have no uncommitted, or discretionary, income. Marginal changes in income become very important in such circumstances, since the purchases made with any discretionary income are also likely to yield a high utility – there are, of course, many examples of people in straitened circumstances spending apparently unwisely, as on drink, but quite what the utility considerations are in these circumstances is not entirely clear. It is understandable, therefore, if individuals are very conscious of, and attach considerable importance to, *differences* in absolute incomes. This will be especially so in the case of any difference between a person and those with whom he habitually compares himself, i.e. his reference group(s). Even a modest increase in a reference group's income relative to that of the person may enable those in the reference group to consider consuming many goods not available to the person. The utility which the person is obliged to forgo might then be quite disproportionate to the difference in income.

If *all* incomes increased in the same proportion at the same time, consumer choice might, of course, be widened without any changes in *relative* incomes. This would be the case where the goods in question, although expensive to produce, were in elastic supply, so that consumers could increase their consumption without affecting price greatly, if at all. Even if real incomes increase over time, however, relative money incomes still matter to the consumer, because a person on a given income will still have available a wider choice of goods than someone on a lower income, and therefore a greater opportunity to purchase goods yielding a high utility in relation to expenditure.

The importance of relative income to the consumer can be demonstrated still more forcefully by reference to what Hirsch (1977) has called 'positional goods', i.e. goods which 'are either (1) scarce in some absolute or socially imposed sense or (2) subject to congestion or crowding through more intensive use.' One obvious example is Old Masters, works of art whose supply cannot be increased (not in the original form at least) because the artists are dead. In many countries, land is also scarce in relation to the size of the population, so that not all can aspire to a house with a garden. Access to many desirable leisure facilities, such as golf clubs, or country clubs, may also be restricted to those on relatively high incomes. In all these cases, increases in absolute incomes would not make the goods much more accessible to the general public, since their price would rise as absolute incomes increased. It is then the *relative* incomes which determine which consumers are fortunate enough to indulge their preferences. Once again, the potential gains in utility to a consumer from having even a slight increase in absolute income, and moving up the income hierarchy, might be quite disproportionate to the amount of the increase in income.

We can carry our argument forward yet another stage. Although we have brought in some of the social influences bearing on consumer behaviour, these social influences are even more pervasive than we have so far allowed. We have said nothing about the influence of government, both central and local. In all countries, governments provide services centrally, and in some countries these services are a substitute, in part or in whole, for the expenditure of individual consumers. Education is one of the most obvious examples. In the more advanced industrial countries, basic education is provided without charge (other than through the tax system) and consumers may make use of it or provide for private education for their children from their own means. Health and social services are also provided on the same basis in many countries. Those on low incomes may also have their incomes supplemented in many ways, through direct receipt of goods, such as foodstuffs, or by means of financial benefits to them.

A great many people – the majority in some countries – are net beneficiaries of government expenditure, after allowing for their contributions to taxation. The amount of government expenditure, and changes in it, and also in the way it is allocated, must therefore have an important influence on the manner in which consumers decide to allocate their disposable incomes. Government expenditure, in so far as it affects consumers' spending decisions, and the utility derived therefrom, ought therefore to feature in a consumer's utility function, in addition to the interpersonal influences on consumption noted earlier.

Despite the redistribution of income which takes place through the tax and benefits systems, sizeable income disparities remain in most countries. These disparities determine not just the direct choice of goods available to the consumer, they also affect the availability of an associated range of goods and services. Income has an important bearing, for example, on the house one can afford, and therefore the neighbourhood in which one lives, which is in turn often linked to the quality of local schools, health and social service provision, recreational facilities available, and so forth. Relative income, in other words, is important in determining people's whole lifestyles, and quality of life, and we can hardly be surprised that they attribute so much importance, not only to their own place in the income hierarchy, but also to that of others, especially those with whom they compare themselves.

For the reasons outlined above, relative incomes are of the greatest importance to consumers, and since for most people pay accounts for the bulk of their income, pay comparisons will be among the most important social comparisons made by the individual. We saw in our discussion of social comparisons in section 2.6 that some writers have suggested that the concept of reference groups is appropriate to such comparisons, while others have stressed the importance of comparisons without formalizing the process in terms of these groups. We believe that the use of reference groups is indeed wholly appropriate in the contexts of both consumer spending and income and pay comparisons, and we shall be examining the empirical evidence relating to them in subsequent sections. Using the concept of reference groups, we are now in a position to set out below what we consider to be a more accurate specification of the utility function. It is as follows:

$$U_i = u\,(W_i,\ W_i/\overline{W}_{r_1},\ W_i/\overline{W}_{r_2}, \ldots\ W_i/\overline{W}_{r_n},\ G_c,\ P) \qquad (3.2)$$

where, U_i is the total utility obtained from consumption by individual i; W_i is the money wage of i, representing the income at the disposal of the individual, and therefore the budget constraint imposed on his consumption of commodities; $W_i/\overline{W}_{r_1}$ represents the money wage of i relative to the average wage of individuals in reference group r_1, denoted by W_{r_1} (similarly for reference groups r_2 to r_n, should there be groups other than r_1); G_c is that portion of government expenditure having an influence on the utility derived by i from his own consumption; P is the general level of prices, which affects the real purchasing power of wages.

In equation (3.2), which is expressed in the form of an indirect utility function, it is the relative wage variables and the government expenditure variable which catch the important effects on consumer utility omitted from the standard treatment. We are not in any way suggesting here that there are no other relevant variables – Morgan (1978) for example, has suggested others, including uncertainty and ignorance of facts – but we are trying to fill one glaring gap. Note, finally, that we have not addressed the question of whether it would be possible to add the utility functions of individuals, as expressed in equation (3.2), to obtain an equation for a group of people. To the extent, however, that individuals act as a coherent group in matters of consumption and pay, it would not seem unreasonable to express a group function in the same form as equation (3.2), with W_i becoming the wage rate of the group.

One must wonder at the failure of the standard utility function to take account of such fundamental influences as social comparisons and the social nature of needs and wants. The answer, as we suggested earlier, seems to be that by concentrating on the common denominator of utility it was hoped to escape from all the problems associated with the subjective, psychological underpinnings of utility. In so doing, however, it is assumed that utility is acquired in a very specific manner, which does not allow for any influences arising from consumption of others in society. The standard treatment of utility is not, therefore, value-free. It is based on a view of the consumer which is no more than a special case, and is so unrepresentative of the actual circumstances in which consumers live and take decisions as to be of very limited value. Yet the special case is presented as the general case. In the theory of the firm, perfect competition is at least represented as one extreme among a number of possible market structures. No such alternatives are offered in the theory of the consumer.

The next obvious question is, what implications, if any, does our recasting of the utility function have for the goals of consumers, including utility-maximizing behaviour? We shall be re-examining this question in the following section, but if for the moment we assume utility-maximization to be the consumer's goal, then it seems that consumer preferences could be affected in a number of ways. Changing needs, the satisfaction of existing needs and wants and the development of new ones could all be expected to alter consumer preferences and the utility derived from consumption of the goods affected. Among the most fundamental influences on the pattern of consumer spending have been rising living standards and the growing leisure time available. Together these make it possible for many people to satisfy a range of existing wants and to develop new ones which permit a greater degree of 'self-actualization'.

Changes in reference groups may also greatly affect consumer preferences. Reference group choice may tend on the whole to be reasonably stable, but it does alter over time, and it may even be subject to short-term change. One possible reason for an alteration in reference groups would be a change in a person's relative income; such a change might also, of course, affect wants *directly*. The alteration in reference groups might not take place immediately, but if the new position in the income hierarchy were to evolve, then a change in reference groups could eventually follow. This, in effect, was the argument deployed by Duesenberry (1949). Although he did not use the term 'reference groups', social comparisons were central to his arguments explaining both the long-term stability of the consumption function and the tendency for current consumption to be influenced by the highest level of income previously attained. Our analysis suggests that his hypotheses were soundly based, and we shall have more to say on this matter later.

With a given set of preferences at any point in time, the income constraint will still operate in determining the maximum utility attainable by the consumer; but the conventional analysis does not bring out the dynamic nature of the forces at work, nor the rapidity with which these may change. Consumer preferences may well be in a state of continuous flux – not necessarily all preferences, but some at least – as indeed is the income of many people. It follows that the so-called 'changes in tastes', far from being relegated to an anonymous supporting role, ought to be centre stage in the analysis of consumer behaviour.

3.2 CONSUMER GOALS

In section 2.4.3 we examined Simon's reasons for believing that the assumption of maximizing behaviour on the part of consumers and entrepreneurs was untenable. One of the principal reasons he advanced was man's bounded rationality, or limited ability to grapple with the complex problems of the real world. He also noted that the knowledge and information required in order to make rational decisions was often simply not available to the consumer. Where decisions related to the future, the uncertainty was also often such that only someone with perfect foresight could hope always to make the right decision. Simon's answer was to suggest that, faced by the need to take complex decisions, economic agents engaged in satisficing, i.e. they settled for a course of action that was satisfactory, or at least acceptable. This view of consumers and businessmen seems much more in keeping with the social and psychological traits of human beings we outlined in section 2 than the traditional representation of economic man, for which, as Simon (1979) points out, no empirical evidence has ever been produced. It is therefore a view of man to which we are happy to adhere.

Abandoning utility-maximizing man immediately confronts us, of course, with the dilemma that satisficing behaviour may not enable us to predict with any certainty how a consumer will behave in any given situation. That does not mean that we are adrift and rudderless, however, since satisificing behaviour is entirely consistent with motivated behaviour, and indeed is likely to be closely associated with it. Can we, therefore, drawing on our discussion of intervening variables in section 2, be any more precise in predicting the likely nature of consumer behaviour, and the goals which will influence it?

We saw in section 2 that one of the principal forces motivating human beings was the desire to satisfy needs, and their associated wants. This will therefore be one of the principal goals of the consumer. Acting within the usual budget constraint, he will direct his expenditure towards those goods to which he attaches highest priority (obtains highest utility) in the satisfaction of his needs. His first priority will be the satisfaction of the basic essentials for survival, in particular those for food and drink, followed by clothing and shelter. Only when these have been satisfied (we are talking now of needs, rather than wants) is the consumer likely to turn his attention to the so-called higher-order goods. Here any idea of a hierarchy common to all consumers breaks down – given our present state of knowledge, at least. Even this sketchy idea of hierarchy is sufficient, however, to indicate that, as consumer incomes increase, lower-order needs are likely to absorb a decreasing proportion of income, since they are by their nature largely fixed in quantity. Even if the associated wants exceed needs, the ability to absorb food, in particular, is limited.

The relevance of our approach is further strengthened when we recall that, in the standard neo-classical consumer theory, 'the consumer' is for the most part a disembodied entity without age, sex or family status, and the effects of changes in these variables are therefore lumped together in the convenient catch-all of changes in 'tastes'. Age only enters the standard analysis in so far as it is essential to know the consumer's lifespan, in order that consumption may be spread more evenly over the life remaining. Sex does not enter the standard model at all. The consumer is either asexual or unisexual. 'Household' behaviour is usually represented by a single consumer who takes decisions on behalf of the family, and the possibility of changes in the number of persons in the household is generally ignored. Even the so-called lifecycle hypothesis, as presented by Modigliani and Brumberg, does not allow for the presence of children, as Fisher (1956) and Tobin (1967) have noted.

The introduction of needs as an explicit basis for motivated behaviour sheds a much fuller light on consumer decision-taking. We can predict with a high degree of certainty that, since the needs of children differ greatly from those of adults, their consumption of many goods, such as foodstuffs, will also differ, both in quantity and type, according to the number of persons in a household, their ages and their sexes. Even for single adults, a needs-based approach enables us to predict that consumer demand for certain types of product – sports equipment, for example – will tend to fall as consumers become advanced in years (even if personal incomes and the prices of products remain unchanged). We must, in sum, take account of physiological and psychological differences between consumers if we are to explain fully the pattern of consumer spending and changes in that pattern.

The desire to satisfy needs, and the associated wants, within a given budget constraint, implies that our consumer will still remain sensitive to changes in prices and income. Our approach is therefore quite consistent with a downward-sloping demand curve for a product, and indeed with much conventional consumer analysis. The essential difference, however, is that we no longer assume that the consumer always acts in a wholly utility-maximizing manner (he might not, for example, have all the necessary information to enable him to do so) nor that the utility-maximizing goal is *always* achieved. In conventional theory, goal-*setting* and goal-*attainment* are one and the same, since there is no room for failure; but in the real world, 100 per cent success is far from being assured – a point also heavily stressed by Earl (1987). We would therefore expect consumers to be repeatedly reassessing their purchasing behaviour in the light of their success, or otherwise, in meeting their needs-satisfaction goals.

Our discussion of intervening variables also indicates that we can expect consumer decisions to be influenced by social comparisons. Needs and wants are in some measure influenced by environmental factors, including the influence exerted by reference groups. The goals adopted by consumers will, therefore, in turn, reflect these influences. If we take, once again, the obvious example of clothing, purchases by those in a consumer's reference group of a particular article may make that article fashionable and desirable. Purchase of the article will therefore become a goal in the eyes of that person. If there are many such articles, then we are talking, in effect, of the consumer pursuing a desired lifestyle – the keeping-up-with-the-Joneses syndrome.

We can also predict with some certainty the nature of the reference groups consumers will adopt. Discussion in section 2.6 suggests, first, that they will be *relevant* to the consumer's buying decisions. A person totally uninterested in sporting activities, for example, would be unlikely to choose sportsmen, or women, as a reference group. *Similarity* is likely to be a further consideration. There would be little point in a consumer using persons in a much higher income bracket as a reference group, certainly not for items of clothing, say, which were very costly to buy. *Saliency* appears to be yet another requirement of consumer reference groups, determining not just the choice of a reference group but the relative importance attached to it. Proximity of time and place will be considerations in this context.

In most of the remainder of section 3 we shall be considering the empirical evidence available to see how well it matches up to the sorts of consumer goal we have specified.

3.3 HIERARCHY AND THE IRREDUCIBILITY OF NEEDS AND WANTS

Some time ago, Georgescu-Roegen (1954) drew attention to the importance for consumer behaviour of the principle of the irreducibility of wants. Bread, he pointed out, could not save someone from dying of thirst, nor a luxurious palace constitute a substitute for food. He also noted an important fact, now more widely recognized, that there was no one-to-one correspondence between wants and goods, and that water, for example, could satisfy several wants. Later writers have spelled out how the irreducibility of needs and wants casts doubt on the assumption in consumer analysis of indifference between goods, on which the notion of indifference curves rests – Lutz and Lux (1979) provide a recent example. We can illustrate the point by reference to irreducibility at its most basic level – the needs of the individual for mere survival, to which we alluded earlier in section 2.2 when discussing needs and wants.

If we assume that a certain number of calories is required for survival, then different foods might satisfy this need, and the consumer might be indifferent between them. But the consumer would not be indifferent between food supplying the requisite calories, say bread, and another good, say cricket balls – much though the consumer might enjoy a game of cricket. We illustrate the situation in Figure 3.1, where O_{y_1} represents the minimum consumption of bread required to provide the minimum intake of calories essential to survival. The conventional indifference curve linking the goods would be convex to the origin, sloping downward from left to right. Since the consumer in our example is not indifferent, however, we have instead what is sometimes referred to as a *quasi-indifference curve*. Below O_{y1}, the consumer would not be prepared to exchange any bread for cricket balls. At the level O_{y_1}, point *b* would be preferred to point *a*, since the consumer would be better off the more cricket balls he had – cricket balls do wear out. Generally speaking, the further the consumer moves along the x axis at the level O_{y_1}, the better off he will become.

The above analysis can be extended to cover other minimum survival needs. If, for example, a certain amount of roughage were required in the food intake in order to help keep the body functioning normally, then we could add a further dimension to the figure. Roughage we represent by the discontinuous line in Figure 3.1. We now have two minima to satisfy instead of one. Any level of consumption above O_{y_1} satisfies the calorie requirements, which are the first priority, but consumption must be increased further to satisfy roughage needs, say to the level represented by point *c*. The latter point then represents a further restriction on the extent to which the consumer would be prepared to swap bread for cricket balls. Other criteria, in order of priority – a so-called *lexicographic ordering* – and further dimensions could be introduced, restricting choice still further.

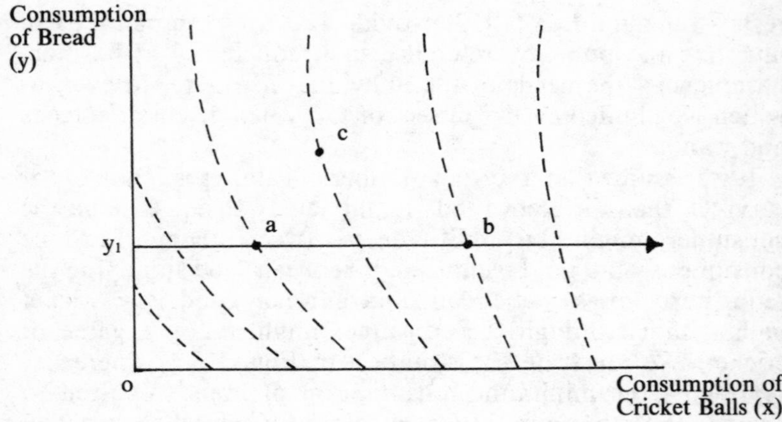

Figure 3.1: Hierarchy and its implications for indifference between goods

We can see, therefore, that the assumption of consumer indifference is not universally applicable. The important question is, how extensive are such constraints in practice? At most it seems possible to talk in terms of the requirements for mere survival being non-negotiable (and even these will vary from one person to another) and, beyond these, possibly certain higher-order needs without which some individuals might consider life not worth living – in the apt words of the old saying, 'Man cannot live by bread alone.' We may conclude that the idea of a hierarchy of needs does indeed limit the application of conventional neo-classical consumer analysis, although probably not to the extent some would apparently have us believe. Only further empirical analysis, however, will enable us to say just how important the principle of hierarchy is in limiting consumer choice in practice.

3.4 EXPLAINING THE PATTERN OF CONSUMER SPENDING AND CHANGES IN THE PATTERN

The neo-classical theory of consumer demand can be given a forward-looking, more dynamic structure by bringing the element of time into the decision-making process, along the lines first suggested by Irving Fisher (1930). The consumer then becomes concerned with the allocation of his income not only amongst current consumption goods but in future time-periods as well. In extending his time-horizon, he will be influenced by his expectations, especially about his future income. Becker (1965) and others have added a further dimension with their production function approach to consumer spending decisions. Even with such modifications and developments, however, there is still a sense in which the neo-classical theory is essentially static. It still does not provide us with anything like a satisfactory explanation of *why* so-called 'tastes' change over time. In the present section we examine in greater depth this dynamic aspect of consumer behaviour, and also some of the main reasons for the widespread variations in the pattern of consumer spending between individuals.

Some of the serious gaps in our knowledge of consumer behaviour were noted by Ferber in his extensive surveys in the field in 1962 and 1973. Since his comments remain just as valid today, they are worth quoting at some length. Three of the deficiencies he remarked on are closely related to the objectives of the present study. First, Ferber stressed the need to unify the different theories of the consumption function:

> Each of the theories ... seems to 'work' under some circumstances. No one is superior to the other in all circumstances, though some are more frequently superior than others. The evidence would seem to point to the desirability of combining the unique features of each in a more general theory, but how to do this remains to be determined. Any such theory would have to allow for the effects on consumption (and on saving) of both human and non-human capital.

Some progress has been made in the direction advocated, principally, it seems, by treating the lifecycle in income as the common link between the lifecycle and permanent income approaches to the consumption function. Duesenberry's relative income hypothesis has not appeared to fit comfortably into this stable, however, and has therefore, as we remarked earlier, tended to be dropped from the reckoning. Our analysis in the present section will maintain that Duesenberry's general approach remains valid, and ought to feature as part of a unified theory of the consumption function.

Ferber's surveys were also helpful in drawing attention to the anomalous position of the *ceteris paribus* variables, particularly the socio-economic variables, in consumer analysis. Among the socio-economic variables listed by Ferber were age, sex, education, occupation, family size and the 'lifecycle'. His conclusions were that:

> . . .socio-economic variables remain the stepchildren of consumption theory. They are invariably introduced as the extra, though essential, ingredient – like pouring salt on french fries – with no theoretical basis except to highlight other relationships (and using what variables of this type are available).

Ferber (1973) further noted the need to incorporate in economics the knowledge about consumer behaviour available in other social sciences.

> Most consumption economists seem to have reacted to the growing popularity and usefulness of interdisciplinary approaches by, if anything, drawing blinkers about their eyes even more tightly lest they be contaminated by other disciplines. Many of these other studies have not been at the same level of sophistication as some in economics. Nevertheless, they are of great relevance to consumer economics and suggest variables and types of data collection, which may lead to more meaningful analysis.

Ferber advocated, finally, the further development of the theoretical basis for the analysis of human and non-human capital, and the integration of these two types of capital. He also saw a need for a greater application of consumer economics analysis to the public sector.

3.4.1 The lifecycle of needs and wants

We have seen that in the neo-classical theory of consumer behaviour the consumer is assumed to have a set of preferences between goods which are generally stable. The main emphasis is therefore placed upon income and price changes as the explanatory variables accounting for variations in the demand for goods. Furthermore, investigators have noted that personal income tends to follow a particular pattern over the lifetime of individuals – usually referred to as the 'lifecycle' – rising in the early years when a worker is still gaining knowledge and skill, reaching a peak in middle age and falling in retirement. This lifecycle in income is, of course, one of the principal foundations of the consumption function, and has been the subject of a great deal of theoretical and empirical research. Much less attention has been paid in standard economic theory, however, to another equally important lifecycle: *the lifecycle of needs and wants*, or, what we might call for convenience, *the consumption lifecycle*, in contrast to the income lifecycle.

Studies have shown that the income and consumption lifecycles in fact follow a similar pattern over most of the age range. The findings of a number of these studies are shown in Figures 3.2 to 3.4. The data for Figures 3.2 and 3.3 were extracted from the US Bureau of Labor Statistics Survey of Consumer Expenditures, 1960–61, whereas Kotlikoff and Summers (1981) used, in addition, the corresponding survey for 1972–73, together with the National Income and Expenditure Accounts and other sources. Although the definitions used differ somewhat, and therefore the findings

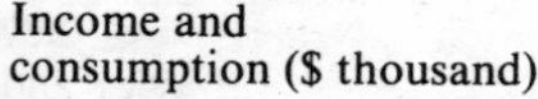

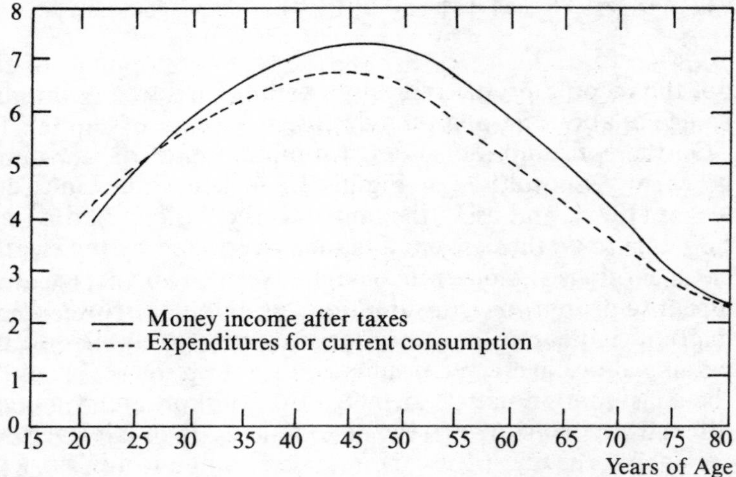

Figure 3.2: Average money income after taxes and expenditure for current consumption

Source: Thurow, L. (1969).

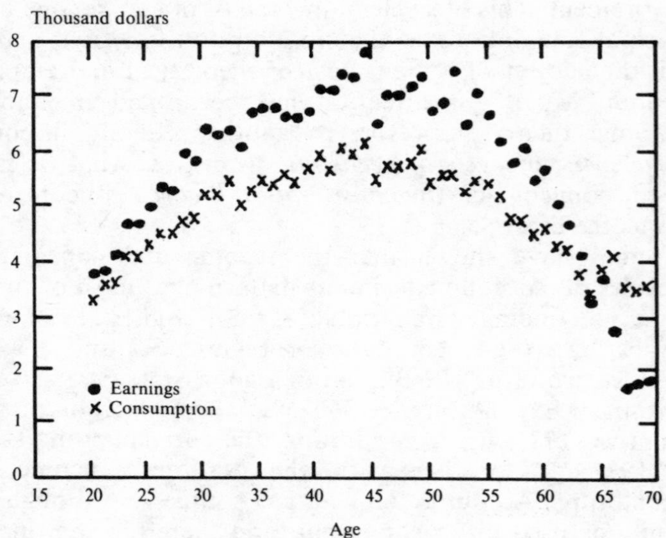

Figure 3.3: Family consumption and earnings by age of head, all education levels combined.

Source: Ghez, G. R. and Becker, G. S. (1975).

too, the income profile typically exhibits a rising trend up to the age of about 50, and then declines.

On the consumption side, consumption exceeds income in the early years (although Figure 3.3, taken from Ghez and Becker (1975), and using the family as the basic unit, does not show this to be the case), but is then overtaken by the steeper rise in earnings and other income. Between 60 and 65, earnings appear to drop below consumption, although Thurow's (1969) diagram indicates that average income from all sources remains above average consumption right up to the age of 80. The consumption pattern depicted by Kotlikoff and Summers differs from that shown in the other studies, in that it levels out from about the mid-fifties and remains around its highest level right into the seventies age range. Quite why this should occur is not clear, but it may be related to their longitudinal approach, which used a cross-sectional profile of relative

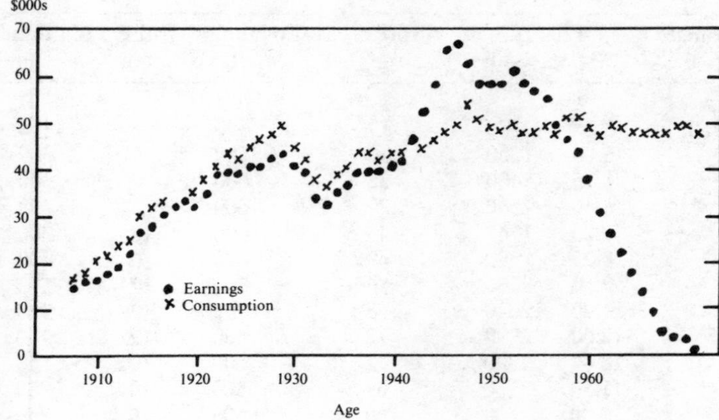

Figure 3.4: Sum of male and female longitudinal average earnings and average consumption profiles, age 18 in 1910, age 82 in 1974.

Source: Kotlikoff, L. J. and Summers, L. H. (1981).

consumption by age and sex to distribute aggregate US consumption in each year to different age-sex cohorts.

While the income and consumption profiles resemble each other, we can see from the diagrams that there are a number of important differences. First, at early ages consumption appears to exceed income, with young people probably still being supported by their families. Second, the peaks in income and consumption do not exactly coincide – the consumption peak appears to come somewhat earlier than the income peak, despite the fact that the direction of causation is generally taken to run from income to consumption. Finally, consumption in the later stages falls less rapidly than income.

Similar work in the United Kingdom by Fisher (1956), using cross-section data for different occupational groups, found that for managers and those in clerical and sales occupations, the peaks in consumption and income fell within the age group 45–54. In the case of manual workers, the peaks came rather earlier, between ages 35–44; while in the case of the self-employed, peak consumption was at ages 45–54, but peak income not until ages 55–64. Fisher also attempted to adjust

Table 3.1: Recommended family amounts of nutrients

Age range	Energy MJ[1]	Kcal[2]	Protein g[3]	Calcium mg[4]	Iron mg	Vitamin A μg[5]
Males						
Under 1	3.25	780	19	600	6	450
1	5.00	1200	30	600	7	300
2	5.75	1400	35	600	7	300
3–4	6.50	1560	39	600	8	300
5–6	7.25	1740	43	600	10	300
7–8	8.25	1980	49	600	10	400
9–11	9.50	2280	56	700	12	575
12–14	11.00	2640	66	700	12	725
15–17	12.00	2990	72	600	12	750
18–34[6]	12.00	2900	72	500	10	750
35–64[6]	11.50	2750	69	500	10	750
65–74	10.00	2400	60	500	10	750
75 and over	9.00	2150	54	500	10	750
Females						
Under 1	3.00	720	18	600	6	450
1	4.50	1100	27	600	7	300
2	5.50	1300	32	600	7	300
3–4	6.25	1500	37	600	8	300
5–6	7.00	1680	42	600	10	300
7–8	8.00	1900	48	600	10	400
9–11	8.50	2050	51	700	12	575
12–14	9.00	2150	53	700	12	725
15–17	9.00	2150	53	600	12	750
18–54[7]	9.00	2150	54	500	12	750
55–74	8.00	1900	47	500	10	750
75 and over	7.00	1680	42	500	10	750

Source: Ministry of Agriculture, Fisheries and Food (1986) *Manual of Nutrition*, London, Her Majesty's Stationery Office.

Notes:
1. megajoule (= 1,000 kJ)
2. kilocalories (= 4.184 kJ)
3. grams
4. milligrams
5. micrograms (1,000 = 1 mg)
6. moderately active males
7. most occupations

the data to yield a pattern of consumption and income over time. The results tended to push back the peaks in consumption and income to higher age groups.

Although the lifecycle approach to the consumption function makes consumption a dependent variable, with income and wealth the explanatory variables, we shall show below that if we examine personal needs, and the associated wants, there are a good many reasons why consumption should follow the inverted-U pattern apparent in the diagrams, quite independently of the influence exerted by income. One of the most important reasons why this should be so is that many personal needs and wants, and the associated consumption, vary according to age.

If we take, first, the major category of food (which in the United Kingdom forms about 20 per cent of average household expenditure), calorific requirements and the essential intake of vitamins and minerals is not the same at all ages. In the United Kingdom, the Department of Health and Social Security has published recommended average daily intakes of energy, protein and certain minerals and vitamins for different age groups – similar recommendations have been made by the National Research Council Food and Nutrition Board in the United States. Table 3.1, which reproduces some of these recommendations, shows quite clearly the inverted-U shape of the lifecycle in food *needs*.

The figures quoted, it should be stressed, are averages, and will vary according to differences in height, weight and sex, the amount of physical activity throughout the day, and the rate of internal body activities, such as heart beat. They will also vary according to environmental differences, such as climate. Because the recommendations have to cover this range of possibilities, they are higher than the *actual requirements* might be in specific instances. They are also higher than the requirements for mere survival, in most circumstances. Despite the qualifications, however, the lifecycle pattern of food need is indisputable.

Studies of the *actual* consumption of foodstuffs have tended to concentrate on trying to explain changes in the *quantity* of food purchased, or *expenditure* on food, but there have also been some investigations of the factors determining consumption of food *nutrients*. One of the most comprehensive of these is the study by Adrian and Daniel (1976), based upon an analysis of data from the 1965–66 nationwide household food consumption survey, conducted by the Consumer and Economics Research Division of the US Department of

Agriculture. The quantities of the different nutrients consumed by individual households were calculated by multiplying the quantity of each foodstuff consumed by the nutrient content of each unit of food. Since some food may have been discarded rather than consumed, this is not an ideal measure, but allowance was made for the loss of nutrients during preparation. The possible use of nutrient supplements was ignored.

The findings of the study showed that if a range of other possible socio-economic variables linked with consumption of nutrients were held constant, nutrient consumption did vary with income, but was not highly responsive to income changes. In the case of each nutrient there was a large positive constant, indicating that consumption would have been appreciable even at zero levels of income – and this was so even when the other variables were free to alter. The obvious explanation, as we have seen in Table 3.1, is that individuals have food needs which have to be met even in the absence of any income if they are to survive.

The investigation by Adrian and Daniel also showed that the degree of urbanization, race, educational attainment of the homemaker, stage of the family in the family lifecycle, family size, meal adjustment (the influence of home, guests, skipped and away meals, etc.) and employment status of the homemaker all had an influence on the consumption of at least some of the nutrients. No test was made, unfortunately, of the possible effect of age, which, as we noted earlier, is linked to disposable income, and, as Table 3.1 shows, is also likely to have a bearing on nutrient consumption.

The effects of age on consumption generally is most apparent, as one might expect, at the extremities of the age range, i.e. in the case of both the young and the elderly. The young, especially the very young, have many special needs. Not only the quantity of food eaten by the young, but the type of food required differs – generally it must be more easily digested than food for adults. Again the smaller stature of young people imposes different clothing needs from those of older people. Expenditure on health care also tends to be above average in the early years, and leisure activities are, of course, very different from those of adults.

In the case of the oldest age group (say those above the age of 60) their physical and other needs differ from those of other adults. We shall examine these special needs further below. It is sufficient to note only one or two examples here. Physical changes mean that the needs of the elderly for such things as health care and heating are likely to be greater than for other adults. The greater time available to pursue leisure activities in retirement may also mean that self-actualization is pursued in rather different forms.

Finally, Wells and Gubar (1966), drawing on data compiled by the National Industrial Conference Board, covering expenditure on services and non-durable goods as well as on durables, have shown that expenditure on luxury goods and services tends also to increase with age, although dropping sharply at retirement. Expenditure on numerous other products and services tended to peak among those aged under 25, or in the middle-age ranges between 25 and 44.

The role of the family lifecycle Although many needs and wants are undoubtedly age-related, and others are determined by sex, most attention in studies of the lifecycle of needs and wants has focused on the influence of the *family* lifecycle on consumption expenditure. As one would expect, age and sex influences on consumption are closely interwoven with influences originating in the family lifecycle, but, as we shall see, there are good grounds for distinguishing the separate effects of all these variables.

First use of the notion of a family lifecycle is usually attributed to Rowntree (1903) in his study of poverty in England. The term is now widely used, since it has been found useful in both theoretical and empirical work in a variety of disciplines. It must be confessed, however, that while there is general agreement that the family lifecycle begins with the marriage of a couple, and that certain events, such as the birth of the first child and retirement, mark important stages in the cycle, there is much less agreement when attempts are made to break the cycle down into more detailed stages, or to take account of the more recent social changes affecting family life. The family lifecycle has nevertheless become an important tool of analysis in many fields within the social sciences, and even beyond.

Murphy and Staples (1979) give a useful summary of the development of ideas about the classifications used to study the family lifecycle. They identify three major eras in its development. The first of these, the 'foundation era', mainly encompasses the 1930s, when the concept was first studied seriously by a number of writers. Most of these writers identified only a few (generally four) stages in the cycle. Sorokin *et al.* (1931) placed an emphasis on changing family membership, with the first stage represented by newly married couples without children, and the last stage by couples in their old age, again without children. Two intervening stages were inserted, one with dependent children and the other with one or more adult, self-supporting young people. Another study by Kirkpatrick (1934) based the cycle on the position of children in the educational system: pre-school, grade school, high school and adult. Yet another criterion, that of the children's age, was used by Loomis (1936).

The second era in the development of the family lifecycle concept is referred to by Murphy and Staples as the 'expansion era', because the number of stages identified in the cycle tended to increase. Several writers now maintained that there were seven main stages. Bigelow (1942), like Kirkpatrick, used school as the main basis of his classification, but extended it to include college and a more refined analysis of the post-children phase. Duval and Hill also developed a seven-stage cycle for the US National Conference on Family Life in 1948, again based largely around the role of children in the family. A study of consumer finances by Lansing and Morgan (1955), using the annual Surveys of Consumer Finances conducted by the Survey Research Center of the University of Michigan, also found that a seven-stage lifecycle based on changing family composition was helpful in explaining changes in consumer behaviour.

Finally, Murphy and Staples cite a 'refinement era', beginning in the early 1960s. The refinements generally entailed still further breakdowns in the number of stages (the most detailed being that by Rodgers, 1962) and the use of employment as another useful criterion for delineating stages. One of the most comprehensive analyses of the family lifecycle, linked specifically to consumer behaviour and marketing, is the study of Reynolds and Wells (1977). It contains a wealth of data and it is worth examining at rather greater length the reasons they advance for picking out particular stages of family development, in order that we can form our own judgements about the family lifecycle. We do not attempt to cover all aspects of the cycle, but concentrate rather on those with the principal economic implications.

Starting with what they call the 'early years', Reynolds and Wells note how early childhood (from birth to around five years of age) is marked by rapid physiological change, requiring rapidly growing food intake and changes of clothing, as old clothes are worn out or become too small. With regard to food requirements, the need alters from milk and soft foods to a more solid diet. At this stage, illnesses are quite common, and medical needs tend therefore to be high. Psychological and conceptual development is rapid, revealing itself in a desire for playthings. Most children also seem to enjoy the company of other children, so that socialising probably begins to exert its influence from an early age.

In later childhood (from around five years to the early teens) rapid physical growth is still a marked characteristic, and food and clothing needs still tend to be increasing, although the pattern of expressed wants changes. Playthings remain important, but their nature changes too – more complex and sophisticated (and more expensive) toys being popular. At this age, sex roles tend to become more clearly established, often as a result of pressures exerted at home, in the school, and sometimes through peer reinforcement. Status and status symbols also become important, as does social acceptability.

From the early years, Reynolds and Wells move on to the 'young consumers', which they subdivide into early adolescence (puberty to about the age of 15) and later adolescence (from about 16 to 20 years). The former is still marked by rapid physical change. A wider range of goods is now demanded, and some, such as sweet foods, tend to be consumed in smaller quantities. Greater interest is shown in games and sports, doubtless because physical prowess has improved and there may therefore be a need to 'let off steam'. Amongst those in later adolescence, greater importance is attached to personal appearance, which will often be associated with a growing interest in the opposite sex. An important development at this stage is the increased influence exerted by peer groups, which to some extent now replace the influence of parents. Young people of this age-range appear to experience a strong need to relate to their peers, to be accepted by them and to meet with their approval. These developments find their expression in demand for products which are fashionable and in accordance with particular lifestyles.

The third main stage of the lifecycle identified by Reynolds and Wells is that of 'young adults', covering the age range of 18 to 35. This is an age range which exhibits both continuities with the past and also major discontinuities. The continuities are most apparent up to about the age of 25, although this 18–25 age sub-group is by no means homogeneous, since it includes those starting college as well as those going directly into the labour force and young people leaving college. The pre-marrieds are closest in activities and interests to adolescents, one indication being that they are still most interested in money for immediate use rather than long-term planning. Further important behavioural differences between the sexes also emerge at this stage, with a higher proportion of females than males becoming married, and a higher proportion of males in college and in the labour force. Income for the 18–25 age group remains relatively low, as one would expect with so many at college and others not long started working, but Figures 3.2–3.4 suggest that incomes still rise sufficiently to establish a better balance with expenditure, and may even overtake it.

The *family* lifecycle usually starts with the young marrieds prior to their having children. Marriage has an important bearing on people's needs, and even more, it seems, on their wants. Marriage itself appears to help meet human needs, including that for belonging, and having a closer, and generally more stable, relationship with a member of the opposite sex. Needs for food, accommodation, and perhaps even clothing in these uni-sex days, are also likely to alter. We cannot, for example, simply assume that the sum of the food needs of two persons living independently will give us the combined needs of a two-person family unit. Both the quantity consumed (there may be less wastage) and the variety of food purchased may alter. The biggest single change, however, will probably concern accommodation. Prior to the arrival of the first child, most young marrieds, certainly in the United States, still rent their accommodation, but whether renting or buying, young people at this stage often seem to feel a need for more space in which to live and follow their pursuits.

A further important consequence of setting up home life is, of course, an associated requirement for durable goods. To what extent some of these purchases can be regarded as satisfying needs, and to what extent they venture beyond this to become merely wants, is a matter likely to be difficult to solve. The effect on purchases of consumer durables is, however, indisputable. Reynolds and Wells quote figures to the effect that over one-half of sterling flatware, about one-quarter of bedroom furniture sales, around 40 per cent of stereo and hi-fi equipment, and high proportions of many other durables are purchased by those who are just about to be, or have just recently, married. The rate of family formation clearly has an important bearing on both the quantities of durables sold and the pattern of personal consumption.

One further feature of the young marrieds without children is the working wife. Much more common today than in past eras, the reasons for wives continuing to work appear to be mainly twofold. There is, first, a desire for more 'discretionary' income, i.e. income which is not tied to covering the overheads and essential running costs of a home, but can be disbursed as the young marrieds see fit. Second, working may for many women be described, in Maslow's terms, as a process of self-actualization. Not all feel that they wish to centre their lives entirely on the home, certainly not at this stage of life. The greater financial freedom of young marrieds leads, it seems, to their being typically optimistic with regard to their finances, and desirous of material goods.

The arrival of the first child has further important repercussions on family life, as anyone who has moved through this stage in the lifecycle will confirm. Personal behaviour has to adjust to the new arrival, and the needs of the household increase. The most obvious additional needs are food and clothing, but parents also look to the future, and the most far-reaching repercussion of the larger household is often a desire for larger accommodation. The desire for more space, not just short-term but also in the longer term, persuades a high proportion of couples to buy their first home. The mother will, of course, also have to give up work, even if only temporarily. Not surprisingly, this in turn results in a deterioration in the household's financial situation. Reynolds and Wells note that the use of credit and charge cards is highest during this stage of the family lifecycle, and that the proportion with instalment debt outstanding is also at a peak. Since, however, purchase of a house by instalments is one form of saving, and since contributions may well also be made towards pension and other forms of retirement provision, it is not surprising that Figures 3.2–3.4 still show income exceeding expenditure over the age range associated with this stage of the family lifecycle.

After young adulthood come the 'middle years'. Reynolds and Wells again subdivide this into middle adulthood, or the 'full house' period (covering approximately the age range 35–44) when all the children tend still to be at home, and later adulthood (approximately age 45 to 54), the 'emptying of the nest' period when children are leaving home. The former is generally the period of reasonable stability, but there is a drop in financial optimism and heavy use of credit to help meet the costs of the expanding needs of children growing up. As durable goods are replaced, the emphasis shifts towards comfort rather than other considerations, such as fashion.

In later adulthood, the departure of the children helps ease the financial situation, so that, although earnings and average income after tax peak and begin to fall (Figures 3.2–3.4), expenditure falls even faster, making this the most affluent stage of the lifecycle for most people – Figure 3.4, as we mentioned earlier, shows consumption levelling off, but the margin between earnings and consumption at this stage is still substantial. It should be remembered, however, that for some occupations, often those involving manual work, ageing may now be associated with growing insecurity of employment. This period is also marked by the return of many wives to the labour force. The main reasons for so doing, according to Reynolds and Wells, is the goal of ensuring security (one of Maslow's list of needs), both currently and in old age. A further factor, which they do not mention, may be a desire to help meet the high costs of further education when children decide to go on to college or university. It seems, too, that there is often a desire to refurbish the home, or move to a new one. The home and its contents now often assume greater importance as status symbols.

We come, finally, to the 'old customers', a category of growing importance in the field of consumer behaviour, as the proportion of elderly people in the population increases in many countries. Sixty is a common age for distinguishing the older from younger age groups (Reynolds and Wells prefer 55), even though retirement may be delayed until 65 or thereabouts. Attitudes towards the age for retirement do, however, differ appreciably. In some European countries at present the pressures of unemployment are such as to cause many to retire before 60 – and redundancy often means enforced retirement, in effect.

The mental and physical changes accompanying old age lead to still further changes in personal needs and wants. As one might expect, there is an increased need for medical care and labour-saving devices. Interests and activities, partly through necessity, become increasingly home-based. The need for social contact is widely felt, but sadly not always satisfied, since a high proportion of widows and widowers now live alone. Mobility remains surprisingly high, if finances permit.

The most important turning point in this age group is retirement, since, as we can see from Figures 3.2–3.4 it is accompanied by (a further) sharp drop in income. For a variety of reasons, however, expenditure may also fall. Any mortgage on the house is now likely to have been paid off, the children will in most cases have left home and finished their education, no state social security contributions will now be required, and the costs associated with working no longer have to be met. While, therefore, the drop in income might otherwise have forced a reduction in expenditure, with expenditure tending to fall anyway, the income constraint may not, on the whole, be so tight as economists have tended to assume. Increasingly, the elderly seem better prepared for old age from the financial point of view, and what is happening on the expenditure side should not be overlooked. Indeed it has been suggested (see, for example, Kotlikoff and Summers, 1981) that saving during the lifecycle may now have as a goal the provision of bequests rather than the financing of consumption in old age.

The above examination of the different stages in the family lifecycle seems to bring out a number of important points. It is apparent upon closer examination that, while key events such as marriage, birth of the first child, and retirement mark key stages in the cycle, there is room for argument about whether it is necessary, or desirable, to break the cycle down into more detailed stages, and, if so, what the appropriate cut-off points should be. With regard to several of these stages, Reynolds and Wells are unable to do more than use their best judgement, indicating that the age ranges selected, for example, are only approximate.

Further research may make it possible to delineate stages in the cycle more precisely, but the complexity of the cycle is such that the stages chosen to explain one form of behaviour, say purchases of clothing, need not help in explaining the purchases of other goods, say, certain consumer durables. It may well be the case that modified versions of the cycle have to be devised to suit individual goods. It is interesting, however, that even with the standard models, a number of studies have been successful in showing that the family lifecycle approach does help explain particular types of purchases. We shall be looking at some of these studies below.

The use of age to help define certain stages of the family lifecycle means that, even if it is not the only criterion applied, the family lifecycle influence on consumer behaviour reflects, in some degree at least, the effects of age. The two are intertwined. Depending on the good in question, one or the other might be dominant, although there is no reason why both should not contribute to explaining consumers' spending decisions.

A further notable feature of the family lifecycle is that the family at the centre of most work on the cycle has been the conventional one of father, mother and one or more children. a number of writers have become increasingly concerned, however, about the fact that this no longer represents the realities of life for many consumers. Following their examination of the development of the family lifecycle hypothesis, Murphy and Staples (1979) for example, went on to suggest the need for what they termed a 'modernized family lifecycle', which takes account of social changes in family consumption and lifestyle. They noted, first, that there had been an overall decline in the average family size. With children tending to be born within a few years of each other, this shortened the middle stage of the family lifecycle, leaving parents with a longer period of freedom from looking after children – making it easier, amongst other things, for the mother to return to work for lengthier periods, if she so wished.

A further trend noted by Murphy and Staples was the tendency to delay the time of the first marriage, with many women postponing it until their late twenties rather than early twenties. The effect is to lengthen the period during which young people remain single. When added to the smaller size of families, greater opportunities are available to females for career development, and probably also for increased earning potential.

Lastly, Murphy and Staples drew attention to the increasing incidence of divorce – in a number of countries, including the United Kingdom, around one third of first marriages now end in divorce – and to the tendency for divorce to occur earlier in marriage. The great majority of first-time divorcees remarry, but a consequence of the higher incidence of divorce has been an enormous increase in the number of one-parent families. The social and financial circumstances of such families generally differ markedly from those of the standard 'nuclear' family.

In addition to the important developments listed above, one could add the growing number of separated couples, those who cohabit without marriage, unmarried mothers, etc. Murphy and Staples finally suggested a modernized lifecycle with five stages ('young single, young married without children, other young, middle-aged and older people) and thirteen additional sub-categories, in contrast to the nine stages advocated by Wells and Gubar. Both these models have been popular in analytical work, and it is interesting that both have been found helpful in explaining consumer expenditure on particular goods and services.

Turning now to look at a number of other empirical studies which have used the family lifecycle as an explanatory variable, it is worth noting, first, a study by Lansing and Kish (1957) which had the specific objective of comparing the explanatory powers of the age and family lifecycle variables. Using data drawn from the 1955 Survey of Consumer Finances conducted by the Survey Research Center of the University of Michigan, the authors were able to show that the family lifecycle was more successful than age in explaining variations in six dependent variables: home-ownership; consumer indebtedness; the proportion of spending units housing a working (income-earning) wife: the proportion of spending units with income over $4000; new cars purchased; and purchases of TV sets. While these results are interesting, it has to be recognized, of course, that much more extensive testing would be required before any *general* conclusions could be drawn about the relative efficacy of age and the family lifecycle as explanatory variables. It could well be the case, for example, that consumption of certain foodstuffs is more closely related to age than the customary lifecycle variables.

In another study which is of interest, Hisrich and Peters (1974) used multiple regression techniques to test not only for the possible effects of age but also for the influence of income and social class on the use of entertainment facilities. The family lifecycle was divided into four stages: under 40 without children, under 40 with children, 40 and over without children in the household and 40 and over with children. The use of 40 as a dividing line was felt to be appropriate, in that it would give some indication of whether or not there were pre-school children at home, which would necessitate babysitters if the parents were to go out, thereby making sorties more difficult – an example of the family lifecycle being adapted to the specific use in mind, although the age of 40 might be considered on the high side in this instance. The results of the study showed that stage in the family lifecycle and income were more closely related to the use of leisure facilities than age or social class. Further tests of the *frequency* of use of the same facilities (a better indicator of regular, as opposed to just occasional, use) showed a strong association with all four explanatory variables. It would seem, therefore, that, for certain types of expenditure at least, income does not provide the sole explanation of consumer behaviour.

A further study, by Fritzsche (1981), tested simultaneously for the effects of income and the family lifecycle on consumer spending on energy consumption. While earlier work, such as that of Newman and Day (1975) had shown energy use to be related to income, the increase in consumption had been less than proportionate to the increase in income – since, like food, there are limits to energy needs, and therefore probably also to the amount of energy one can usefully consume even in an era of consumer durables – and it seemed possible that the family lifecycle might have something to contribute towards explaining both total consumption and the pattern of use. Fritzche's study is also of interest in that it tested slightly modified versions of both the Wells and Gubar and Murphy and Staples models of the lifecycle.

Fritzsche's results clearly demonstrated the usefulness of the family lifecycle approach. Both the models tested showed that total energy consumption followed an inverted-U pattern, being lower amongst the younger married without children, reaching a peak in the middle-aged married with children stage, and declining thereafter. The inverted-U pattern was also apparent among the individual types of fuel consumed, although to differing degrees. The family lifecycle was also found to be useful in predicting consumption at the regional level. A word of caution should be inserted, however, in so far as the data were drawn from the 1972–73 Consumer Expenditure Survey of the Bureau of Labor Statistics, and therefore pre-dated the oil price rises of 1973–74 and subsequent years. The study was also based on samples from cross-section data, which are an imperfect substitute for the longitudinal data required for family lifecycle analysis.

Using the same 1972–73 CES database to try to explain family clothing expenditures, Wagner and Hanna (1983) introduced a jarring note into discussions of the lifecycle. In an attempt to cater for some of the criticisms of the family lifecycle approach, they tested not just the basic models of Wells and Gubar and Murphy and Staples, but a variety of alternative models. To take account, first, of the criticism that the family lifecycle variable obscures the effects of both family size and the age-sex structure of the family (not wholly true of all models) they devised a *family composition model* using age and sex categories. A further model attempted to incorporate what was referred to as 'socio-economic and demographic variables, especially income'. The variables in the latter model included the occupation and education of the household head, the employment status of the spouse, race, geographic region, city size and total consumption expenditure (used as a proxy for income). One difficulty with this approach, it would seem, is that the role of a number of these variables is somewhat ambiguous. Occupation and education of the household head, for example, are likely to be related to household income. The employment status of the spouse may, too, in fact be a function of the family lifecycle. Furthermore, while the use of total consumption expenditure as a proxy for income is now a well-established procedure, one cannot be entirely happy about using an independent variable which includes the dependent variable as one of its components, even if a relatively small one.

The results of the tests by Wagner and Hanna suggested that neither the basic lifecycle models nor the family composition model were very good predictors of total clothing expenditure. The results with these models improved appreciably, however, when controlled for socio-economic and demographic variables, and were then able to explain rather more than half the variation in clothing expenditure. The socio-economic model on its own also yielded similar results, with total consumption expenditures having the dominant influence. Wagner and Hanna concluded that, independently of income, as represented by the proxy variable total consumption expenditures, family lifecycle and family composition models had little ability to predict clothing expenditure – when either gross income or personal disposable income were used instead of consumption expenditures, the explanatory power of the family lifecycle variables did, however, improve slightly.

Our discussion has served to show, it is hoped, that while problems remain, and a good deal more research is required, the use of the lifecycle of needs and wants – or the consumption lifecycle as we have called it – can make an important contribution towards explaining variations in certain categories of consumer expenditure. The need for food – still a major component of consumer spending, even if diminishing in importance – is clearly related to age (and to a lesser extent to sex) and therefore the lifecycle. Numerous other items of personal consumption are also age-related, such as expenditure on health and certain *types* of clothing – such as children's clothing. The evidence relating to the *family* lifecycle of needs and wants, it must be admitted, is more mixed. Critics are right to insist that tests of the hypothesis ought, so far as possible, to try and separate family lifecycle variables from the effects of other variables, such as age, sex and other socio-economic influences, which, while linked to the family lifecycle, are by no means identical to it. That said, there do seem to be good grounds for believing that the family lifecycle influences at least certain kinds of needs-linked expenditures, even if only their timing. The effect of marriage and the arrival of the first child on the setting-up of new homes and the purchases of certain consumer durables cannot, for example, be ignored. It may, nevertheless, be the case that, the more aggregated the data, the more difficult it will be to find a family lifecycle variable which exerts a significant influence.

We go on now to look at other ways in which intervening variables can help improve our understanding of consumer behaviour, and in so doing draw attention to further respects in which the conventional approach based primarily on income and price effects is inadequate.

3.4.2 The development of new needs and wants and the growth of consumption

We have already seen in the present section on consumer behaviour how the lifecycle of needs and wants – the consumption lifecycle – can help us understand the changing demands for many products and services. Needs and wants may also help us understand certain other features of the pattern of consumption, including some of a longer-term nature. Much of the extensive body of empirical evidence in economics on the changing pattern of consumers' expenditure has been built upon the pioneering work of Engel (1857). Expressing the demand for goods as a function of household income, he was able to establish relationships (so-called Engel curves) showing how rapidly consumption of individual goods increased in relation to rising income. One of his principal findings was that the proportion of expenditure allocated to food decreased as the standard of living of a household increased. Work by later economists, using a variety of functional forms, has confirmed this particular finding and suggested a number of other 'laws' relating to consumption of certain essential goods. Houthakker (1957) in an extensive survey of budget studies carried out in thirty-three countries, at different times, found that the income elasticity of food was always less than one (although the elasticity did vary appreciably between countries), and that the same was generally true of housing (including fuel and light). The income elasticity of demand for clothing, on the other hand, was usually slightly greater than unity. The findings relating to other goods were more mixed.

Brown and Deaton (1972) have drawn attention to the way in which the standard theory of consumer behaviour is concerned with a single consumer purchasing a large number of homogeneous goods, whereas household budget studies entail a measure of aggregation across individuals. Most studies have passed over the consequent aggregation problems, and 'have used utility functions or the constants of the theory as if average *per capita* data were generated by one single consumer possessed of average *per capita* income and behaving according to demand theory'.

A further problem with household budget studies – a problem recognized by Engel – is that if they are to be at all realistic, they must take into account not only income, but also the effects of household *size* on consumption. Later studies have also found it necessary to allow for differences in family *composition*, i.e. the age and sex of household members. Standard utility theory does not allow for such differentiation, even though it is now generally recognized that adults and children do have different needs. The solution has been to weight household members differently according to a scale. This approach may be represented as follows:

$$q_{ir}/n_r = f(y_r/n_r) \qquad (3.3)$$

$$\text{and } n_r = \sum_j w_j n_{jr}$$

where, q_{ir} is the quantity purchased of the ith good per head of household r, n_r is the number in household r and y_r is money expenditure per head of household r. The weights w_j are an adult-equivalent scale, one commonly used example of which is the so-called Amsterdam scale (Table 3.2) – employed by Stone (1954) in his analysis of food expenditure – which takes an adult as the basic unit.

Table 3.2: The Amsterdam Scale

Age Group	Male	Female
Under 14 years	0.52	0.52
14–17 years	0.98	0.90
18 years and over	1.00	0.90

A variety of these scales exists, with different basic units and weightings. Some of the scales are based on the nutritional requirements of persons of different ages and sex, others on differences in expenditure behaviour between households of different sizes and composition. Later studies have also become more sophisticated, recognizing that weightings ought to be commodity-specific, since children's needs, as for baby food, differ from those of adults in kind as well as in quantity. Much attention has also been paid to the possible welfare uses of such data, since they permit calculations of the expenditure required to support families of different sizes and composition.

Although the points tend not to be made explicitly, we have in these studies the recognition, first, that the standard neo-classical theory, as presented, is inadequate for the purpose of analysing household consumer behaviour, and, second, that the underlying basis of utility is personal needs. Unfortunately, the logic of accepting needs as the basis of utility is not pursued so far as it might be, since it can help us make more sense of some of the principal findings of the household surveys to which we briefly referred above. If we take, first, the case of foodstuffs, we saw in Table 3.1 that individuals have certain nutritional requirements. While the associated wants for food, and therefore food purchases, may exceed the stated requirements, the capacity of the body to absorb food is limited, and we would not therefore expect food consumption to increase indefinitely in line with the growth of income. Consumers may, of course, switch their spending between foodstuffs, on the lines of the traditional textbook examples, and there are gourmets who live for their food, and are prepared to spend large sums on it, but a needs-based approach to food consumption would certainly predict that this item of consumption should grow less rapidly than income – as indeed the empirical findings confirm.

In the case of two other basic necessities of life, housing (including fuel and light) and clothing, the position is less clear-cut. In the industrialized countries at least, most people already have access to more than would be included in any reasonable definition of 'basic needs' – although there are undoubtedly still sizeable minorities in some countries which live in dire poverty. Moreover, demand is not finite, as it is, in the short term at least, with food. The *need* for housing and clothing is, however, limited, and while wants may be considerably in excess of needs, this is likely to have more to do with other, higher-order needs, such as that for esteem, than with any physical needs. While, therefore, it is not possible from the standpoint of needs to predict with certainty on housing and clothing, there is no reason why everyone should wish to continue spending even more on these items of consumption once their basic requirements have been met. In the aggregate, therefore, one might reasonably expect housing and clothing to be among the more slowly increasing items of personal expenditure, and it is hardly surprising that this should be so in practice.

The preceding discussion suggests that consumers experience declining marginal utility as their consumption of lower-order goods increases. Since at the early stages of economic development consumption is overwhelmingly of lower-order goods, this raises a question of some importance: what features of the economic system provide the dynamism which persuades consumers to go on adding to their consumption of goods, despite the general experience of declining marginal utility? This apparent contradiction seldom receives the attention it deserves, perhaps because, up to the present at least, there has been little sign that consumers are becoming sated – the average, aggregate propensity to consume having remained remarkably stable over the long run, despite the enormous increase in income which has take place in the industrialized countries in recent decades. It is important, however, to appreciate the factors underlying the drive towards ever higher levels of consumption, if only because we might wish at some stage to try and control them – not necessarily solely in order to stifle them.

The neo-classical economic model, it might be claimed, provides a number of good reasons why consumers could be expected to go on consuming growing quantities of goods. Consumers are assumed to want to maximize total utility, which would mean continuing to consume more even if the marginal utility of all goods consumed were declining, but still positive. The neo-classical model also provides, however, for the appearance of *new* goods, and therefore new opportunities for beneficial consumption. Technological progress may lead to the development of new products which are attractive to the consumer. Good examples are provided by the advent of new means of transport, such as the railways, aircraft and automobiles, leading to increased expenditure on automobiles and travel. The discovery of television and the telephone afford similar examples in the consumer durables field, and numerous others could be cited. Some of the technological developments may come in response to perceived consumer demands, but others may be the brainchildren of brilliant minds able to conceive of ideas beyond the ken of ordinary consumers.

Consumption of new products may be expanded still further if, instead of producing a single version of a new good, competing suppliers make available different versions of the product which appeal to a wider range of customers – automobiles again being a good example. Product differentiation, in other words, as well as possibly giving one supplier an edge over his competitors, may serve to expand the total market for a new product.

Pursuing the basic example still further, producers may *improve* their products, thereby generating repeat orders, perhaps even before the original purchases have worn out. One such example would be the development of colour television, which persuaded many to abandon their old black and white sets in favour of the improved images which could be obtained with the new sets. Numerous forms of electronic equipment, such as computers and video recorders, are also subject to frequent, sometimes marginal, improvements which serve at the very least to sustain demand for these products, and probably also to keep it increasing – for a time at least. Lancaster's (1966) characteristics approach, as he noted, lends itself to an analysis of improvements in products which result in added benefits to consumers.

Galbraith (1969) has remarked on a further aspect of the neo-classical model which is relevant to our discussion at this stage. Whereas continued accretions of a good at any given point in time are likely to exhibit diminishing marginal utility to the consumer, the same is not necessarily true if the consumer acquires the additional units *over a period of time*. For one thing, goods may wear out and need to be replaced. Consumers' wants (and perhaps even their needs) may also increase over time – in the case of food consumption, to take but one example, stomachs may expand, even if not indefinitely.

Galbraith is not impressed by such arguments, however, and he has advanced his own powerful reasons for the continued upward trend in personal consumption. Arguing that additional consumption must be to meet less pressing wants, he explains the continued urge of consumers to purchase more goods by the role of producers in artificially stimulating wants. The central function of modern advertising and salesmanship is 'to create desires – to bring into being wants that previously did not exist.' Wants are therefore actively encouraged, and even created, by persuasion in order to sell more wares. In addition to this active creation of wants, Galbraith notes that there may also be a 'passive' aspect to want-creation: 'wants are increasingly created by the process by which they are satisfied.... Increases in consumption, the counterpart of increases in production, act by suggestion or emulation to create wants.' The aim is prestige: 'The more that is produced the more that must be owned in order to maintain the appropriate prestige.' This manner in which wants depend on the process by which they are satisfied, Galbraith refers to as the 'Dependence Effect'.

Although expressed in too extreme a form to be universally acceptable, many economists probably suspect that there is more than a grain of truth in Galbraith's thesis. After reviewing the empirical evidence available, however, Albion and Farris (1981) have concluded that 'it remains to be shown that [advertising] is a significant factor in determining the ultimate size of an industry or market.' Their conclusions with regard to the effects of advertising on the aggregate propensity to consume were equally agnostic. Galbraith's arguments have nevertheless remained influential, and they are also of interest to the present study, since they clearly have links with the framework we have developed, through the emphasis placed on the hierarchy of wants and want-creation, and the importance Galbraith attaches to social comparisons. The latter aspect we shall be looking at again in the following section. We wish to look first at other ways in which a needs-based approach to consumer behaviour may provide us with insights into the reasons for the development of new wants, and for the changing pattern of consumer spending over time. These reasons have more to do with consumers themselves than with the producers of goods and services.

We noted earlier how wants for even the basic essentials of life may considerably *exceed* needs. This might be due to a natural predilection on the part of many people to demand more than they need, or it might be due to the persuasive powers of advertising and salesmanship, as Galbraith avers. Wants associated with certain lower-order needs, such as housing and clothing, may, however – as we have again remarked – also help intensify another important need: that for esteem (self-esteem and/or esteem by others). Larger houses, or houses in the more expensive areas, perhaps with sizeable gardens, are often a measure of status. Glossy journals are devoted to singing the praises of desirable houses and flats, and to ways of improving one's own accommodation and lifestyle. In the case of clothing, appearance and style probably count for even more. It is difficult to believe that the clothing industry could flourish the way it does without the benefit of advertising. Here, perhaps more than anywhere else, it might be claimed that we have an example of the artificial stimulation of demand envisaged by Galbraith. Skirts rise and fall, ties broaden and narrow, but new fashions do not seem to be imposed upon a wholly unwilling public – even if there is sometimes talk about the 'dictates of fashion'. To understand more fully what is happening we almost certainly have to add to the pressures of advertising the need felt by many people for esteem – it is not being implied, of course, that the need of esteem takes only this form, but it is one obvious example, and it is associated with one of our more basic needs, that for clothing.

We have already remarked on the manner in which the widely felt need for esteem, or status, may even affect the wants associated with such lower-order needs as those for clothing and accommodation. The accumulation of goods in order to try and impress one's fellows may, however, take a much wider variety of forms, of which the purchase of consumer durables offers perhaps the greatest scope for most people. Among those with even more funds to dispose of, the acquisition of works of art, land, expensive means of transportation, and so forth, provide larger-scale outlets. Social comparisons play an important role in the process, providing much of the spur. Duesenberry in this context talked of a 'demonstration effect', with people coming into contact with superior goods, which they then wished to possess. Once again, advertising might also have important effects. There is clearly almost limitless scope here for the stimulation of wants, or for wants to increase of their own accord.

We saw earlier that the income elasticity of demand for lower-order needs, such as that for food, housing and clothing tends to be relatively low. An economy dependent solely upon meeting such needs would not receive much stimulus from consumers' expenditure. What, therefore, of the likely effects on personal consumption of the wants associated with the other needs which have been identified? Scitovsky (1987) has recently suggested that additional demand for the 'positional goods' identified by Hirsch (1977) has almost the same economic impact as hoarding money. Since these goods and services are in inelastic supply, increased demand simply siphons off additional funds in the form of higher prices. Researchers in the field of needs seem to be agreed, however, that there is one form of higher-order need which becomes especially important once the individual is able to satisfy (not necessarily 100 per cent) his lower-order needs. Maslow described it as the need for 'self-actualization'; McLelland talked of the need for achievement, and Alderfer of the need for 'growth'. The general consensus seems to be that once men and women are able to satisfy their most pressing needs they turn their attention to ways of developing their human potential more fully.

The desire to develop one's potential may, of course, take many forms, and it is not possible to predict which will be selected by any particular individual. Some are more interested in developing their physical potential, others their mental abilities. Most, however, will probably wish to foster some combination of the two. With regard to the development of physical potential, there is plenty of evidence of increased participation in activities such as sailing, skiing, athletics and team games like football. Other pursuits of a less physical nature which may also enable people to develop their talents are too numerous to mention, but they would include education, in the broadest sense, and music, drama, literature, foreign travel and so forth. Some might regard these as no more than leisure pursuits, but for many they also contain the potential for human development. It is no surprise, therefore, to anyone who adopts a needs-based approach to consumer spending, to find that consumer expenditure associated with the sorts of activities listed is developing very rapidly. It may be objected that our approach is no more than *ad hoc* rationalizing of the use of the growing leisure time available as machines take over from men and real incomes continue to rise. In these conditions, however, people still have the option of trying to find further work or simply doing nothing. The fact that so many *prefer* to engage in the sorts of pursuit listed strongly suggests that doing so meets a felt need.

A process of self-actualization through the means discussed above is time-consuming, and since there are no more than twenty-four hours in the day, one's ability, and capacity, to indulge in activities will be limited. It may well be the case, therefore, that in the longer run producers will have to rely on the need for esteem to provide the impetus to consumption of an ever-increasing quantity of goods. The role of advertising and salesmanship would then assume even greater importance, and we might yet find ourselves in the situation which Galbraith maintains is already with us.

3.4.3 Social comparisons and consumer behaviour

Much of the empirical work relating to the influence of social comparisons on consumer behaviour makes use of the concept of reference group, which we examined in section 2.6. It is not surprising to find, therefore, that many of these studies talk in terms of the normative and comparative influences of such groups, although a variety of other influences have also been identified, many of which would appear to be covered by the terms 'normative' and 'comparative', such as 'socialization', development of the 'self-concept' and 'value-expressive' (the latter being characterized by the need for psychological association with a person or group). Some work also attributes an important informative role to reference groups, in the way they may be used to disseminate knowledge about the goods on offer. Advertising and salesmanship, as Galbraith (1958) noted, may also exert their influence through the process of social comparisons.

Although psychologists have for some time been investigating group behaviour, and the influence which groups exert, it is only relatively recently that these findings have been applied to the study of consumer behaviour. Two examples of studies of small group activities which have been influential in helping to explain certain aspects of consumer behaviour are those by Asch (1951) and Sherif (1936). Asch, using a control group for the purposes of comparison, was able to demonstrate how the views of a majority of group members exerted an influence on a minority (especially if the minority consisted of only one person) even when the views of the majority were contrary to the facts of a situation. Personal character did count for something, however, since some individuals showed themselves to be less easily influenced than others.

In his much earlier study, Sheriff showed how individuals, when asked to sit in a dark room (without any points of reference) and estimate the distance moved by a point of light (which in fact remained stationary throughout the experiment) modified their estimates when put in a group situation. The tendency of individuals when brought together in a group was to structure the situation by converging towards a common norm in their judgements. The process, it is interesting to note, was not in all cases a conscious one.

Two important conclusions emerge from these studies which have a bearing on consumer behaviour – and the findings are supported by other studies in the field (see Howard, 1963). First, group pressures may exert an influence on what the individual believes he perceives. Second, in the absence of objective standards or norms (and sometimes even when such standards or norms are available) the individual will turn to other people for guidance on what the norms should be.

Product and brand selection In an attempt to study the effect of group pressure on the consumer decision-making process, Venkatesan (1966) experimented with individuals' choices between men's suits (presented individually) which were identical in style, colour and size. In the absence of group pressures, choice did not differ significantly from a chance distribution. When, however, an individual was confronted with a unanimous choice by other members of his peer group (in this case male college students not majoring in psychology) individuals tended to conform to the group norm. In less rigid tests in which members of a group did not present a united front, but rather attempted to influence an individual indirectly in favour of a particular selection, there was less evidence of conformity. A modified version of these tests by Sims (1971) produced similar results.

So far we have not attempted to distinguish between different types of product in assessing group influence. Bourne (1957), however, has maintained that reference group influence varies with the 'conspicuousness' of a good, i.e. it depends upon how exclusive a good is and how readily recognized it is by consumers. In a follow-up study, Bearden and Etzel (1982) interpreted 'exclusive' to mean a distinction between luxuries and necessities, and 'recognition' to signify those goods consumed publicly, as distinct from those which tended to be consumed in private. A combination of the luxuries-necessities and public-private distinctions yielded a 2 × 2 matrix of categories: (1) publicly-consumed luxuries; (2) publicly-consumed necessities; (3) privately-consumed luxuries; (4) privately-consumed necessities. Taking each of these in turn, Bourne's approach when applied to product and brand decisions suggested the following:

(1) *Publicly-consumed luxuries*
Strong reference group influence on *product* purchases because it is a luxury, and also *strong* influence on choice of *brand* because the product will be seen by others. A suggested example – golf clubs.

(2) *Privately-consumed luxuries*
Strong product influence, but *weak brand* influence, because the product will not be seen by others. Suggested example – a waste compactor.

(3) *Publicly-consumed necessities*
Weak reference group influence on *product* purchases because the products are widely owned, but a *strong* influence on the *brand* selected because the product is widely seen by others. Suggested example – an automobile.

(4) *Privately-consumed necessities*
Influence on *product* choice again *weak*, and so too is their influence on *brand*, since the product will not be seen by others. Suggested example – a mattress.

The results of the investigation confirmed the value of the four-fold distinction between luxury and necessity and publicly and privately consumed goods, and of the need therefore to take account of the differing impact of reference group influence according to the type of good being considered. The findings also indicated that although reference groups influenced both product and brand choice, the effect was greatest in the case of the latter. It might be the case, therefore, that need satisfaction requires products with specific characteristics, whereas the particular brand selected of a good is more often due to the persuasive influence of reference groups. We shall return to the question of reference group influence on brand selection below.

Yet another example of reference group influence on product choice is the study by Moschis (1976) of female users of cosmetics (perfume, face make-up base, hand cream or lotion, lipstick and eye make-up) – this study also investigated the use of reference groups as an information source, a further topic to which we return below. Based on a combination of a direct approach to shoppers and a mailed questionnaire, data were assembled which confirmed once more that reference groups – both those with whom the subjects were in some direct form of interaction and those with whom the relationship was comparative and less direct – did influence product choice. Moschis's conclusion was that 'informal groups exert a great influence on their members' purchasing behaviour when there is a high degree of similarity among members on various attributes relevant to products under consideration.'

A word of caution has been introduced by Park and Lessig (1977) into discussions of the role of reference groups in determining product choice. They have remarked on the fact that many of the studies in this area have used college students as respondents, and when comparisons have been made between students and other groups – frequently housewives – no unequivocal conclusions have been drawn. Their own study results indicated that although the differences between the two groups were not marked in respect of all products, students were nevertheless likely to be more receptive to reference group influence on product choice. Among the reasons suggested for the divergence were that students might be subject to more peer pressure, the differences in average ages, and the possibly more hedonistic attitude to life of the students. It would certainly be interesting to have more information about the reasons for divergences in behaviour between groups, but for present purposes the main conclusion is that the Park and Lessig study provides still further evidence that reference groups do indeed influence consumers' product choices.

Turning now to the studies concerned with the influence of reference groups on *brand* selection, one of the earliest investigations was by Stafford (1966), who tested three hypotheses. First, that small, informal social groups did exert an influence towards conformity in member brand preference. Second, that the degree of influence exerted on a member by the group was directly related to the cohesiveness of the group.

Finally, that the group 'leader' (selected on the basis of attractiveness, expertness and the central role played in communications between members) had the greatest individual influence on group choice. Membership of each group studied was based on personal nominations by housewives (who were themselves randomly selected) of other housewives with whom they would like to, or were willing to go shopping. In this way groups of women were gathered together who were friendlily disposed towards each other, who interacted, and who had been selected with a view to shopping together. The tests related to different brands of one product – white bread. Analysis of variance confirmed the first hypothesis, but in attempting to explain *how* group influence was exerted, no statistical significance could be found between cohesiveness and brand loyalty. Only when cohesiveness and leadership were combined (a link between the two having been noticed) was a relationship with brand selection established. The degree of brand loyalty by the leader was also found to influence group member choice.

A later study by Witt (1969) of four products used by undergraduate students (beer, aftershave lotion, deodorant and cigarettes) again found group cohesion to be a factor influencing brand choice, together with a knowledge by group members of the frequency of use of brands by other members of the group. The findings also showed that the strength of these influences varied appreciably between products, being strongest in the case of beer and deodorant, and relatively weak in the case of cigarettes and aftershave. The existence of important product differences was confirmed in a subsequent study by Witt and Bruce (1970).

A recent investigation by Reingen *et al.* (1984) has drawn attention to a number of criticisms of the work on reference group influence on product and brand choice. They note, for example, that Hansen (1969) was unable to support the existence of a relationship between group cohesiveness and brand congruence, and that Ford and Ellis (1980) were unable to replicate the findings of Stafford (1966). They have also cast doubt on the procedures used to select and define the informal groups used by researchers such as Stafford and Witt. They advocate instead the use of groups whose sociological and formal properties are systematically and precisely controlled. They also doubt whether all types of social relationships used as a basis for studying reference group influence, such as those of friends, neighbours and fellow students, are necessarily appropriate to consumer decisions about some at least of the products and brands investigated.

In an effort to overcome the problems, Reingen *et al.* used techniques of social network analysis to study the stated brand preferences of individuals in several kinds of basic sociological structures or groups – such as close friends, room-mates, neighbours and fellow participants in sporting activities. The analysis covered both tangible and intangible 'products' (e.g. shampoos and TV shows). The overall results suggested strongly that brand congruence depended heavily upon a complex mixture of type of product, social mix and social structural units. The findings of the earlier studies by Stafford, Witt, etc. were therefore confirmed despite the different methodological approach used. Furthermore, the Reingen results also suggested support for the more specific findings of earlier studies that group cohesiveness influences members' brand choices.

The communication of information In section 2.6 we remarked that Ofshe (1972) had identified a third form of reference group additional to comparative and normative groups, which he referred to as an 'informational reference' source. To take one example, an individual wishing to solve a problem (which is in effect the situation facing a consumer required to choose between different products and brands) or attain a goal might use a reference individual or group as a source of useful information which was of assistance to him. In our earlier discussion of product and brand selection, it is possible therefore that as well as using reference groups to help establish a norm for behaviour, the individual was also using the groups as a source of information which was helpful in the selection of products and brands – views on the respective merits of the products and brands, for example, which are especially important in the case of complex, expensive durable goods which are purchased infrequently.

The 'informational' aspect of product and brand selection

has been investigated by Burnkrant and Cousineau (1975). After a study of the choice of different brands of instant coffee, they concluded that people use other's product evaluations as a source of information about the product:

> It seems that, after observing others evaluating a product favourably, people perceive the product more favourably themselves than they would have in the absence of this information. They use the evaluations of others as a basis for inferring that the product is, indeed, a better product.

Rather than the subjects' complying with the norms of a reference group, it may be, therefore, that agreement within a group may be due to qualities the individuals are able to attribute to products as a consequence of the observed reactions of others. The reactions, in effect, may serve as a basis for inference about a product's characteristics. In the survey by Moschis (1976) of the factors determining the choice of cosmetics to which we referred earlier, it was also found that the groups to which individuals turned for information were more likely to be composed of friends with whom they had similar attributes than persons with whom they had little in common.

McGuire (1976) has suggested a useful classification of the socio-psychological factors influencing consumer choice which helps put our discussion to date in context. He distinguishes, first, between the external and internal factors having a bearing on choice. Among the former he includes product-relevant communications received from other persons, either by means of face-to-face contact or via the mass media. The internal factors he subdivides into a 'directive aspect' and a 'dynamic aspect'. The directive aspect he describes as 'the structural characteristics of one's personality that channel the information processing of one's own experiences and of communications from other people through successive steps ... to the ultimate purchasing act and consumption behaviour.' The directive aspect is therefore concerned, in effect, with processing the external communications received from other people and the influences of stored past experiences. Finally, the dynamic aspects of personality are the motivating forces which energize, direct, sustain and ultimately terminate the information processing. McGuire formulated his own classification of motives, based largely on the cognitive and humanistic approaches to motivation, and a distinction between those theories which stress the goal of the individual as being the maintenance of equilibrium and those which stress a person's need for further growth.

A summary of the literature on the information-processing approach to consumer choice is given by Bettman (1979), who also attempts to devise his own detailed, integrated framework of analysis, based on human motivation and the setting of goals by consumers. His framework, as he notes, is compatible with that outlined by McGuire, and his approach is very much in the same vein as that of Herbert Simon, which we looked at earlier. Individual consumers are depicted as having a very limited capacity for processing information:

> ... consumers do not typically undertake complicated computations or analysis or engage in extensive processing. Rather, consumers use simpler heuristics, or rules of thumb, to help them in dealing with potentially complex choice situations. Such heuristics as 'buy what I bought last time' or 'find the brand with the highest protein content' may be used to select an alternative.

It is the communications received by individuals as part of the raw material for processing which is our immediate concern, however, and we now turn to examine the importance of social comparisons to advertising, which is among the most powerful of the 'external' influences on consumer behaviour.

Advertising and social comparisons Advertising frequently makes use of social comparisons as a means of triggering the decision to buy a good. An example of the informative role of a reference group is the common use of respected figures, say in the world of sport, to point out the virtues of particular goods, perhaps on television or in newspaper advertisements. The message has greater impact because it comes from someone who is widely regarded as an authoritative source, and who is doubtless also considered trustworthy. There may be a feeling, too, that if one or more top ranking tennis players, for example, use a particular brand of tennis racket, then the norm for those aspiring to play good tennis is to use the same brand of racket. This normative role of the reference group is also frequently made use of by advertisers. Other examples are commonly provided by advertisements for clothing, drink and cigarettes, with the products being linked to groups of people with whom consumers wish to identify themselves. In such instances, conformity on the part of a consumer might well be rewarded through closer association with a group. Lack of conformity, on the other hand, could lead to sanctions, perhaps even exclusion from the group.

A number of writers have also stressed the part advertising may play in the development of a consumer's 'self-concept' (see, for example, O'Brien *et al.*, 1977; Lessig and Park, 1978), i.e. the way the consumer perceives himself, what he thinks of himself, how he values himself and how he sees himself in relation to others. Self-enhancement (the process of improving one's self-concept over time) depends in part on the reactions of those whose opinions the person values. The purchase of goods may be strongly influenced by the image the buyer wishes to convey, and the extent to which the goods help foster this image.

In their study of the advertising implications of reference group influence, Lessig and Park (1978) found, as one might expect, that there was an appreciable difference between products in the degree of influence exerted by reference groups. Some showed no discernible influence, others only limited influence, but a third set of products – which included colour television, automobiles, refrigerators, clothing and furniture – appeared to be influenced by informational, normative and self-concept reference groups. Such findings give helpful guidance to advertisers about the factors which they should stress in their advertisements, and the types of person who should feature in adverts.

The above discussion gives an indication of some of the ways in which advertising may serve to stimulate wants, and therefore the demand for products. The normative and self-concept influences of reference groups, in particular, appear to offer enormous scope for the promotion of goods, and almost certainly help explain why consumer spending keeps on increasing, yet still leaves many wants unsatisfied.

3.5 FROM MICRO TO MACRO: THE CONSUMPTION FUNCTION

The transition from microeconomics to macroeconomics is generally an uneasy one, since what holds true for the individual or firm need not hold true for individuals or firms in the aggregate. We have already seen that even in shifting the analysis from the individual to the family, problems of aggregation arise. It is not possible simply to assume that a family of four people will consume the same as the four would do living separate lives and acting individually. Expenditure per head to meet the basic needs for food, heating, lighting, accommodation and perhaps also clothing will almost certainly vary according to whether persons live independently or communally. Individual preferences also differ, and, in the case of reference groups, overlapping may well occur. There is nothing in our analysis to suggest, however, that our general approach is inapplicable at an aggregated level. Motivational forces, such as needs, the desire for equity and the importance of goals do not suddenly become irrelevant when individuals group together, even if joint needs, notions of equity and goals may well differ somewhat from those of individuals. In any reasonably democratic society at least, individuals will, after all, have a say in aggregate decisions. We can also expect that the importance of social comparisons will be reflected to some degree in these aggregate decisions. We move on, therefore, to examine the relevance of our previous analysis to the consumption function.

We look first at the lifecycle and permanent income versions of the consumption function, which are now frequently grouped together because of the common stress they place on the need to take account of expected lifetime income, not just current income, in determining individuals' consumption. Both approaches rest on the assumption that individual consumers attempt to maximize a utility function, subject to an income constraint. From our earlier analysis we would therefore expect that consumers' expenditure would be determined by factors associated both with the consumption lifecycle and the income lifecycle. In the case of the permanent income hypothesis, Modigliani and his associates recognize in presenting their hypothesis that there are, 'systematic variations in income and in "needs" which occur over the lifecycle, as a result of maturing and retiring, and of changes in family size – hence the name Life Cycle Hypothesis' (Modigliani, 1986). In other words, the existence of both income and consumption lifecycle effects is explicitly recognized.

In the original article setting out the theoretical foundations of the lifecycle hypothesis (written in 1952 by Modigliani and Brumberg, but not published until much later in Modigliani, 1980), the aggregate consumption function was derived by summing the *average* consumption of each age group over the life span as follows:

$$c^T_t = (1/L_t)\, y^T + [(N-t)/L_t] y^{eT} + a^T_t/L_t \tag{3.4}$$

Where, N–t is the balance of the earning span at age t;
L_t denotes the remaining life span at age t;
T is the calendar year or period (used also as a superscript to date a variable);
a_t average net worth of the age group in the year T;
Y^T average income, other than from assets, per household in the earning span;
y^{eT} average income expected in any later year, by consumer in year T;
c^T_t average consumption of non-durable goods and services plus current depreciation of direct service-yielding durable goods by the age group of age t in the year T.

Summing over all age groups, the aggregate consumption function was given by:

$$c^T = \sum_{t=1}^{L} n^T_t\ c^T_t = \sum_{t=1}^{N} (n^T_t/L_t) y^T + \sum_{t=1}^{N} [n^T_t (N-t)/L_t] y^{eT} + \sum_{t=1}^{L} (n^T_t a^T_t)/L_t = \sum_{t=1}^{N} (n^T_t/S^T_1 L_t)\, Y^T + \sum_{t=1}^{N} [n^T_t (N-t)/ S^T_1 L_t]\, Y^{eT} + \sum_{t=1}^{L} (n^T_t a^T_t)/L_t$$

or,

$$c^T = \alpha^T Y^T + \beta^T Y^{eT} + \lambda^T \tag{3.5}$$

where,

$$\alpha^T = \sum_{t=1}^{N} n^T_t / S^T_1 L_t, \; \beta^T = \sum_{t=1}^{N} [n^T_t (N-t)]/S^T_1 L_t \text{ and}$$

$$\lambda^T = \sum_{t=1}^{L} n^T_t a^T_t / L_t$$

and where n_t is the number of households in age group t;
S is the total number of households;

$$S_1 = \sum_{t=1}^{N} n_t \quad \text{the number of households in the earning span.}$$

The above rests on a number of simplifying assumptions, for example that every age group within the earning span has the same average income in any given year T, and that the average expected income by any age group t for any later year within the earning span is the same. These assumptions were later relaxed without materially altering the equations, and the consumption function for the purposes of empirical testing 'over a not-too-long stretch of time' was approximated by an equation of the form:

$$C^T = \alpha Y^T + \beta Y^{eT} + \delta A^T \tag{3.6}$$

Modigliani and Brumberg expected the coefficients α and β to change only slowly, if at all, over time, since most of the variables affecting the coefficients were thought to change slowly. Among these variables they included the lengths of the earning and retirement spans, and the relationship between them, the age distribution of the population and of assets, and 'the typical life pattern of income and consumption'.

Statements of the lifecycle hypothesis do not, unfortunately, always spell out these important qualifications in respect of the constancy of α and β, and tend therefore to present the hypothesis almost entirely in terms of the income and assets aspects of the hypothesis, despite the fact that there have in most advanced industrial countries been major changes in the age distribution of the population, and in the ages of marriage and retirement, the average size of the family, etc. in the period since the end of the Second World War – a period covered by many empirical studies of the consumption function. Many of these social changes have a bearing on needs, and therefore on the consumption lifecycle. Since they may be important enough to affect the coefficients α and β in equation (3.6) they ought certainly to feature in tests of the consumption function.

The failure of the lifecycle hypothesis to allow for the effects on consumption of changes in the composition of the family prompted Fisher (1956) to refer to the hypothesis as 'the bachelor theory of saving'. Tobin (1967), as we remarked earlier, has also commented on the failure of the Modigliani-Brumberg lifecycle to take account of children. He found it, 'implausible to assume that parents spread consumption evenly over adult life, independently of the number of mouths to feed'. In empirical tests of the lifecycle hypothesis, White (1978) found that, when allowance was made for family size, the effect was to reduce aggregate household saving – despite this adjustment, however, the lifecycle hypothesis still proved rather poor at explaining aggregate personal saving in the years in question.

Turning to the permanent income hypothesis, we may summarize it in the familiar system of three simple equations used by Friedman (1957):

$$c_p = k\,(i, w, u)\, y_p \qquad (3.7)$$

$$y = y_p + y_t \qquad (3.8)$$

$$c = c_p + c_t \qquad (3.9)$$

Equation (3.7) defines the relationship between permanent income (y_p) and permanent consumption (c_p), specifying that the ratio between them is independent of the size of permanent income, but dependent upon the rate of interest (i), the ratio of non-human wealth to permanent income (w) and a portfolio of variables (u) which determine the consumer unit's tastes and preferences for consumption versus additions to wealth. According to Friedman, u includes, 'the number of members of the consumer unit and their characteristics, particularly ages'.

Equations (3.8) and (3.9) are simply the identities denoting that total income and consumption are made up of transitory and permanent components, indicated by the subscripts t and p, respectively.

Since equation (3.7) relates to what Friedman calls a 'consumer unit' (which is a collective of individuals rather than a single person, and seems to be akin to a family) it has to be decided whether, for the purposes of aggregation, equation (3.7) is also applicable to an aggregate of consumer units. Friedman argues that the variables w and u are designed expressly to allow for differences among consumer units. If, furthermore, we assume that the distribution of consumer units by income is independent of their distribution by i, w and u, then we can reduce equation (3.7) to:

$$c_p = k^* \, y^*_p \tag{3.10}$$

where, aggregate permanent consumption (c^*_p) is a constant proportion (k^*) of aggregate permanent income (y^*_p). As a description of the real world, Friedman admits that equation (3.10) is false, in that age and size of family, for example, which are included in u, are known to be related systematically to the distribution of income. Friedman maintains, nevertheless, that equation (3.10) is a good approximation of the relation among observed magnitudes, and that interdependence must therefore be of only secondary importance. This conclusion, he notes later, however, appears to owe more to offsetting tendencies among the factors which influence the constancy of k^*, than to any definite indication that they are unimportant. This happy coincidence of offsetting tendencies is not, however, something which can be relied upon in all periods, and the possible influences on k^* ought not, therefore, to be ignored.

In his 1973 survey of consumer economics, Ferber remarked on the neglect of the theoretical underpinnings of socio-economic variables in the consumption function (other than the lifecycle). The usual criterion for the selection of variables for testing, he noted, tended to be, 'the very pragmatic one of throwing in all such variables available'. Many of these variables turned out to be statistically significant, and there the matter was allowed to rest.

We have seen above that the lifecycle hypothesis and the permanent income hypothesis do not ignore socio-economic and psychological variables, although the former hypothesis assumes that they exert an effect only very slowly, and can therefore be ignored for practical purposes, while the permanent income hypothesis reaches much the same conclusion due to a coincidence of offsetting factors. Only Duesenberry's relative income hypothesis accords a central role to socio-economic and psychological variables, and we therefore now turn to see how it relates to the framework of analysis we have adopted so far in the present study.[2]

Duesenberry's thesis is not, of course, that relative income alone determines personal saving. He recognizes that asset holdings, interest rates, expectations and other factors must also play a part, but relative income, he maintains, is the dominant influence. The basis of his argument is that the preference system of analysis of consumer behaviour lacks a theory of consumer motivation. Indeed, he claims that the preference system, as it has been developed, 'is a more or less deliberate attempt to sidestep the task of making any psychological assumptions'. Duesenberry's own theory is in essence needs-based, although he also allots a key role to social comparisons. Writing prior to the development of the current theories of needs, he distinguished three main reasons for consumers' desires for the things they buy: to maintain physical existence or physical comfort; to participate in activities which are an essential part of the consumer culture; the maintenance of social status. People, he observed, 'do not, for the most part, desire specific goods but desire goods which will serve certain purposes.' He goes on to recognize that a variety of goods may be suitable for one purpose, but that some will be better for that purpose than others – an early recognition of goods' characteristics, which draws attention once more to the close link between the needs-based approach and the analysis of goods' characteristics.

The form of the decision-making process is important in Duesenberry's theory. Spending decisions have to be related to each other because of the income constraint. The mechanism connecting these consumption decisions is not, however, one of rational planning as the preference theory assumes, but rather one of learning and habit formation. The example is given of a man suffering a (permanent) 50 per cent reduction in his income. Initially, habit dictates that spending decisions are not adjusted immediately to the lower level of income. With the passage of time, however, the consumer learns that adjustment is unavoidable, and how best to make the adjustment, in terms of what is bought. Once the adjustment is made, force of habit tends to reassert itself.

Purchasing habits can be broken, however, without any accompanying change in income or prices. One of the foremost influences in changing habits, according to Duesenberry, is contact with goods of superior quality to those already in use by a consumer. Increased expenditure by those with whom the consumer comes into contact will give rise to the 'demonstration effect' we referred to earlier, causing the consumer to desire goods of higher quality. One of the principal goals of society is to raise living standards (in which higher quality goods play an important part) and this driving force is further strengthened by the widespread desire in society for social status: 'every individual makes comparisons between his own living standard and those of his associates in higher or lower status positions.' Social comparisons are therefore crucially important in Duesenberry's model, tending to drive consumption upward in the pursuit of both higher living standards and high social standing. Dissatisfaction with *current* consumption standards also affects *future* consumption, thereby introducing intertemporal features to the model.

Taking the above factors into account, Duesenberry advocates a revised form of the utility function, which he expresses as:

$$Ui = fi\,(Cil/Ri, \ldots Cin/Ri, Ail/Ri, \ldots Ain/Ri) \qquad (3.11)$$

Where, Ui is the utility index of the ith individual, and Ci and Ai are the consumption expenditure and value of assets, respectively, of i in the kth time period. $Ri = \Sigma\alpha\ ij\ Cj$ is a weighted average of the consumption expenditures of other individuals, with α ij the weight attached by i to the consumption of the jth individual.

If, as Duesenberry assumes, the individual attempts to maximize his utility, he will choose a current level of consumption, and plan future consumption, in order to maximize Ui, subject to the restraints of actual and expected incomes, interest rates and assets. This leads to a set of equations for each individual, the number of equations depending upon the number of time-periods and the number of consumption goods and assets. To obtain current consumption in a system of x individuals, we then have x equations of the form

$$Ci/Ri = f\,(Yil/Ri, \ldots Yin/Ri, Ai/Rirl, r2 \ldots rn) \quad (3.12)$$

where the Yi's are expected incomes, the r's interest rates and A current assets. Since there are x unknown C i's and x equations, there is an equilibrium value for each individual's consumption.

Looking now at the relationship between these hypotheses (our remarks generally also apply to Keynes' absolute income hypothesis) we can see that all three posit an aggregate utility function based on utility-maximizing behaviour by individual consumers. According to our earlier reasoning they are therefore all ultimately needs-based theories. Duesenberry's hypothesis is, however, the only one to incorporate the additional element of social comparisons, which we would argue is indispensable to a theory of consumer behaviour.

While all three hypotheses are ultimately needs-based, only Duesenberry attempts to pursue the implications of the needs approach at any length. The other two theories concentrate very largely on the income lifecycle, relegating the consumption lifecycle to the role of an also-ran. The reasons advanced for playing down the importance of consumption lifecycle variables are far from convincing, and we believe their possible importance ought at least to be tested in empirical work on the consumption function.

Since all three hypotheses are clearly out of the same stable, yet emphasize different, but essential, aspects of consumer behaviour, they ought to be regarded as complementary rather than competing theories. A comprehensive theory of the consumption function must inevitably include the central features of all three theories, as well as many of the more recent developments relating to the consumption function, including, for example, those which have attempted to place it in a more dynamic setting – generally still concentrating, however, only on the income lifecycle.

While it complicates the analysis still further, the notion of reference groups should also be introduced when trying to allow for the influence of interdependent preferences on consumer behaviour. There is certainly sufficient evidence now that they are important at the micro-level. Attempting to catch their influence at the macro-level would, admittedly, pose difficult practical problems, but no greater problems than those already posed by the concepts introduced in the other main hypotheses – finding suitable proxy variables is a *general* problem in macroeconomic work. As Ferber (1973) noted when commenting on the permanent income concept:

> However formulated, it is surprising to note how often the testable and successful form of the hypothesis reduced to the inclusion of lagged consumption as the manifestation of income effects.

Finally, in those countries in which transfers from central government have grown to be a significant source of consumer income, their possible consequences for personal consumption, as we suggested in equation (3.2), should also not be disregarded.

3.6 CONCLUSIONS

The analysis of consumer behaviour tends to be approached at present from two apparently different viewpoints. In neo-classical economics, the analysis rests mainly on utility theory, the use of indifference curves and the revealed preferences of consumers. The principal emphasis is placed on income and price changes in explaining consumer behaviour, with other possible influences relegated to minor supporting roles. A feature of this approach is that, even at the micro-level, a strict demarcation line is drawn between consumer utility, or satisfaction, as a tool of analysis, and the socio-psychological foundations upon which the notions of utility and satisfaction must ultimately rest. Such a restricted approach to consumer behaviour entails a high degree of risk, because it means that one of the cornerstones of economic theory rests on constructs which are not properly understood by economists, and whose nature can only be appreciated by close examination of their socio-psychological foundations. The dangers of misinterpretation are obvious. Rather than face up to this problem, however, economics simply makes a number of convenient, simplifying assumptions, with little or no attempt to justify them. There the matter rests, despite repeated criticisms over many years of this deplorable state of affairs.

The other main approach to the analysis of consumer behaviour draws its inspiration principally from those relevant studies in the fields of sociology and psychology which economics so wilfully ignores. This approach is also strongly influenced by microeconomic theory, but there has been only limited progress in integrating the economic and behavioural theories which have been found useful. This approach places a heavy emphasis on empirical investigation, and the findings have frequently been found of value to those in business. It is not surprising, therefore, that this approach tends to be well represented in courses designed for those with an interest in business affairs.

The present study, it is hoped, shows that the differences between these approaches are more apparent than real. Both approaches are ultimately needs-based, and they already incorporate, or ought to incorporate, an important element of social comparisons. In order fully to appreciate the importance of needs, we have to distinguish between the consumption lifecycle and the income lifecycle. The latter is related to age, since those in employment tend to become more skilled, knowledgeable and experienced with the passage of time, and perhaps also acquire greater seniority with added years. Moreover, earnings only begin to accumulate after one is old enough to start work, and they end on retirement at an advanced age. The consumption lifecycle, on the other hand, whilst inevitably influenced by the income constraint, also has a rhythm (one might even say a life) of its own, with age and the family life cycle being dominant influences.

While at the micro-level it would be difficult to deny the

importance of the consumption lifecycle, at the macro-level its consequences are less easily described, partly because they may be submerged in longer-term trends, and partly because of the difficulties of testing for the effects of some of the relevant variables. These difficulties do not seem insurmountable, however, and the inadequate attention paid to them probably owes more to a lack of conviction about, or a failure to appreciate, their theoretical significance, than to the practical problems they pose.

The evidence that social comparisons are important to consumers is now overwhelming, and the conventional neo-classical theory of the consumer will remain unconvincing so long as it refuses to recognize this fact of life. Once again, it is difficult to catch the effects of such a factor at the macro-level, but it is not impossible, as Duesenberry's work demonstrates.

We conclude, then, that intervening variables, in particular needs and social comparisons, can help provide us with a more unified framework for analysing consumer behaviour. The theory which emerges is also immeasurably richer and more dynamic, and applicable to a much wider range of circumstances than will ever be possible using conventional economic analysis.

4 The Labour Market

The analysis in the preceding sections has important implications for the workings of the labour market, and is also helpful in understanding some of the developments which have taken place in the labour markets of the main industrial countries in the period since the Second World War. One of the principal developments has been the increase in the supply of labour, associated not only with growing populations, but also with rising participation rates. The neo-classical economic model explains such a growing labour supply in terms of rising real wages, but this explanation appears unconvincing to many economists, and it fits ill with the widespread downward inflexibility of wages which is all too evident in the real marketplace.

It can always be argued, of course, that the adjustments necessary to remove imbalances in the labour market will take place in the long run, and that the labour market does therefore still work like a commodity market. It is already evident, however, that many industrial countries are now faced with highly persistent unemployment on a scale which can no longer be put down to temporary malfunctions of the marketplace. Just as the labour market repercussions of the Great Depression in the inter-war years lead to a questioning of the then current orthodoxy, so ought we now to be re-examining the dominant economic theories to see if they match up to the realities of the present time.

4.1 THE SUPPLY OF LABOUR

We begin the present section by looking at the main trends in the supply of labour, and the explanation offered by orthodox theory for these trends. The trends are divergent, and it seems unlikely that any unicausal explanation will be adequate. The demand for labour is also examined, but only in so far as it relates to changes in labour supply. As we shall see, there are strong grounds for believing that the growth in labour supply has been, in part at least, a response to the forms which labour demand has taken.

4.1.1 Trends in the supply of labour

It is helpful before embarking on an explanation of changes in the supply of labour to identify the main trends which we need to explain. Many of the major trends are common to all, or most, of the more advanced industrial countries. One of the most pronounced trends (other than that for total populations to increase due to demographic factors) has been the rise in the participation rate among females of working age. Table 4.1 shows how widespread this has been. An important exception to the rule is Japan, which, however, had an exceptionally high female participation rate in the 1960s compared with other countries: it has now been overtaken by the US and the UK.

In the case of males, countries generally show a declining participation rate in the aggregate, with the decline being most pronounced in West Germany and Italy, and among the smaller countries of the OECD. Combining both male and female participation rates, experience is very mixed, with the US, the UK and Canada, among the larger OECD countries, showing some increase, and the others a decline – again treating the smaller OECD countries as one bloc.

Trends in the aggregate participation rates disguise a number of important developments related to the age of the labour force participants. In a good many countries, including the United Kingdom, West Germany, France and Italy, the proportion of males under the age of 25 working in the labour force has tended to decrease (Table 4.2) although since the late 1970s the rate has shown signs of recovery in a number of countries, of which Japan is one. In the United States, the rate

Table 4.1: Labour force as a percentage of the population from age 16 to 64

	Annual Average		
	1960 – 67	1968 – 73	1974 – 81
Males			
United States	89.6	86.9	85.5
Japan	90.1	89.6	89.4
West Germany	94.4	91.5	85.1
France	90.8	87.3	83.7
United Kingdom	96.9	94.0	91.3
Italy	92.0	86.7	83.5
Canada	89.0	85.9	85.9
Smaller OECD countries	96.3	92.9	87.3
Females			
United States	43.9	49.0	56.5
Japan	57.6	54.8	53.5
West Germany	48.9	48.4	49.7
France	45.5	47.4	51.3
United Kingdom	48.1	51.1	56.7
Italy	36.4	33.5	37.4
Canada	36.9	44.1	53.2
Smaller OECD countries	42.0	43.0	46.4
Males and females			
United States	66.5	67.7	70.8
Japan	73.5	71.9	71.2
West Germany	70.4	69.2	67.1
France	68.1	67.4	67.6
United Kingdom	72.2	72.5	74.0
Italy	63.3	59.5	59.9
Canada	63.1	65.1	69.6
Smaller OECD countries	68.8	67.8	66.9

Source: OECD Economic Outlook, Historical Statistics, 1960–1981 (Paris, OECD, 1983).

has risen marginally in recent years, but there has still been a decline over the longer term.

In the case of females under 25, there are again national differences, with the participation rate declining appreciably in Japan, but rising slightly in the UK and the US. Among those aged 65 and over, the general trend in participation is downwards, amongst both males and females.

Table 4.2: Participation rates by age and sex

	Percentage				
	1965	1970	1975	1980	1985
United States					
Males 16–24	70.9	71.8	73.2	74.5	73.1
25–54	95.7	94.8	93.8	93.4	93.1
55–64	82.9	80.7	74.6	71.2	67.9
65 and over	26.6	25.7	20.7	18.3	15.7
All males	91.5	90.1	88.2	87.8	87.0
Females 16–24	43.6	50.7	57.1	61.7	62.9
25–54	45.1	49.7	55.0	63.8	68.1
55–64	40.3	42.2	40.7	41.0	41.5
54 and over	9.4	9.0	7.8	7.6	7.0
All females	45.7	50.4	54.9	61.3	64.3
United Kingdom					
Males 16–24	77.4	74.7	67.9	70.5	72.3
25–54	98.4	97.8	96.1	96.1	94.8
55–64	92.7	91.3	87.8	81.8	69.2
65 and over	23.7	20.2	15.8	10.5	7.8
All males	96.0	94.4	90.9	89.2	86.1
Females 16–24	61.0	56.7	56.4	62.2	63.5
25–54	48.1	53.2	61.3	64.0	64.5
55–64	35.6	39.3	40.3	39.2	34.6
65 and over	6.5	6.4	4.9	3.6	3.8
All females	50.0	52.8	57.6	60.1	59.9
Japan					
Males 16–24	59.0	57.7	50.2	42.9	43.3
25–54	96.7	97.3	97.4	97.0	97.0
55–64	86.7	86.6	86.0	85.4	83.8
65 and over	56.3	49.4	44.4	41.0	37.6
All males	88.5	89.2	89.7	89.0	88.4
Females 16–24	51.8	53.4	45.6	43.9	44.3
25–54	56.0	55.1	52.3	56.7	60.0
55–64	45.3	44.4	43.7	45.3	45.0
65 and over	21.6	17.9	15.3	15.5	15.9
All females	55.8	55.4	51.7	54.9	57.2

Source: *Labour Force Statistics, 1963–1983* (Paris, OECD, 1985).

In the middle age ranges we also find major divergencies. In the age bracket 25–54, covering the bulk of the active labour force, most countries, including the US and the UK, have experienced a downward trend in male participation rates in recent years. Japan is once again a major exception to the rule, with the rate there remaining fairly level. It is amongst females in this age bracket, however, that the most dramatic changes have occurred. Between 1965 and 1984, the female participation rate in this age range rose from 45 per cent to 68 per cent in the United States. In the United Kingdom over the same period the corresponding figures were 48 per cent and 65 per cent. Even in Japan there has been some increase overall, although it has mainly taken place during the 1980s.

The only major working age group we have not yet mentioned is that between 55 and 64. There again seem to be grounds for treating this category separately from the others. First, as males increase in age, it is over this age range that male participation first shows signs of falling appreciably. It is also noticeable that female participation rates in this age group have tended to level out in both the US and UK, and show no signs of increasing further. In Japan, too, the participation rate has been level since the 1960s.

It is apparent from the many divergent labour supply trends noted above that it is going to be very difficult for any one theory to explain simultaneously the events which have occurred. Indeed, Killingsworth (1981), in the conclusions to his very extensive survey of the literature on the labour supply, noted that there appeared to have been no comprehensive study which had attempted a simultaneous explanation of the trends in male and female participation. When we add to participation rates the changes which have taken place in hours of work, the picture becomes even more complex.

At the same time as the participation rate has been rising overall in most countries, the average number of hours worked has been declining. In the United States, the average number of paid hours of work in private non-farm industries has fallen from around 58 at the turn of the century to about 35 hours at the present time. The number of hours *actually* worked in manufacturing industries shows a slightly less steep decline, but the same general trend is evident. Since the Second World War the pace of decline has slackened considerably, and even levelled out during certain periods. In many of the other industrial countries, the trend in hours worked still seems to be slowly downwards (Table 4.3).

Table 4.3: Actual hours worked per week in non-agricultural activities

	1965	1970	1975	1980	1984
United Kingdom – total	"	"	"	"	42.5
– males	47.0	45.7	43.6	43.0	43.4
– females	38.7	37.9	37.4	37.5	38.2
W. Germany – total	44.3	44.0	40.5	41.6	40.9
– males			41.2	42.1	41.2
– females			38.3	40.0	39.7
France – total			42.7	| 41.1	39.1
Japan – total	44.5	| 43.1	| 39.7	| 40.6	| 40.7
– males			40.6	41.8	42.1
– females			37.6	37.9	37.9

Source: *Year Book of Labour Statistics, 1985* (Geneva, International Labour Office). Vertical lines separating years indicate changes in method of compilation.

4.1.2 The neo-classical explanation of labour force trends

The development of models of the labour supply has been one of the growth areas in economics in recent years. In his excellent survey of the extensive work in this important field, Killingsworth (1983) traces the development of the different types of model and analyses the value of the empirical findings. As in all neo-classical models, the basic assumption is that individuals are motivated by the goal of utility-maximization, and that they make their labour supply decisions accordingly, subject to certain constraints.

The simple static model of labour supply will be very familiar to most readers, but we briefly refer to it here for completeness, using the notation adopted by Killingsworth, since it is convenient to be able to draw on his study. The neo-classical approach to the labour supply envisages individuals making a choice between work, for which payment is received, and leisure. The income from work and other sources is used to purchase goods, and since leisure may also be regarded as a form of personal consumption, the choice facing the individual in any given time-period may be treated as the familiar one between one good (hours of leisure L) and the consumption of all other goods (C).

In making his choice the individual faces several constraints. First, if he desires more leisure, say an additional hour L, then he must forgo W, the wage per hour. Second, since there are

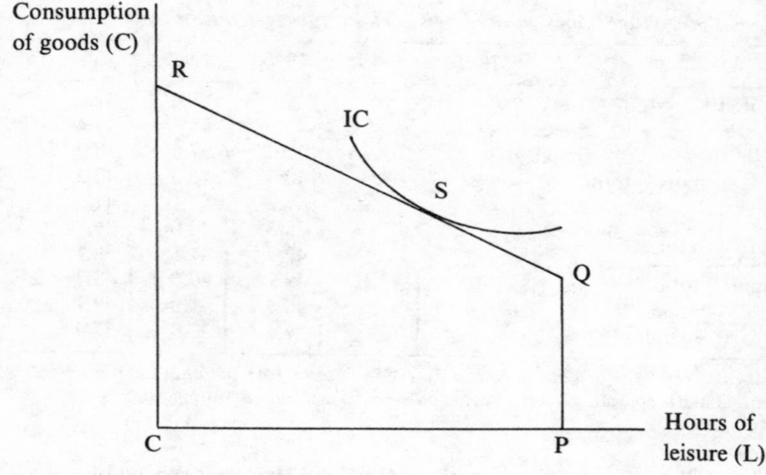

Figure 4.1: The choice of goods and leisure

only twenty-four hours in the day, the total amount of time available T is fixed, and must be allocated between L and hours of work H. Finally, spending by the individual on market goods (i.e. PC, where P is the price of a unit of C) must equal the total of income from work WH and income from other sources V, such as property. The individual's choice between the different combinations of C and L available is determined by his tastes, or preferences, represented by an indifference curve IC. The maximization process is depicted in Figure 4.1, where PQ represents consumption made possible by the non-labour income of the individual and QR represents his budget line, based on his total income from work and other sources. The point S denotes the individual's chosen combination of leisure and other consumption goods, determined by his preferences. The combination represents the maximum attainable, given the budget constraint.

The precise form in which the labour supply function is specified may differ, but the various forms derive ultimately from the utility function, and for empirical purposes most tests of the basic model use a labour supply function for an individual of the form

$$H = a + bW + cV + \epsilon \tag{4.1}$$

in which the hours worked are said to be primarily a function of labour and non-Labour income, with ϵ an error term. Some studies add control variables for age, race, etc., and equation 4.1 may also be expressed in a form in which the hours worked by an individual are influenced not only by his own income but by the total income of his family, including the wages of other family members.

Killingsworth (1983) identifies what he refers to as a 'second generation' of static labour supply models, which spell out more fully the utility-maximizing function, and incorporate, for example, decisions about both labour force participation and hours of work. These later studies also attempt to investigate some of the influences on labour supply which were not very fully analysed in first-generation studies, or were simply caught up by the error term, including the effects of taxes and the costs of entry to the labour market. Possible discontinuities in the labour supply were also examined more fully in the second generation models.

Yet a further generation of labour supply models attempts to place the discussion of labour supply in a dynamic, multi-period setting. Some of these models treat wages as an exogenous variable, others extend the analysis by allowing for endogenous wages and for the accumulation of human wealth, or capital. Given the wide variety of models which has been used, it is difficult to talk in terms of representative models, but most of the models contain common features. Killingsworth concludes, for example, with regard to the specification of dynamic models with exogenous wages, that 'In many cases, the result is an expression that is strikingly similar to a static labour supply function.'

Labour supply models generally recognize explicitly that, in addition to labour and non-labour income, and other relevant observable variables, there are what Killingsworth refers to as 'unobservable taste factors' which are also likely to bear on labour supply decisions. The treatment of wage variables as endogenous in some models also means that 'unobservable' variables relevant to wages may be important to the labour supply schedule – and, as Killingsworth points out, even the estimation of a dynamic labour supply function with exogenous wages may require estimation, and therefore specification, of a dynamic wage function. Moreover, many of the models allow for discontinuities in the labour supply schedule, such as might be imposed, for example, by reservation wages. It is precisely in these 'black box' areas of labour supply analysis that the framework developed in the present study may make a contribution to a better understanding of the forces at work. Before turning to these questions, however, it is useful to see how well existing models have shaped up to the task of explaining the principal labour market trends to which we drew attention at the outset. Here we are indebted once more to Killingsworth (1983) for his comprehensive and very thorough analysis of the empirical work on the various models.

Killingsworth finds that three main conclusions emerge from the empirical evidence: first, that 'pecuniary variables –wage rates and property income – do generally seem to have something to do with labour supply'; second, and of almost equal importance, female labour supply, whether measured by labour force participation or hours of work, is considerably more wage and property income elastic than male labour supply; finally, 'as second generation research has begun to recognise explicitly, unobservable factors – taste differences, nonpecuniary components of pay, hard-to-measure pecuniary influences – play a substantial role in labour supply.'

The first of these conclusions is rather hesitant, and with good reason, since Killingsworth goes on to note that, on the whole, the evidence on the determinants of labour supply is rather imprecise, with the quantitative estimates of labour supply elasticity varying over a wide range. Moreover, far from helping to narrow the range of these estimates, recent research seems if anything to have widened it.

The conclusion with regard to the elasticity of labour supply is, on closer examination, even more disturbing. Many studies find, in fact, that in apparent contradiction with the theory, the wage and property elasticities in respect of males are negative. In the light of the data in Tables 4.1 and 4.2 this is hardly surprising, since they clearly show that male labour force participation in the US and UK has declined in recent years, even among prime age males in the age bracket 25–54. The trend in average hours worked by males has also been downwards. Given the nature of the evidence, Killingsworth is finally obliged to conclude that, 'various important questions about past secular trends in labour supply are still very much open'. The introduction of intervening variables to the analysis, we will maintain, helps fill at least some of the gaps in the standard explanations of labour force trends, and also helps explain the reasons why the labour market does not function in practice like an efficient commodity market.

4.1.3 Other reasons for the trends in the labour force

The lifecycle of labour force participation In section 3 we saw how personal needs are determined in part by the age of individuals and by the family lifecycle, the two being closely interlinked. It is no surprise to find, therefore, that there is also a close association between labour supply decisions, in particular as they affect participation rates, and the age and family lifecycle variables. Tables 4.2 and 4.4 show that male and female participation rates by age typically follow the familiar inverted-U pattern which we encountered earlier when we examined the consumption lifecycle. Further aspects of the link with age emerge if we break down the age categories in greater detail. Figure 4.2, which also brings out interesting differences between countries, shows that a fall in female participation rates occurs in many countries after the ages of 40–45. In a number of countries, however, the decline starts somewhat earlier – after the ages 35–39 in West Germany and the Netherlands, and earlier still, after the ages 25–29, in France, Belgium and Italy. The United Kingdom and Japan are unusual, in that female participation rates in these two countries follow a bimodal pattern, falling appreciably at ages 25–29 and then rising, before falling once more from about the ages of 45–49 onwards.

An age profile of participation rates is apparent among both married and non-married females, although, as one would expect, there are differences in the profiles. Table 4.4, based on data for Great Britain, shows that participation rates are generally lower at all ages for married females than other females (including not only single women, but also those

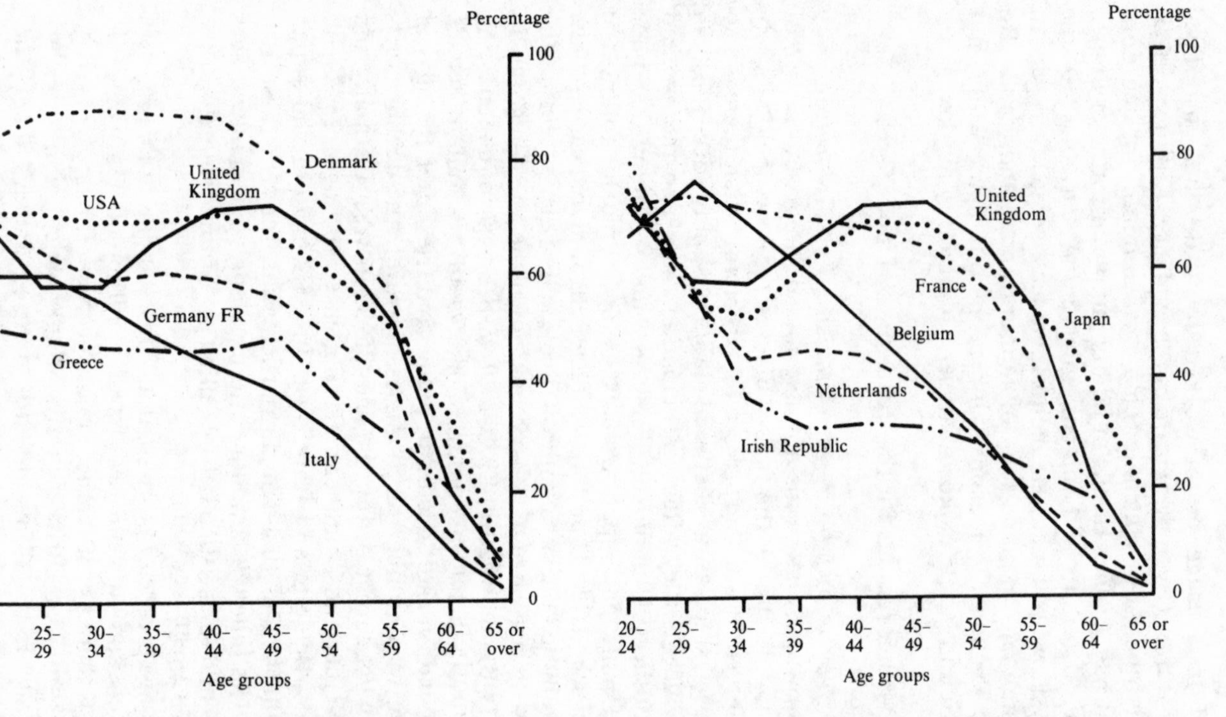

Figure 4.2: Female economic activity rates: by age, international comparison, 1983

Source: Social Trends, 1985 (London, HMSO, 1986).

Table 4.4: Age, marital status and participation in the labour force, Great Britain, Spring 1985

Age	Males	Females	Married females	Other females
			Percentage	
16–19	72.3	67.9	38.4	69.7
20–24	90.5	70.9	58.4	81.4
25–34	95.8	61.4	57.9	75.5
35–49	95.8	72.1	71.5	75.2
50–59	86.8	58.6	58.4	59.0
60–64	54.4	18.6	19.4	16.9
65 and over	8.4	3.2	3.9	2.6
Total over 16	75.4	49.3	52.2	44.3

Source: Department of Employment, *Labour Force Survey, 1985*.

widowed, divorced or legally separated[1]) with the exception of those aged 60 or over. The disparity between participation rates of married and other females is greatest in the younger age groups, and then narrows progressively until the middle years between 35–39, when the differences are relatively small.

The nature of the relationship between married and other female participation rates is not, of course, merely a chance occurrence. Since young children are the most dependent on their mothers, and since many mothers like to be close to their children when young, it is hardly surprising that a smaller proportion of married women is willing, or able, to work during the earlier years, when childbearing is most frequent. It seems to be the case, however, that as women progress to the age ranges when children tend to be older, they feel inclined to re-enter the labour force, or in some cases to enter it for the first time. It is noticeable that the participation rate of married women jumps sharply in the age range 35–49, and is also at a peak at this time, when most children will be in school, some will already be in their teens, and others may even have left home. It is therefore a time when it is much easier for married women to go out to work.

The effects of young children on female participation rates have been well demonstrated by Martin and Roberts (1984) in their very useful study of the lifetime pattern of female

Table 4.5: Current economic activity by number of children under 16: all women except full-time students

Economic activity	Number of children under 16				All women with children under 16	No children under 16	All women except full time students
	1	2	3	4 or more			
	%	%	%	%	%	%	%
Working full time	21	14	12	11	17	54	35
Working part time	35	38	32	25	35	20	28
Total working	56	52	44	36	52	74	63
'Unemployed'	5	3	4	6	4	7	6
Total economically active	61	55	48	42	56	81	69
Economically inactive	39	45	52	58	44	19	31
	100	100	100	100	100	100	100

Source: J. Martin and C. Roberts, *Women and Employment: a Lifetime Perspective*, (London, HMSO, 1984).

employment, carried out for the UK Department of Employment. Table 4.5, based on their results, shows that women with dependent children under the age of 16 (the school leaving age in the UK) were much less likely to be in the labour force than those without children under 16. Moreover, each additional child under 16 reduced the rate of participation still further. Martin and Roberts also found, however, that the age of the youngest child was even more important to determining activity rates than the number of children under 16. Table 4.6 shows that there was virtually no difference in total participation rates between women with only one child and those with two children, once the age of the youngest child was taken into account. Nor was there any significant difference in participation rates among those with a youngest child under 5, until there were at least four children under 16.

Since the age of females, marital status and the age of the youngest child are all interwoven, Martin and Roberts went on to calculate the effect of each in turn, while standardizing for the other two variables. The results are given in Table 4.7, showing, first, that the participation rates for married and unmarried women were identical when differences in age distribution, the presence of children and the age of the youngest child were taken into account. On the other hand, the standardized proportion of women working, classified according to the age of the youngest child, still revealed large differences between the three groups of women with children under 16. It seems, therefore, that differences in participation rates according to the age of the first child have little to do with the age or marital status of females. Finally, when the proportions of women working in different age groups were standardized for marital status, the presence of children and the age of the first child, the differences in participation rates were reduced, but by no means entirely removed. A further interesting point to emerge was that the standardized age data showed a fall in the female activity in later years, especially in the fifties age range-well ahead of the UK retirement age of 60 for females.

The main conclusions from the above evidence, which are supported by other research in the field, are that the presence

Table 4.6: Current economic activity by number of children under 16 and age of youngest child: all women with children under 16 except full-time students

Economic activity	Number of Children under 16									
	1 child aged			2 children youngest aged			3 children youngest aged*		4 children youngest aged*	
	0–4	5–10	11–15	0–4	5–10	11–15	0–4	5–10	0–4	5–10
	%	%	%	%	%	%	%	%	%	%
Working full time	11	16	32	4	17	28	5	15	8	14
Working part time	16	49	44	23	49	48	22	43	10	41
Total working	27	65	76	27	66	76	27	58	18	55
'Unemployed'	5	5	4	3	3	7	2	6	4	9
Total economically active	32	70	80	30	69	83	29	64	22	64
Economically inactive	68	30	20	70	31	17	71	36	78	36
	100	100	100	100	100	100	100	100	100	100

*Base for those aged 11–15 too small to show percentages.
Source: J. Martin and C. Roberts, *Women and Employment: A Lifetime Perspective*, (London, HMSO, 1984).

Table 4.7: Estimated proportions of women working: a comparison of standardised and unstandardised proportions

By marital status[1]	Estimated standardised proportion of women working %	Unstandardised proportion of women working %
Married	63	60
Not married	63	75
By age of youngest child[2]		
0–4	24	27
5–10	57	65
11–15	73	76
16 or over	74	65
childless	83	83
By age[3]		
16–29	65	60
30–39	71	61
40–49	67	74
50–59	50	60

Source: J. Martin and C. Roberts, *Women and Employment: A Lifetime Perspective* (London, HMSO, 1984).
Notes: [1] Standardized for age and age of the youngest child.
[2] Standardized for age and marital status.
[3] Standardized for age of the youngest child and marital status.

of children and the age of the youngest child are much the most important determinants of female labour force participation. It is the children rather than marital status as such which greatly influence labour force decisions. Age also plays a role, although a secondary one. The combined results, in a lifecycle setting, are summarized in Table 4.8. Similar conclusions to these were reached in a study by Joshi, Layard and Owen (1981) based on an analysis of age cohorts. They found that the pattern of childbearing, and to a lesser extent age, provided a remarkably accurate explanation of the pattern of female lifecycle participation.

Changes over time in the lifecycle of participation rates The lifecycle of participation rates is of particular interest to the present study, since there have over time been changes

Table 4.8: Current economic activity by life cycle stage: all women except full time students

Economic activity	Lifecycle stage: Childless women aged:		Women with youngest child aged:			Women with all children aged 16 and over, aged:		All women except full-time students
	Under 30	30 or over	0–4	5–10	11–15	Under 50	50 or over	
	%	%	%	%	%	%	%	%
Working full time	82	67	7	16	31	40	27	35
Working part time	3	12	20	48	45	37	32	28
Total working	85	79	27	64	76	77	59	63
'Unemployed'	11	6	4	4	5	5	5	6
Total economically active	96	85	31	68	81	82	64	69
Economically inactive	4	15	69	32	19	18	36	31
	100	100	100	100	100	100	100	100

Source: J. Martin and C. Roberts, *Women and Employment: A Lifetime Perspective*, (London, HMSO, 1984)

associated with that cycle which have had a crucial bearing on variations in the labour supply. These changes have principally affected females, since the overall male participation rates in most countries, as we saw earlier, has not altered to anything like the same extent. Both the studies by Martin and Roberts (1984) and Joshi *et al.* (1981), to which we have already referred, were able to demonstrate that the secular increase in female participation rates has not occurred evenly at all stages of the lifecycle. It has instead been particularly marked among women over the age of thirty, including those in their fifties, although the latter is not shown by Table 4.9. We can also see in Table 4.9 the sharp drop in participation rates among teenagers since the 1960s.

Two developments appear to have been important in facilitating the growth in participation of women in the labour force, although both have really only exerted a major influence in the period since the Second World War. First, fertility rates have dropped in most countries, and so too, consequently, has the average size of family, and therefore the length of the period during which very young children make it difficult for wives to go out to work. These factors, as we saw earlier, do have an appreciable effect on female participation rates. In the United Kingdom, although there has been a large fall in the fertility rate since the mid–1960s, there have been periods when fertility was actually rising at the same time as participation rates (the late 1970s, for example). Factors other than the change in fertility must therefore also have been at work, but the upsurge in participation rates during the 1970s would certainly have been facilitated by the earlier trend towards small families. Joshi *et al.* (1981) estimated that one child less per family has the effect of raising the participation rate for females aged 20–59 in Great Britain by about 7 percentage points.

A second factor facilitating female participation in the labour force has been the enormous growth of part-time employment, which is especially popular among women with children. Table 4.10, relating to Great Britain, shows how the growth in part-time employment has occurred mainly since the 1950s, and has been overwhelmingly amongst women; however, 6 per cent of men now also work part-time, and the

Table 4.9: Proportions of women working full and part time at different dates by age*

Age at date	Work status	Date (end December)								
		1939	1944	1949	1954	1959	1964	1969	1974	1979
%	%	%	%	%	%	%	%	%	%	%
15–19	Full time	89	88	89	93	90	89	86	84[+]	75[+]
	Part time	1	1	1	–	1	1	2	1[+]	3[+]
	All working women	90	89	90	93	91	90	88	85[+]	78[+]
20–24	Full time		70	60	62	61	56	60	57	57
	Part time		1	3	3	5	4	6	11	6
	All working women		71	63	65	66	60	66	68	63
25–29	Full time			35	31	33	30	29	30	32
	Part time			5	8	6	11	12	20	17
	All working women			40	39	39	41	41	50	49
30–34	Full time				24	27	23	25	23	22
	Part time				13	13	16	21	27	34
	All working women				37	40	39	46	50	56
35–39	Full time					27	30	28	29	30
	Part time					19	21	23	36	39
	All working women					46	51	51	65	69
40–44	Full time						29	33	34	32
	Part time						26	29	36	41
	All working women						55	62	70	73
45–49	Full time							34	37	36
	Part time							29	33	37
	All working women							63	70	73

table 4.9 cont.

Age at date	Work status	Date (end December)								
		1939	1944	1949	1954	1959	1964	1969	1974	1979
%	%	%	%	%	%	%	%	%	%	%
50–54	Full time								34	31
	Part time								32	34
	All working women								66	65
55–59	Full time									26
	Part time									29
	All working women									55

Source: J. Martin and C. Roberts, *Women and Employment: A Lifetime Perspective* (London, HMSO, 1984).
Notes: *Excluding full-time students.
+Age 16–19.

proportion is still growing. In Table 4.9 we can see that the growth in female participation rates in Great Britain has been associated almost entirely with the growth of part-time employment, since the full-time participation rate has remained fairly level overall. When we recall that part-time working has increased most noticeably among females over 30, and that it has also risen sharply among women with young children (Table 4.11) especially those of school age, it seems clear that part-time employment has been instrumental in permitting many women with children to take jobs who might otherwise have been unable, or unwilling, to do so.

Since employment decisions involve employers as well as employees – something which seems to be forgotten in many studies of the labour supply, with employers too frequently being treated merely as passive agents – it is not possible to explain what has been happening to the labour supply without also looking at developments affecting the demand for labour. The two are inextricably intertwined, and the enormous increase in female part-time employment certainly could not

Table 4.10: Growth of part-time employment in Great Britain, 1951–81

	Employees in employment, all industries (thousands)							
	Male				Female			
	FT	PT	All	%[3]	FT	PT	All	%[3]
1951[1]	13,438	45	13,483	0.3	5,752	754	6,508	11.6
1961[1]	13,852	174	14,026	1.2	5,351	1,892	7,243	26.1
1971[1]	12,748	572	13,320	4.3	5,166	3,152	8,318	37.9
1971[2]	12,840	584	13,424	4.4	5,467	2,757	8,224	33.5
1981[2]	11,511	718	12,229	5.9	5,304	3,781	9,085	41.6

Source: O. Robinson and J. Wallace, 'Growth and Utilisation of Part-Time Labour in Great Britain', *Employment Gazette*, September, 1984, pp. 391–7.

Notes: 1 Census of Population
2 Census of Employment
3 Part time as percentage of total employment.

have taken place unless it had also suited employers. Much of the increase in part-time employment, as is well known, has been in a wide range of service industries, including not only such industries as catering and tourism, but also banking and finance, education, health and welfare services. The distinction between manufacturing and service industries is becoming increasingly blurred, however, and part-time employment is now widespread in manufacturing as well as in services, especially among manual workers. The 1980 *Women and Employment Survey* in the UK found that 34 per cent of female manual workers in manufacturing were part-time (70 per cent in the service industries), compared with 21 per cent of non-manual workers in manufacturing (35 per cent in services).

The 1980 *Survey* concluded, in fact, that a woman's occupation was a more important indicator of her employment circumstances than whether she worked in manufacturing or services. The less skilled nature of much part-time work and its heavy concentration in particular types of occupation is well documented in Table 4.12, taken once more from the 1980 *Women and Employment Survey*. One-fifth of the representative sample were found to be working in semi-skilled domestic occupations, such as waitresses, child-minders, home helps, etc., while as many as 17 per cent were in unskilled occupations, like cleaners. The proportions in clerical jobs (20

Table 4.11: Proportion of women with dependent children working full and part time at different dates by age of youngest child

Age of youngest child	Work status	Date (end December)						
		1949	1954	1959	1964	1969	1974	1979
		%	%	%	%	%	%	%
0–4	Full time	9	6	8	8	8	6	7
	Part time	5	8	7	10	14	20	19
	All working women	14	14	15	18	22	26	26
5–10	Full time		21	20	21	23	22	18
	Part time		19	24	30	33	43	45
	All working women		40	44	51	56	65	63
11–15	Full time			36	33	31	31	31
	Part time			30	32	29	42	47
	All working women			66	65	60	73	78

Source: J. Martin and C. Roberts, *Women and Employment: A Lifetime Perspective*, (London, HMSO, 1984).

Figures for the earliest dates in each row will be biased because women in these groups are younger than average for women with a youngest child of the given age at the date in question.

per cent), semi-skilled factory jobs and professional and other intermediate non-manual jobs, although sizeable, were still well below the corresponding proportions of those working full-time. The survey also found that 45 per cent of women taking a part-time job on re-entering the labour market after childbearing experienced downward occupational mobility.

Table 4.12: Occupational group and social class of full- and part-time working women

Occupational group	Social class	Full time		Part time		% All working women	
Professional	I	1		1		1	
Teaching		8		3		6	
Nursing, medical and social	II	7	24	6	12	7	19
Other intermediate non-manual		9		3		6	
Clerical	III non-manual	39	45	20	32	30	39
Sales		6		12		9	
Skilled manual	III manual	8		6		7	
Semi-skilled factory		13		7		10	
Semi-skilled domestic	IV	4	20	20	32	11	25
Other semi-skilled		3		4		4	
Unskilled	V	2		17		9	
		100		100		100	

Source: B. Ballard, 'Women Part-time Workers: Evidence from the 1980 Women and Employment Survey', *Employment Gazette*, September, 1984, pp. 409–18.

Robinson and Wallace (1984), in case studies of 21 organizations, explored the reasons why employers hired part-time workers. The manner in which such labour was used provided cost savings, the nature of which differed between service and manufacturing industries. In service industries, part-time labour gave managers great freedom in matching their labour demands with changing patterns of operational or customer requirements. It enabled them, for example, to cover peak trading times during the week, or at weekends, and to meet fluctuations in orders. In manufacturing industry, the benefits derived mainly from maximizing the use of capital equipment, for example by maintaining production during lunch-breaks, or by maintaining unbroken production over a 15 or 16-hour day without incurring premium payments for overtime or shift working. Part-time workers were also used temporarily to fill vacancies for full-time workers. Robinson and Wallace also found a strong belief among employers that the productivity of part-time workers was greater than that of full-time labour. On the debit side, greater expenditure was incurred in recruiting and administering a large labour force.

Yet another important reason for the use of part-time workers was to circumvent legislative requirements. In the United Kingdom, if gross weekly or monthly earnings are below a certain level, and if the number of hours worked per week is kept below a certain threshold, the national insurance payments may be avoided, and a number of Acts of Parliament, such as the Redundancy Payments Act and the Employment Protection and Consolidation Act, do not apply to the workers concerned. Freedom from the restrictions obviously saves employers a good deal of money and gives them much greater labour flexibility.

We can see, therefore, that there are a good many sound reasons, from the employers' point of view, why part-time workers should be hired. The fact that part-time employment has continued to expand even when unemployment has been high and there has been no shortage of full-time workers, indicates clearly that much of the spur to part-time work has come from the employers' side, and that the growth in labour supply has therefore, in large measure, had as much to do with demand factors as supply factors.

On the one hand, then, we have a growing demand for part-time labour, as employers struggle to keep down their costs, and on the other a growing supply of willing part-time labour, particularly among women over 30 with children. We still do not have an adequate answer, however, to the question of what factors are ultimately the source of women's desire for part-time employment. For further insights into this key question we are fortunate in being able to draw once more on the 1980 *Women and Employment Survey*. A central aim of the survey was to determine why women do or do not work, and in particular to distinguish women whose reasons for working were principally financial from those for whom financial motivation was of secondary importance. In order to obtain an indication of the reasons for working, respondents were asked to examine a selection of possible motives, and to select all those which best described their own motivation. They were then asked to choose from the selected reasons the one which represented the *main* reason for working. The results are given in Table 4.13, distinguishing between full-time and part-time female workers.

Looking first at the financial motives, 55 per cent of full-timers and 35 per cent of part-timers gave as a reason for working the need to earn money for basic essentials, such as food, rent or mortgage. These proportions dropped to 41 per cent and 28 per cent, respectively, when only the principal reason for working was listed, but it seems that the desire to satisfy basic, or lower-order, needs was still the single (more accurately, the first equal, as we shall see below) most important driving force.

The finding is consistent with the evidence that, in the United Kingdom at least, female lifecycle participation, after dipping in the age range 25–30, rises again to a very high level between the ages of 30 and 50, just when the consumption lifecycle is also at its highest levels, and when there is therefore likely to be most pressure on family budgets. The link between the consumption and work lifecycle differs, it seems, from country to country, according to local family customs – in the United States, West Germany and France, for example, the major decline in activity rates appears to start somewhat earlier than 50, while in Italy and Belgium activity rates seem to decline steadily after marriage and the birth of children. There appear, nevertheless, to be grounds for arguing that, in some countries at least, the lifecycle pattern of female labour supply is in large measure a reflection of the lifecycle pattern of family consumption – interrupted to some extent by the demands of childbearing – and therefore essentially needs-based.

We are, however, principally seeking an explanation of the *growth* in female labour supply, and unless it can be shown that there has been a long-term increase in the number of

Table 4.13: All reasons and main reason for working of full- and part-time working women

Reasons for working	*All reasons*			*Main reason*		
	Full time	Part time	All working women	Full time	Part time	All working women
	%	%	%	%	%	%
Working is the normal thing to do	20	7	14	4	1	3
Need money for basic essentials such as food, rent or mortgage	55	35	47	41	28	35
To earn money to buy extras	35	51	47	13	28	20
To earn money of my own	38	36	37	15	13	14
For the company of other people	40	49	44	4	11	7
Enjoy working	55	48	52	15	14	14
To follow my career	24	7	17	7	2	5
To help with husband's job or business*	1	2	1	–	2	1
Other reasons	2	2	2	1	1	1
				100	100	100

Source: J. Martin and C. Roberts, *Women and Employment: A Lifetime Perspective* (London, HMSO, 1984).
*Not listed on the prompt card.
Percentage for 'all reasons' do not add to 100 as women could have more than one reason for working.

families unable to purchase the basic essentials of life, or unless the term 'basic essentials' has been redefined over time because of the influences of the social comparison process, we have to look elsewhere for an explanation of the rise in female participation rates. Both these factors may indeed have operated (see, for example, Morris and Preston, 1986) the former being associated with the large increase in unemployment in many countries, especially during the 1970s and 1980s (giving rise to a sort of 'additional worker hypothesis' in a long-term context). Governments, as in the US and the UK, have also tended to redefine poverty to take account of rising living standards and expectations. If, however, we look again at Table 4.13 we can see that two additional financial motives for female labour force participation are also indicated.

Among part-timers, where the growth in participation has been most marked, the reason given must frequently for working, along with that of the need to buy basic essentials, was to 'earn money to buy extras' – 28 per cent gave this as their *main* reason for working, exactly the same proportion as listed the purchase of basic essentials as their principal reason. A further 13 per cent of part-timers worked mainly to 'earn money of my own'. Neither of these reasons sits easily with the neo-classical explanation of labour supply growth, in which the central emphasis is placed on a trade-off between real income and leisure. Rather than being seduced into the labour force by rising real wages, rising real income could instead remove the necessity of working for these two ends, and therefore serve to *decrease* the labour supply.

A much more convincing explanation of the desire for money to buy extras, or to have money of one's own, is that it will tend greatly to increase the range of choice available to the consumer, for the reasons we outlined in section 3, especially if it increases a person's *relative* income. We have also stressed the pressures which social comparisons, including the effects exerted through advertising, place upon consumers. If those in a consumer reference group are able, perhaps because of part-time work by the mothers in certain households, to afford the purchase of desirable goods – holidays abroad have, for example, become a form of status symbol in Britain in recent years – then there will be pressures for other mothers to work as well.

When we examine the other principal reasons advanced in Table 4.13 for females working, we find that they too fit into the framework we have adopted in the present study. The neo-classical model treats work as a form of disutility, for which payment is received, and it is contrasted with the utility gained from leisure. Many employees, however, obviously do not view work wholly in this light. Table 4.13 shows that 11 per cent of part-time workers (but only 4 per cent of full-time workers) worked *principally* because it enabled them to enjoy the company of other people (much higher percentages included it among their lists of main reasons for working). Since children may severely restrict parents' social activities (especially if they are also short of funds) this finding is not surprising. Work clearly may satisfy the need for companionship, or belonging, noted by Maslow and others. Table 4.13 also shows that many people simply enjoy working, and obtain a great deal of satisfaction from it. Once again, work seems to be meeting deep-seated needs, perhaps for self-actualization, which it would be difficult, perhaps even impossible, to satisfy in any other way.

The overall picture which emerges, then, is quite consistent and is one which many social commentators would recognize. Essentially it is one in which an increasing proportion of females has defied the old conventions which confined them solely to home and children and they have done so in order to lead a much fuller life. In the terminology which we have adopted, needs which previously had to be suppressed are now being satisfied by work itself and the financial freedom which it has brought.

The labour supply of young persons and the elderly Certain developments of special relevance to the youngest and oldest age groups in the labour force make it worthwhile examining these groups separately from the others. Looking first at the young, the proportions of those aged 16–19 and 20–24 in the labour force are heavily influenced by decisions about whether or not to stay on at school and, after school, whether or not to go into full-time higher education. The proportion staying on in full-time education, rather than entering the labour force, differs appreciably from one country to another, being relatively high in Japan and the US, for example, and relatively low in the United Kingdom, but the general trends are quite consistent. In most countries there has been a tendency for the proportions of both males and females in full-time education to increase in the post-war period, and a corresponding tendency for labour force participation rates in the relevant age groups to fall.

The decision about whether or not to stay on at school, or in higher education, may be analysed in terms of investment in human capital, as Becker (1975) and others have shown, and therefore fits in well with the neo-classical approach to labour supply. Empirical studies have confirmed the usefulness of this approach in explaining changes in school enrolment (see, for example, Pissarides, 1981), but in the late 1970s and early 1980s, when labour force participation rates dropped quite sharply in a number of countries, the rapid increase in youth employment appears to have become a major factor. Increased school enrolment associated with rising unemployment might, of course, be interpreted as one aspect of the human capital approach, since improved education could reduce the likelihood of unemployment and lost earnings, but in the case of the United Kingdom, at least, the scale of the increase in unemployment suggests that the main influence on school enrolment in recent years has been the lack of sufficient jobs for young people (Baxter and McCormick, 1984).

The changed job outlook has also affected those in the labour force nearing retirement age – and even some well short of the retirement age. Since the Second World War, substantial improvements in both state and private pension provision, and the lowering of the official age of retirement, have resulted in a general reduction in participation rates of men and women in the age range 65 and over. This tendency has been reinforced in many countries, especially in the late 1970s and early 1980s, by the very rapid increase in unemployment which has so severely affected so many young people. The participation rates of the oldest and the youngest age groups have in fact become interlinked, as the pressures to provide new jobs for the young have led to measures to persuade those approaching retirement to retire early. In sum, while unemployment is not a variable which features prominently in many models of labour force participation, its effects have become too important to ignore in the case of certain age groups in recent years, especially the very young and the elderly.

4.1.4 Conclusions

Labour supply decisions constitute yet another field of economics in which the standard theory appears to provide a less than satisfactory explanation of what transpires in practice. Probably few would quarrel with Killingsworth's conclusion that 'pecuniary variables – wage rates and property income – do generally seem to have something to do with labour supply', but the fact that Killingsworth was unable to be more specific in the face of the available evidence is an indication of the state of affairs in this field. Trends within the aggregate labour supply are widely divergent, and it has not yet been demonstrated that they can all be accommodated simultaneously within the neo-classical framework. There is, of course, a sense in which the income–leisure trade-off can be advanced to 'explain' just about any trend in labour supply – and that must surely be a central weakness as well as a strength of this approach. If people do not wish more income, they wish more leisure, or vice versa, so the argument runs. But such a simple dichotomy is inadequate to capture the full complexities of the numerous factors which may influence the supply of labour during any given period.

A further weakness of neo-classical theory is that it has until relatively recently largely ignored the important lifecycle of labour supply. Work by Heckman and MaCurdy (see, for example, their 1980 study) and others has gone some way towards rectifying this deficiency, but the analysis is still presented within the unduly restricting confines of the income-leisure trade-off model.

One important conclusion from our own analysis is that we must distinguish at least three important lifecycles, all of which are interlinked, but not identical in their time scales. We noted, first, that there was a largely needs-based consumption lifecycle, associated with the age of consumers and the family lifecycle. This consumption lifecycle results in very heavy commitments for families in the middle and later years of the parents. It is not surprising to find, therefore, that this concentration of family needs in turn influences the work, or activity, lifecycle of the parents (and, in the less well-off families, probably of children too) with participation rates being highest around the age when family commitments are greatest. The *growth* in female participation – by far the most dominant of the labour force trends – has also been concentrated principally in the age group associated with this phase of the consumption lifecycle. Parents are not, of course, always entirely free – or do not feel themselves entirely free – to decide just when and when not to work. The age of the youngest child appears to be an important consideration. The work lifecycle is therefore in large measure dictated by family needs. We should not, however, overlook the fact that the growth of the labour supply, especially the part-time element, has also been demand-induced, in that it has been greatly encouraged by employers, who have used it as a convenient means of reducing their labour costs.

The work lifecycle has, in turn, an important bearing on family income. Since earnings from employment are the most important source of income for most families, it is again hardly surprising that family income follows the familiar inverted-U pattern of both the work lifecycle and the consumption lifecycle. It would seem, therefore, that while income must ultimately act as a constraint on consumption, that constraint is to some extent flexible, in so far as families have a measure of discretion over how much they work (assuming that work is available), and that in turn is partly a reflection of their consumption needs. The direction of causation, in other words, runs from consumption (based on needs and social comparisons) to income, as well as from income to consumption.

There is also strong evidence that the reasons for working, and for the growth in labour force participation, extend beyond that of pecuniary gain and the satisfying of the more basic needs of households. Working helps satisfy a number of other needs which do not feature in the income–leisure model. Two of the most important of these appear to be the need for companionship, or belonging, and for the pleasures inherent in work itself – not for all, but for a sizeable proportion of the workforce – which for many could be described in Maslow's terms as a form of self-actualization.

Among the various labour force groups whose behaviour we have felt it worth examining separately are the very youngest and the oldest age groups. While it is certainly possible to rationalize the labour force participation trends of these groups in terms of the work–leisure model, there are grounds for thinking that, in recent years at least, the rapid increase in unemployment which has affected most countries has also had a particularly important bearing on participation rates in these age groups. These groups provide another good illustration of how difficult, and probably also how unwise, it is to generalize about labour supply trends, or to try to find a simple, unicausal explanation of these trends.

4.2 WAGE BEHAVIOUR

In this section we wish particularly to examine two outstanding features of wage behaviour: first, the tendency for money wages to be 'sticky', or inflexible, in a downward direction; second, and in distinct contrast, a tendency for money wages to edge ever upwards, even in economic circumstances which might be expected to inhibit such increases. This asymmetrical wage behaviour lies at the very heart of economics, since it helps explain both unemployment and inflation, yet there has been only limited progress in explaining the reasons for this phenomenon, certainly within a unified theoretical framework. Our analysis can help shed a good deal of additional light on the forces at work. There is no great mystery, it turns out. Wage asymmetry follows quite naturally from the behavioural characteristics of individuals which have been at the centre of our study.

4.2.1 Motivation and wage behaviour

In recasting the utility function (equation 3.2) we maintained that utility derived ultimately from the satisfaction of needs and wants, in which the influence exerted by an individual's reference groups(s) played a part. Specifying the utility function in an indirect form, as in equation 3.2, serves to emphasize the importance to the individual not just of his own wage but also of his *relative* wage. Personal motivation is therefore already linked to wages in the framework we have developed. Before we can analyse wage behaviour satisfactorily, however, we must introduce the other powerful motivating forces to which we earlier drew attention, namely, equity and goals. We shall look at each of these in turn.

Equity considerations influencing wage behaviour In our discussion of equity in section 2.3 we saw that the issue has tended to be treated at two levels: first, equity and inequity in exchange relationships, as in the work of Adams; second, at an aggregated level concerned with the principles which govern, or ought to govern, the distribution of rewards in society. Both are relevant in matters of pay, since each may influence people's perceptions about pay; but given that most decisions on pay are taken at a disaggregated level, and that there has been a failure so far to devise any generally acceptable criteria of distributive justice, we shall concern ourselves in this section principally with equity in exchange, without however entirely neglecting distributive justice. The notion of relative deprivation, which is not bound to any particular form of transaction or situation, will also play an important role in our analysis.

Among the theories of equity, or inequity, in exchange relationships, that of Adams stands out as one of the most fully developed and convincing. It has not been without its – generally constructive – critics, but it seems well suited to the analysis of wage behaviour, especially as it relates to relative pay. In Adams' formulation, it will be recalled, equity exists for an individual when

$$\Sigma O_{ip} / \Sigma I_{ip} = \Sigma O_{ia} / \Sigma I_{ia}$$

i.e. when the weighted sums of Person's perceived outcomes relative to his inputs are equal to Other's outcomes in relation to his inputs. Included in Person's outcomes will be a level of pay which is considered equitable (W*) both in relation to Person's other outcomes and his inputs and in relation to the inputs and outcomes of Other (an individual with whom Person compares himself, and therefore a reference group, which following our earlier notation we represent as r_l).

The equitable wage may, of course, differ from the actual wage (which we denoted by W_i in equation 3.2), in which case Person will be motivated to try to rectify the situation. If $W_i < W^*$, Person has the options of trying to raise W_i, raise his other outcomes, reduce his inputs, or a combination of all these. The evidence available also suggests that if $W_i > W^*$, Person will again be unhappy, and even if he cannot bring himself to take a cut in his money wages, he may try to offset the imbalance in other ways, perhaps by increasing his inputs, or reducing his other outcomes.

The third possible case is that in which Person starts off in a situation of wage equilibrium in which $W_i = W^*$. In this situation Person perceives himself to be equitably treated, and any attempt by an employer, or government, to reduce W_i would, other things remaining equal, produce inequity in the eyes of Person. We could therefore expect Person to resist such a move, or to attempt to rectify the situation if the decision were taken unilaterally by the employer, or government.

At the broader level of society as a whole, the links between inputs and outcomes become hazier, and it is more difficult, as we have seen, to devise generally acceptable criteria by which inequalities may be judged. This is doubtless one of the reasons why such large inequalities are tolerated in most societies – another being the restricted nature of most reference groups. Beyond some point, however inequalities may give rise to resentment, and, since pay is the most important component of income for the great majority of people, it would not be at all surprising if discontent with the extent of inequalities expressed itself in the form of pressures for pay increases, as one means of reducing these inequalities.

Individual pay goals The modified utility function expressed in equation 3.2 indicates that a person's utility derives both from the level of his real wage and the level of his wage relative to those in his reference groups. From the discussion of equity we also know the conditions required for equity in exchange, and that the individual will actively pursue the goal of equity if it has not already been attained. A variety of considerations bear on the pay goals likely to be set by an individual. If we take first the equity aspect, the goal will be a level of W_i which is equal to the perceived equitable W*, which in turn will be a proportion of the wage received by reference group r_1. The first pay goal, therefore, is

$$W_i = W_i^* = k\,\overline{W}_{r_1} \tag{4.1}$$

where W_i is the actual wage of individual i, W_i^* is i's perception of the equitable wage, and $k\,\overline{W}_{r1}$ is i's desired equitable wage expressed as a proportion of the mean wage of reference group r_1.

As the total utility attainable by i depends not only on the absolute level of his real wage, but also on his relative wage position, a second pay goal (assuming the first has been attained) will beto maintain that relative position. This will require a forward-looking stance on the part of i, since (other things remaining equal) he will have to try and anticipate, and match, the wage increases obtained by his reference group(s). We may therefore express the second pay goal as

$$\dot{W}_i = \dot{\overline{W}}{}_{r_1}^{e} \tag{4.2}$$

where $\dot{\overline{W}}{}_{r1}^{e}$ is the expected rate of change of the mean wage in reference group r_1. If, however, the expected rate of wage increase in another reference group, say r_2, were to be greater than that for r_1, then the target rate of growth of money wages would become $\dot{\overline{W}}{}_{r2}^{e}$ rather than $\dot{\overline{W}}{}_{r1}^{e}$. In effect, the target growth of money wages would be determined by the reference group expected to obtain the most rapid growth in pay. This is a familiar situation in pay bargaining, with the most rapid pay increase becoming the standard which other pay groups seek to match. The effect, of course, may be to disturb other pay differentials, such as that between W_i and W_{r1} in the above example, with possibly further consequences for pay claims.[2]

Since a tendency for the price level P to rise faster than the wage level W_1 would cause a reduction in real wages, and therefore in the total utility attainable by the individual i, a third wage goal of individual i is likely to be

$$\dot{W}_i = \dot{P}^{e} \tag{4.3}$$

where $\dot{W}_i$ is the rate of change of i's money wage, and $\dot{P}^{e}$ is the

the expected rate of change of prices. The individual, in other words, will seek to obtain an increase in wages which at least matches the expected rise in prices.

A feature of pay increases in all the major industrial countries since the Second World War has been the steady increase in real wages, with the rise in money wages outstripping inflation. There have been brief periods in some countries when real wages have fallen, but the tendency for real wages to rise has become a well-established norm for most people, most of the time. It would not be at all surprising to find, therefore, that pay claims contained an element of target real growth in wages, based on the rate of growth of real wages to which employees had become accustomed. We saw, too, in section 3 that the pattern of consumers' expenditure has shifted towards new forms of consumption, many of which, such as foreign travel, are expensive. At the present stage of economic development, consumers are still not short of desirable things on which to spend their incomes. Surveys of consumers' views on their incomes generally indicate, too, that most consumers would relish an increase in the incomes. The desire to satisfy needs, and the associated wants, will therefore reinforce any tendency to base claims on accustomed rises in real wages.

An alternative goal for the individual might therefore be

$$\dot{W}_i = \dot{P}^e + \alpha \qquad (4.4)$$

where α is a constant representing the target real rate of growth of wages set by individual i. When such a goal is adopted, it will, of course, supersede that set in equation 4.3 above.

We now have three important pay goals which will be pursued by individual i. The first is aimed at obtaining, and maintaining, a certain differential with respect to a reference group. The other two goals are entirely anticipatory, based on expectations about movements in relevant price and wage variables. In practice, these three goals seem likely to boil down to a unified goal, which would be the lowest rate of pay increase sufficient to enable all three sub-goals to be achieved. A simple example would be the case in which $W_i = W^* = \overline{W}_{r1}$, and $\dot{\overline{W}}^e_{r1} = \dot{P}^e$, so that i's unified pay goal would be that depicted in equation 4.4. Where $W_i < W^*$, and catch-up was required, W_i would have to be greater than that indicated by equation 4.4. If, to simplify matters, we assume that individual i wishes to make good the whole of the shortfall in W_i at time t, and that he also wishes to obtain at time t a level of wages which will compensate for expected inflation, and provide the expected growth in real income, then we may represent i's unified pay goal at time t as W^{**}. Since W^*_i represents only equity in exchange, and might therefore be modified when viewed in the wider context of inequity in society at large, we also assume that any such influence is included in W^{**}.

An important characteristic of the unified pay goal, as defined, is that it represents, in the eyes of individual i, a fair and realistic goal which he might reasonably hope to attain – it would not, therefore, include any part of a wage claim which was introduced simply as a bargaining ploy, or which was included more in hope than in realistic expectation. A failure to achieve the goal would therefore give rise, in effect, to a feeling of relative deprivation, as expressed earlier in section 2.3.

One implication of the pay goals, as expressed above, is that if for some reason they are not realised during a given period, an employee will consider that he has some catching up to do in subsequent periods. Evidence of this desire to catch up has been apparent in post-incomes policy periods, to take one example, and is a major reason why many have concluded that pay policies are a futile exercise. Pay policies give rise to much wider issues, however, to which we shall return at a later stage.

While the pay goals individuals might be expected to adopt follow logically from the modified utility function, as we expressed it, one might well ask whether individuals do in practice formulate their pay objectives in such a precise manner, and whether indeed they have anything other than the haziest of pay goals in mind. Work by Behrend and others in the UK and Ireland has cast some helpful light on such questions. With regard to the matter of fair pay, Behrend *et al.* (1970) found that members of the public do have decided opinions about the relative rates of pay which ought to apply to different occupations. A sample of males, when asked how much men in each of eleven occupations and four occupational groups should be paid per week, showed a very high level of agreement on the ranking of the occupations. Moreover, the rank order corresponded to the then current rates of pay for the occupations. The median rates of pay quoted by the respondents were, however, higher than the actual rates for all but the salaried occupations. The findings also suggested that the higher a respondent's income, the greater the differentials he considered fair at the upper end of the income distribution.

Questioned about their views on low pay, the respondents in Behrend's survey also showed that they had quite clear ideas about what constituted low pay. Moreover, they adjusted their views over time to take account of inflation. There is also evidence that they accepted the 'needs' criterion of fairness, i.e. they recognized that those on low pay with families or other responsibilities required higher levels of pay to satisfy their needs than those without such responsibilities.

When questioned about pay *increases*, employees also had quite clearly defined views. They tend, it seems, to think of pay increases in flat rate terms (Behrend, 1984), perhaps because percentage increases are not very meaningful to all employees, and because flat rate increases are more easily related to weekly or monthly pay receipts. Behrend's evidence 'suggests that there is at any given period of time a perceptual threshold zone for pay increases'. In effect, a pay increase below a certain size is perceived to be 'not noticeable', while beyond another, higher, level the increase is judged to make a 'noticeable difference'. In Britain in 1966 this 'threshold zone' was thought by Behrend to lie between £1 and £2 per week. The results of a survey by Behrend and others in Dublin in 1971 produced equivalent figures of £2.00 and £2.50 per week. Using a somewhat different approach, Daniel (1975) in a survey concerned with pay and inflation, claimed to detect a 'critical point', or pay threshold, of £4 a week.

Further evidence gathered by Behrend from pay surveys in Ireland in 1969 and 1971 suggests that notions of fair pay also include full compensation for inflation. The importance of pay differentials to employees also emerges clearly from Behrend's work. She notes, however (Behrend, 1984) that 'there is no consensus with regard to what are fair pay increase differentials.' If these findings are of general validity, we have here, it seems, the seeds of serious problems in the matter of equity. While the evidence suggests a consensus about the pay rankings appropriate to different occupations, there is apparently no such consensus with regard to the appropriate pay differentials between occupations. Yet both are necessary for reasonable pay stability.

The main conclusion for our immediate purposes, however, is that, despite the intangible nature of fairness, employees do indeed have sufficiently clear perceptions of what, for them, constitutes equitable pay for this to be a major influence on their actions. Before going on to examine the implications of this conclusion for employees' wage behaviour, however, it is necessary to say a word about the problem of aggregation across individuals. Until now we have been concerned with the case of one individual only, but we now wish in much of what follows to deal with pay at a more aggregated level, and we must therefore consider what modifications, if any, are required in order to make this transition.

Aggregate pay goals The notion of an equitable wage plays a central role in our analysis. Is it meaningful, however, to think in terms of such a concept for groups of individuals, and through them for the economy as a whole? There seems to be a variety of ways in which an aggregate concept of equity might emerge. If we consider, first, the case of a group of individuals whose wage is set in centralized bargaining with an employer and we assume that a democratic voting system is in use, then, with equal weighting, individual views of equity would determine both the pay claim and the rate of pay ultimately accepted in the bargaining process. In any given period of time, the group might fail, of course, to attain the group notion of the equitable wage – it might, on the other hand, exceed it – but the main point would be that a *group* notion of the equitable wage existed, and the group's actions were determined by it. The mean wage which emerged as a goal need not, of course, have coincided with any single member's views on equity, but each individual's views on equity would have played a part in determining the group goal.

As an alternative way of proceeding, a pay group might attempt to reach a consensus about the equitable wage. Since W** for each individual is a perception, it is not rigidly fixed, and might be altered in the light of argument and information, including information about the views of others in the group. It might well be possible, therefore, to work towards a view of the equitable wage which was widely accepted within the group.

Yet another possibility, which is common in organized trade unions, is for the setting of pay goals to be left to trade union officials. Generally they will consult with members, or with members' representatives, before deciding on particular pay goals. In such cases, the influence of individual members' views on pay might not be all that great, although generally a trade union seems unlikely to be able to stray too far from its members' opinions, certainly not for a prolonged period. For practical purposes, what really counts, however, is that a group perception of what is fair and reasonable in the circumstances is still likely to emerge, and, once again, as in the other cases cited, group actions in matters of pay will be influenced by individuals' notions of equity.

Where there are many pay groups, each with its own view of equitable pay, aggregate pay in the economy as a whole will be determined by the actions of the groups, and, of course, of employers. Individual notions of equity will, therefore, ultimately have a bearing on the general level of wages which employees are prepared to accept, and on wage increases. Any attempt by, for example, a government to hold pay claims below the rate of inflation, could be expected to meet resistance from employees, unless they had been persuaded to accept such a policy. While, therefore, it must be admitted that at more aggregated levels, individual notions of equity are less easily discerned, their influence is nevertheless still there, and simply to dismiss them as of little consequence would be mistaken and, to say the least, unwise.

Where individuals have a reasonably strong influence on the setting of group pay goals, then, there seems little reason to expect these goals to depart in any significant respects from the individual goals we outlined earlier. Even in the case of trade unions, where the views of union officials may carry a heavier weighting than they deserve, any differences seem more likely to be differences of degree (for example, over the target growth of real wages) than of kind – if other pecuniary (e.g. pensions) and non-pecuniary (holidays, hours of work, etc.) demands are brought into consideration, the scope for differences of view greatly increases, of course. In subsequent sections of our analysis, therefore, we assume that group pay goals are in essential respects similar in kind to those set by individuals.

4.2.2 The downward inflexibility of wages

Even in conditions of excess supply, prices do not always adjust to ensure that all product markets clear. Gordon (1981) has reviewed the numerous ways in which firms' price-setting decisions in product markets contribute to this state of affairs. The labour market, too, in most countries exhibits persistent signs of disequilibrium, and this in turn, of course, also has repercussions on product markets. It is these labour market aspects with which we shall be principally concerned in this section. In particular, we shall be examining why wages tend to be 'sticky' in a downward direction. They move upwards easily enough, but experience has shown that it is notoriously difficult to adjust money wages downwards, even in the conditions of gross excess supply of labour which have characterized many industrial countries in the 1980s.

A variety of theories is already on offer to explain why wages are sticky. Solow (1980) lists a number of examples, including: Keynes' view that workers attempt to defend traditional wage differentials (a factor also stressed by Tobin, 1972); Solow's own hypothesis that employers avoid aggressive wage-cutting if this will antagonize the remaining workforce, harming productivity and making it harder to recruit high quality workers when the labour market tightens; Pigou's recognition that widely-held notions of fairness might play a role; the implicit contract theory; the rigidities imposed by the specifying of wage rates in labour contracts, since this leaves the employer only with the option of varying his demand for labour should costs have to be cut. Solow notes that the various theories are not mutually exclusive – we would, for example, link Keynes' emphasis on differentials with Pigou's attention to fairness. Solow also makes a further significant comment: 'it is quite likely that many of the candidate hypotheses are true, each contributing a little to the explanation of labour market failure.' It is in this spirit that we offer our own explanation of wage stickiness, drawing on the framework of analysis which we have developed.

To understand why money wages tend to be inflexible downwards, even in conditions of surplus labour supply, we have to appreciate the different interests of the parties involved (we draw here on earlier published work – see Baxter, 1987). The three parties are the unemployed, the employed and employers, and we look at each of these in turn. From the point of view of the unemployed seeking work, their utility function is different from those in work, including their former colleagues (if the unemployed have previously been in a job). Instead of earning a wage or salary, they will be living on social security benefits which are likely to be less, perhaps appreciably less, than their previous wage. They will therefore have had to modify their lifestyles – the more so the longer unemployment lasts. Their consumption pattern will be different, with a higher proportion of income now being devoted to satisfying basic needs. The families of the unemployed may even have to move house and live in a different neighbourhood. Inevitably, reference groups will alter. For some time at least, the likeliest standard of comparison will be the individual himself in his previous, employed, state. Comparisons with the wages of other workers may be maintained, but probably less strongly with the passage of time; or comparisons may assume a more general form, in which the financial plight of the unemployed is compared with the general body of those in work. We might therefore represent the utility function of an unemployed person as

$$U_j = u(B_j, B_j/W_j, B_j/\overline{W}, G_c, P) \qquad (4.5)$$

where, B_j is the unemployment or other social security benefit received by unemployed person j, W_j is the wage previously received by j when in employment, $\overline{W}$ is the average wage of those in employment, the assumption being that comparisons with the reference groups previously used have now been abandoned.

Unless the unemployed person blames only himself for his plight, or feels that no one is really to blame, or is totally apathetic, he is likely to feel a sense of grievance, or, in our terminology, of relative deprivation, when he compares his situation with what it was previously, or with that of others still in employment, including perhaps former colleagues. Even if his plight is justified by others on the grounds that it is in the best interests of society at large, that will be little compensation to the unemployed person. Since the most direct way to escape from his predicament would be to obtain employment at a wage comparable with that previously received (although not necessarily in the same line of work) the unemployed will generally seek work. If, however, it should prove impossible to obtain work at the previous level of remuneration, the utility approach to consumer behaviour indicates that it would still be in the interests of the unemployed to accept work at a lower level of payment, so long as it exceeded unemployment benefits by a margin sufficient at least to cover the direct costs of working. In such circumstances, however, a sense of relative deprivation could still be expected to prevail, even if to a lesser extent than when unemployed. The individual's absolute income would be lower than previously, and so too would be his relative income.

In the case of an employed person faced by the threat of a cut in money wages, the situation would be very different. There are a number of reasons why he might be expected to oppose any attempt to reduce his money wage, even in conditions of excess labour supply. First, it would reduce his total consumption of commodities (assuming no compensating fall in prices, and such could not be assured) and therefore his total utility. Equally important, however, it would, in the absence of a proportionate reduction in the money wages of those in his reference groups, reduce his consumption relative to these groups. He would therefore suffer an even greater loss of utility, probably no longer being able to afford as many of those commodities which they enjoyed in common, perhaps even having to forgo some altogether. The reduction in utility could in fact be quite disproportionate to the reduction in income, because at the margin certain goods yielding a high utility for a given financial outlay only become available above a certain level of income, and might be lost if income fell.

There is, too, the question of equity. If we assume that at the outset equity existed, and the employee was being paid the equity wage W**, then any reduction in his money wage relative to that of reference group(s) would be judged unfair, and would be resisted. To the extent that the reduction in pay subjected the individual to greater inequalities in society at large, the resistance would be stronger still. Feelings of relative deprivation would have been created, with inevitable consequences for the third party involved, the employer: we list some of the likely consequences below.

We have assumed in the above analysis that the general price level P remained unaltered. Even if money wages are sticky, real wages can, of course, be reduced if P rises. But then all money wages are affected proportionately, so that relative money wages remain unaltered. Keynes (1936) rightly saw that a reduction in incomes would be less strongly resisted if it occurred through the medium of a rise in prices, with relative money incomes remaining unchanged – the loss of utility would then derive only from the fall in absolute real income. The practical difficulty of a policy designed to reduce real income by deliberately raising prices is, however, that we wish, of course, to avoid inflation, and no one has yet devised a workable alternative which enables all money wages to be reduced at precisely the same time – although there have been examples of all employees in particular firms accepting proportionate reductions in their money incomes.

Turning, finally, to the employer, he has an interest in minimizing labour costs, and therefore in reducing money wages in relation to prices, but he also has a number of other important considerations to bear in mind. If by reducing the money wages of his employees he causes feelings of unfairness and relative deprivation among them, then a number of undesirable (and costly) consequences may follow. Baxter (1973) noted that one consequence of a feeling of RD would be to alter employees' attitudes towards their employer(s). It could be expected to make employees less cooperative, perhaps accompanied by a reduction in effort at work, obstruction and a resistance to change. There might even be a work-to-rule, or strikes, with a consequent loss of output and productivity. We can illustrate these effects by specifying the short-run production function of the firm in the following form (a form closely resembling that used by Annable (1977) although arrived at by a rather different route):

$$Q_A = q\,(L,\ W_i/W^{**}) \qquad (4.6)$$

where, Q_A is the volume of output of firm A, L is the labour input, W_i is the money wage paid by Firm A to individual i, and W^{**} is the equitable wage, as perceived by individual i.

The implication of our analysis is that Q_A will be maximized when $W_i > W^{**}$. When $W_i = W^{**}$, output of Firm A will depend in effect simply on the input of labour, and will be no different from a conventional production function. When, however, $W_i < W^{**}$, the normal functional relationship between Q_A and L will alter, with the value of the coefficient of L falling as output per unit of input is reduced by the actions of the aggrieved employee. This will in turn have implications for the profit maximising output of the firm.

In a situation in which $W_i = W^{**}$, and the employer is offered alternative, or additional, labour at a wage rate less than W_i, an employer will, in purely financial terms, have to weigh the effect of the reduction in labour costs on profits against the possible reduction in output and revenue caused by the sense of RD created among existing employees (RD, as we saw earlier, might also exist even among the new employees, if recruited from unemployed who were previously employed at higher rates of pay). The quality of the labour offered may also be inferior to that of existing labour.

Where $W_i > W^{**}$, it should be possible to reduce W_i without causing a sense of RD, although if it has for long been customary for an employer to pay above the fair wage, then it is possible that employees will have come to consider W_i as the appropriate yardstick and still feel aggrieved if they are paid a lower rate. The reference group in effect becomes the individual in his previous, more highly paid, state.

In a firm paying less than W^{**}, RD will already exist, and reducing W_i still lower could be expected to add to the sense of

RD (whether proportionately to the reduction in W_i, or not, is a matter which can only be resolved empirically).

Finally, in circumstances such as we have been considering, where labour contracts are incompletely specified, there might, of course, be other reasons why an employer would not wish to reduce employees' wages. As Dow and Earl (1982) have noted, if work tasks have idiosyncrasies which require on-the-job learning, a reduction in wages could lead to the loss of valuable staff, some of whom could have been expected to pass on their specialised knowledge. The net result might be a drop in productivity. Nor need wage decisions always be taken wholly on financial grounds. The idea of the implicit contract may also embrace a feeling of moral commitment on the part of the employer towards his staff, perhaps requiring him to pay the equitable wage, or to maintain differentials *vis-à-vis* reference groups.

Before leaving the question of the downward inflexibility of wages, it is also worth noting that public sector employment is now very important in many countries, and, if anything, pay comparisons seem even more important to public sector employees (in, for example, the public utilities) than to those in the private sector. Since productivity and other performance indicators are difficult to construct for much of the public sector, resort often has to be made to comparisons with pay in the private sector. It may be the case, too, that financial considerations weigh less heavily in the public sector, and that greater importance is attached to social considerations (as they relate to employees). The balance of forces then, in both the private and public sectors, seems to be weighted heavily against a policy of reductions in money wages as a means of fostering employment, certainly where the reductions apply only to some, not all, workers – there may also, of course, be demand effects, as Keynes stressed in his *General Theory*.

4.2.3 The upward pressure on wages

In his Presidential Address to the American Economic Association, Tobin (1972) drew attention to a myth of macroeconomics: '... that relations among aggregates are enlarged analogues of relations among corresponding variables for individual households, firms, industries and markets.' He went on to outline how an economy in which wages in different sectors were linked through a system of comparability could be in perpetual sectoral disequilibrium even when it had settled into a stochastic macro-equilibrium. Such a system might also exhibit marked trends over time, and appreciable fluctuations around these trends. A good deal of evidence suggests that this type of system is typical of the labour market. It is also the type of wage system which, on the basis of our earlier analysis, we would expect to find in the labour market. In this section of our study we examine how such a wage system might operate, we look at the empirical evidence available, and we conclude with an assessment of the economic implications.

The wage transmission process Numerous writers, especially those with an interest in labour market institutions and the detailed workings of the labour market, have been impressed by what they have seen as a tendency for the wages of certain groups of employees to move in association with each other, although generally after a time lag. A sizeable literature now exists in which various hypotheses about the nature of this wage linkage, or 'wage spillover', have been advanced and tested. It is not the intention here to provide an exhaustive account of these studies – extensive surveys can be found in Burton and Addison (1977), Mitchell (1980) and Addison and Burton (1984) – but rather to give an indication of the nature of the work and the empirical findings. We shall also try to explain the reasons for this wage spillover process, and its implications for inflation.

In its general form, Addison and Burton (1984) have expressed the spillover process as

$$\dot{W}^{s}_{it} = \sum_{i=1}^{n} \beta_{ir} \dot{W}_{rt} \qquad \beta_{ir} > O \tag{4.7}$$

where, $\dot{W}^{s}_{i}$ is the spillover–induced rate of growth of money wages in sector i, $\dot{W}_{r}$ is the rate of growth of money wages in reference sector r(r = 1, . . ., n, constituting the reference wage set for the ith sector participants) and β_{ir} is a spillover coefficient denoting the degree of pattern following by the ith sector wages consequent upon an increase in rth sector wages. As expressed, the wage spillover all takes place at time t, but, as noted earlier, there is in practice likely to be some timelag before the dependent variable reacts.

Studies of wage spillover generally advance a hypothesis in which the spillover assumes a specific form. Given the large number of studies, it is helpful to try to categorize them, although not all fit readily into categories, and even the different categories have certain common features. There are, however, a number of basic hypotheses, and studies which stand out as examples of particular hypotheses, and we tend to concentrate on these.

Among the early studies of wage spillover was the 'union politics' hypothesis advanced by Ross (1948). His central proposition was that a trade union is a 'political agency operating in an economic environment'. Whilst, formally, a union exists to further the interests and economic welfare of its members, institutional objectives, such as the survival and growth of the organization, take precedence, he believes, should there be a conflict with the formal goals.

Ideas of equity and justice, Ross claimed, have a compelling force in wage negotiations, providing the substance of equitable comparisons, which are important not just to workers and trade union officials, but also to employers. The employers are concerned to avoid 'getting out of line' and being censored by their fellow employers – they are as concerned to ensure that they pay no *more* than is just, than that they pay what is just. Employees carefully scrutinze the outcome of pay bargaining in order to assess how well their negotiators have done. Workers' dignity and prestige are at stake, and if they have done less well than those with whom they can legitimately be compared (for guidance on the legitimacy of comparisons they may rely on union leaders) repercussions may well ensue, with support perhaps being transferred to rival leaders, or even rival unions. Lastly, for the labour arbitrators, the 'going rate' and the 'prevailing pattern of adjustment' are the key standards by which they judge their own performance, and by which they expect to be judged by others.

Such is the importance of equitable comparison, Ross argued, that wage rates and wage changes are transplanted from one agreement to another. But this wage spillover is not a limitless process. It runs in limited circuits, not in a single chain throughout the whole economy. These limited circuits Ross referred to as 'orbits of coercive comparison', determined by competition as well as cooperation among unions, and employers, and perhaps also by the state playing a more active role in setting rates of pay. In such circumstances, even small differences in pay, or pay awards, may assume quite disproportionate importance in the eyes of the participants.

After reviewing the evidence for the later years of the nineteenth century and the inter-war years, Ross concluded that real hourly earnings had advanced more sharply in highly organized industries than in less unionized industries, irrespective of what was happening to union membership. While recognizing that the evidence was not conclusive, it was nevertheless consistent with his thesis.

Dunlop (1957), another early writer in the field, was not impressed by arguments in favour of a 'political' theory of wages, since such arguments still boiled down in the end, he believed, to the central question of what differences, if any, unions made to wage determination. Dunlop's own thesis rests on the concept of a wage structure embracing both the structure to be found within a plant, firm or other grouping in which differentials are set by the same authority (described as an 'internal' structure) and the complex of inter-firm or group structures covered by a number of different agencies (an 'external' structure). The central structures in Dunlop's model are 'job clusters' and 'wage contours'. A job cluster is defined as:

> a stable group of job classifications or work assignments within a firm (wage determining unit) which are so linked together by (a) technology, (b) by the administrative organisation of the production process, including policies of transfer and promotion, or (c) by social custom that they have common wage-making characteristics.

The internal wage is envisaged as being divided into groups of job clusters. Ross cites a tool room in a plant as one example of a cluster.

Wage contours Dunlop defines as:

> a stable group of firms (wage determining units) which are so linked together by (a) similarity of product markets, (b) by resort to similar sources for a labour force, or (c) by common labour market organisation (custom) that they have common wage-making characteristics.

Contours have three dimensions: particular occupations or job clusters; a sector of industry; a geographical location. Dunlop gives as an example the basic steel contour for production jobs, consisting of the producers of basic steel products scattered in communities throughout the country.

Within both clusters and contours there are, Dunlop maintained, key wage rates. The key rates in the job clusters perform the function of linking the internal structure of the firm with the external wage structure among firms forming part of the contour. It is via this channel that external developments in the contour are transmitted to the interior rate structure of the individual firms. As yet another practical example of the sort of wage structure he had in mind, Dunlop chose the case of motor truck drivers in one city – Boston – in a particular month. For what was essentially the same job, the highest rate of pay among one group of employers was approaching double the lowest rate paid by another group of employers. Similar disparities, it was claimed, could be found in other cities. In essence, the rates paid by the various groups of employers represented wage contours – and therefore the crucial wage comparisons were within contours rather than across them, although doubtless some cross-contour comparisons would also be regarded as legitimate (the highest rate of pay, for example, was for those delivering magazines, and the second highest for those delivering daily newspapers, two jobs which would almost certainly be regarded as comparable).

Dunlop's system of wage contours allowed for the effects on key bargains of external factors, such as demand, productivity and price changes, although the response of the different contours to these factors was likely to vary, depending, for example, on the degree of competition, the proportion of labour costs to total costs, etc. within a contour. It might be claimed, therefore, that ultimately it is the usual economic influences which determine wage changes, even if the wage structure as depicted by Dunlop is essential to an understanding of the wage transmission process and the pattern of wages. There remains the question, however, of whether, without the contours, economic variables would exert the same impact on wage rates other than key rates.

Dunlop's wage contour hypothesis makes use, as we saw, of the idea of key wage rates, and therefore key wage changes, which feed into other wage groups via the wage contours and the job clusters. Many other studies of the wage transmission process make use of a similar idea of wage leadership, although with rather different notions of how the transmission mechanism works. Burton and Addison (1977) distinguish five forms of the 'wage leadership hypothesis', and even this list is not exhaustive – in one sense, all spillover hypotheses contain the element of wage leadership. The first hypothesis Burton and Addison identify is referred to as 'national pattern bargaining', since the analysis takes place at the industry level, rather than the firm level, as in Dunlop's hypothesis. Ross (1957) was able to show that a variety of 'hard goods' industries, including basic steelmaking, non-ferrous metals (smelting and refining), engines and turbines, agricultural machinery (excluding tractors) and locomotives and parts, experienced almost the same flat rate increases in hourly wages over the thirteen year period 1939–52. 'Soft goods' industries, such as shoes and textiles, showed much less uniformity, because ability to pay and the possible effects on unemployment appeared to weigh more heavily with negotiators.

In a later study, Eckstein and Wilson (1962) produced evidence which tended to support Ross's conclusions. They found that in a key group of heavy goods industries, including rubber, clay and glass, primary metals, fabricated metals, non-electrical machinery, transportation equipment and instruments, wages since 1948 had moved almost identically. Wages in this key group were explained by the profit rates and the unemployment rates in the group, whereas wages in the other industries outside the group were largely determined by spillover effects from wages in the key group. In a subsequent follow-up article, Eckstein (1968) found that the economic ties linking the key group industries had weakened, but that there was now evidence of new wage spillovers from the construction trades to durable manufacturing. This is a good indication of the changing nature of the spillover process, and how we must expect it to be affected by the changing industrial structure.

More detailed analyses of particular industries have also found evidence of pattern-following behaviour – with, however, divergencies from lead settlements becoming greater the further the pattern moves from the source. Selzer (1951, 1961) and Locks (1955) detected pattern bargaining in the steel industry in the 1940s and 1950s; and Levinson (1960) and Alexander (1961) made similar claims for the automobile industry. It is noticeable that these industries are typified by high wages, strong industrial unions, large corporations with considerable market power, and strong geographical concentration. These are precisely the characteristics noted by Eckstein and Wilson in the pattern-following heavy goods industries which they investigated. Interesting comparisons between wage-setting in these 'non-competitive' sectors of industry and that in 'competitive' sectors, in which wages are more sensitive to market forces, have been made by Wachter (1970, 1974). His findings suggest another interesting feature of pattern-following – that it is the more responsive competitive sector which leads the whole process, with the non-competitive sector adjusting to this lead, but much more slowly, in an effort to restore what are seen as the normal differentials between the two sectors.

A further distinct version of the wage leadership model can be found in the work of Turner and Jackson (1969, 1970) and Jackson, Turner and Wilkinson (1975) based on differences in rates of productivity growth between industries. The reasoning, briefly, is that in the trade or industry where productivity growth is fastest, wages tend to increase in line with productivity, since firms find it easier to grant wage demands than to reduce prices (perhaps because price-cutting, once started, is not easy to control if competitors respond by cutting their prices). The large pay increases in the lead industry generate pressures for similar increases in other industries, the effect of the excess growth in wages over productivity usually being passed on by employers in the form of higher prices.

The productivity growth leadership hypothesis has been criticized on a number of counts, including a failure to test the hypothesis properly, and the hypothesis's implication of a kinked demand curve in the lead industry, when many new, rapidly growing technological and consumer industries, such as computers and video recorders, have demonstrated that prices in such industries may fall. The attempt by Turner *et al.* to extend their analysis to explain international wage and price levels has also been found wanting.

A variant of the productivity growth leadership hypothesis has been proposed by Edgren, Faxén and Odhner (1969, 1973) for a small open economy (in their case Sweden) operating under a system of fixed exchange rates. Their hypothesis rests on the division of the economy into a competitive sector (i.e. one exposed to foreign competition) and a sheltered sector. The movement of prices in the competitive sector, it was claimed, had followed world market prices during the 1960s, both in the case of exports and the products of domestic industries competing with imports. The scope for wage increases was said to be determined by productivity growth in the competitive sector and international price movements. Wage increases in the sheltered sector, it was found, had matched those in the competitor sector, even although productivity gains in the former had been considerably lower. Since the rate of profitability in the sheltered sector had been constant, prices there had risen more rapidly than in the competitive sector.

The productivity growth hypothesis of Edgren *et al.* is clearly more limited in its application, since it is less likely to be relevant to larger economies with smaller foreign trade sectors, especially if they should be operating under flexible exchange rates. The productivity growth leadership nevertheless has considerable attractions, and is consistent with the stability in the industry ranking of average earnings over considerable periods of time noted by many researchers – see, for example, Cullen (1956), OECD (1965) and Turner and Jackson (1969). Inter-industry differentials do change over time, showing some tendency to increase, but only slowly. As Addison and Siebert (1979) note, such stability in the wage structure could also be given a competitive long-run supply price interpretation. If, for example, differences in skill mix and in non-pecuniary advantages and disadvantages did not change much over time, then we could also expect the wage structure to be stable. The relative stability of earnings over considerable periods of time, despite appreciable differences in productivity growth between industries, nevertheless strongly suggests an important element of inter-industry wage spillover.

The possibility of a wage transmission mechanism linking the unionised sector of an economy to the non-unionised sector has been a further subject of study by economists. The theory has been elaborated by Rosen (1969) and Ashenfelter *et al.* (1972). Rosen states the position facing a non-unionized firm, within an industry which has been unionised, in the following terms:

$$E(W) = pWu + (1 - p)Wn \qquad (4.8)$$

where E(W) is the wage a non-union employer expects to pay, p is the probability of unionization of the non-union firm, and Wu and Wn are the actual wages in the unionized firms and the non-union firm, respectively. The firm sets its actual wage Wn to minimize its expected wage, assuming a one-to-one correspondence between the firm's wage and its profits. The value of p is likely to depend upon such factors as the extent to which the union has been successful in raising union wages above the non-union level, and perhaps also on the degree of unionisation already obtained in the industry. If, to simplify matters, we take only the former into account, then the value of p may be expressed as:

$$p = P[Wu - Wn)/Wn] \qquad p' > 0 \qquad (4.9)$$

with p an increasing function of the union–non–union differential.

Rosen's findings confirmed the existence of a 'threat effect', which forced non-union firms to respond to the levels of wages set in the unionized sector. Ashenfelter *et al.* also found their results to be consistent with the hypothesis of significant spillover effects from union to non-union wages in the US. Rather interestingly, they found, too, however, that the spillover operated in the reverse direction during certain periods. This latter finding was a precursor to two studies by

Flanagan (1976) and Johnson (1977) which appeared to indicate that the direction of wage spillover did indeed run from the non-union to the union sector, the reverse of what had been thought. Vroman (1980, 1982) and Mitchell (1980) have demonstrated, however, that these latter findings are very sensitive to the specification of the equations and the data series used, and ought to be treated with caution. While therefore the threat hypothesis rests on a spillover from union to non-union wages, and there is evidence to support this view, it is as well to recognize that, in some periods at least, it is possible that the direction of causation is reversed, with unions perhaps trying to maintain differentials in relation to non-union firms. In both cases, however, the end result may be the same: greater wage increases than would have occurred under market forces alone.

The public sector–private sector divide offers yet another potentially fruitful area for wage spillover research, especially in countries with sizeable public sectors in which employees are represented by powerful unions, and the degree of unionization is high. The United Kingdom is one such country. Studies by Foster *et al.* (1984, 1986) broke down earnings into four sectors – private manufacturing, private non-manufacturing, public corporations and central and local government – and tested whether one or more of these sectors acted as leader, giving rise to subsequent wage increases in the other sectors. The results suggested an influence running from public corporations to the other sectors, with a lead time generally of one quarter.

We come, finally, to a group of studies which has attempted to determine whether wage leadership has taken the form of a regular 'wage round'. Much of this work has been carried out in the United Kingdom and Ireland. Knowles and Thorne (1961), in an early study, identified three types of repetitive pattern: first, the grouping of settlements, or collective bargaining, at periodic intervals; second, similarities of achieved, or negotiated, pay increases; third, 'inclusiveness', i.e. the frequency with which individual bargaining groups appeared in each wage round.

The main findings of Knowles and Thorne, and a related study by Knowles and Robinson (1962) were, first, that there was no regular periodicity, with the settlements of bargaining groups taking place at set intervals, such as a year. Knowles and Robinson noted, however, that there were certain regular coalitions of groups, although they had no regular leaders. Neither study could find a high degree of uniformity, either in money or percentage terms, among settlements – contrary to the conclusions of a 1961 OEEC (now the OECD) study, which had found a marked degree of uniformity in the percentage wage increases obtained in 16 selected British industries. Knowles and Robinson remarked, however, on the fact that the overall spread of wage rates increased only slightly. There was, in other words, more uniformity in the *cumulative* wage increases obtained than in the 'round', or short-period, increases – evidence, it seems, of catching up.

With regard to inclusiveness, Knowles and Robinson also found that about two-thirds of their negotiating groups appeared in at least four of the six major wage rounds they identified (only about one-fifth appeared in all wage rounds). Once again, therefore, there appears to be something in the nature of a wage round, but there is no clearly defined, regular pattern to it.

Much more positive results were reported in the Irish study by McCarthy *et al.* (1975). The authors found clear evidence of a primary process, or wage round, involving virtually every bargaining group. This process did not produce identical settlements, although there was evidence that it did produce a minimum rate of increase, usually in money terms – the tendency to settle for flat rate pay increases resulted in some compression of differentials during the 1960s.

An interesting feature of the Irish wage round highlighted by McCarthy *et al.* was the practice of paying 'primary' and 'supplementary' pay awards. The former ensured that workers generally obtained pay increases which kept pace with inflation and the general growth of the economy. The supplementary awards, on the other hand, appeared to be a response to specific labour market pressures and exceptional status claims, especially those involving powerful bargaining groups.

McCarthy *et al.* went on to carry out a more detailed examination of some of the more important bargaining groups which were said to have negotiated 'key wage bargains' – defined as 'a settlement representing a significant upward departure from existing patterns which had a disproportionate influence on the expectations, claims and settlements of other groups'. They had little difficulty in locating a small number of such groups (two examples being building, electrical contracting). Analysed sequentially, a picture emerged on the union side of 'competitive unionism seeking to restore traditional relativities'. Moreover, in each case a settlement was followed by a chain reaction, as other groups then attempted to restore their relative positions. On the employers' side, there was almost as much disunity, with rivalry rather than cooperation the order of the day.

The only economic influence appearing to exert much sway on bargains was found to be the cost of living, which was the highest scoring single argument used by 'wage followers' – although over half of the respondents ranked it as of less than primary importance. Much more important in total, the authors concluded, was the weight given to various kinds of comparability argument, relating for example to workers doing similar work or receiving similar levels of pay. On comparability, the authors summed up their views as follows:

> Our conclusion was that comparability in all its forms is the major test of relative failure or success in the Irish bargaining process. *It follows that, even if the primary process deals with the cost of living argument, supplementary settlements will be demanded, from time to time, to satisfy notions of relative deprivation. In short, the risk of wage leadership exists regardless of the level of inflation or the extent to which wages are indexed.* (Emphasis as in the original).

Studies of wage rounds have also been conducted in the United States. Some of the works referred to earlier in the context of wage leadership also tested for the existence of wage rounds. Ross (1957), for example, was able to show that a group of 15 hard goods industries had granted very similar pay increases, measured in cents per hour, over the period 1939–52 taken as whole. Ross concluded: 'These figures show equalisation of movement, and preservation of differentials, with a vengeance.' Levinson (1962) also found evidence of the clustering of settlements in time, and, in the case of key industries, in the characteristics of the settlements. Maher (1961) too found evidence of pay rounds and, in their earlier study, Eckstein and Wilson (1962) concluded that wage rounds were an important institutional characteristic of the wage determination process. In their 1968 work, however, they found that 'The key group, wage round technique also has considerable limitations and is becoming more difficult to apply.' These rather disheartening conclusions may have had a dampening influence, since there has been little subsequent US interest in pursuing the question of wage rounds.

Stepping back for a moment to try and assess what we may conclude from this large body of research work, we must sympathize, first, with the task faced by researchers. Given the large number of bargaining units involved, and the complications caused by such factors as changes in hours, holidays and fringe benefits, it is not surprising that there have been difficulties in trying to isolate wage patterns. There seems to be sufficient evidence, however, to justify the conclusion that wage linkage, or spillover, does indeed exist, even if the links are not as regular, nor as clearly defined, as some of the hypotheses suggest. Those directly involved in wage negotiations, or with first-hand knowledge of the institutional arrangements, would invariably support such a conclusion. One interesting piece of evidence of this nature is the experience of Aubrey Jones, one-time Chairman of the Prices and Incomes Board in the United Kingdom, who was so impressed by the evidence he found of strong wage leadership and the importance of comparability arguments in pay bargaining that he felt impelled to write a book about it entitled *The New Inflation* (1973).

Even if interest in wage spillover has waned amongst economists, evidence continues to accumulate that there is a widespread problem (one of the most recent examples being a study of wage spillover in the Australian labour market by Plowman *et al.*, 1986) which will not simply disappear, and we ought therefore to face up to its implications. In order to do this successfully, however, we need a better understanding of the forces underlying wage spillover.

A general weakness of spillover studies, as Wood (1978) has pointed out, is that neither the microeconomic behavioural underpinnings of the models nor the nature of the processes described are adequately formulated. We now go on to offer an explanation of a number of the fundamental influences underlying the spillover process, drawing on the analytical framework outlined earlier. One major attraction of our approach is that it is in the nature of a *general* explanation of the spillover phenomenon, and is not tied to any particular view about the pattern of wage spillover. It does not even imply that there must a be *regular* pattern, other than that one or more pay groups act as leaders, perhaps only briefly, and others tend to follow the leader(s).

Before passing on to give our explanation of wage spillover, it is worth noting, finally, that the spillover hypothesis accords well with the relative stability in occupational and industrial pay differentials over long periods of time which has been remarked upon by a number of investigators. Routh (1980) for example, in one of the most extensive studies undertaken, concluded with regard to the UK, 'The outstanding characteristic of the national pay structure is the rigidity of its relationships.' In the United States, studies have found a tendency for the skilled–unskilled differential to narrow over time (see, for example, Keat, 1960 and Orton, 1976) but the change has occurred principally during wartime – a further factor (usually associated with wars) is exceptionally rapid inflation, perhaps because the effect of flat rate pay increases on differentials is greatest at such times. It is, of course, possible to provide other explanations of relative pay stability, but the importance of pay comparisons in wage bargaining suggests that wage spillover is a key factor.

An explanation of wage spillover We saw earlier why any unilateral move by an employer, or government, to reduce an employee's money wage was likely to give rise to a feeling of relative deprivation. Similar feelings may be aroused even in circumstances in which money wages are increasing. The response to the influence of intervening variables is a perceived wage entitlement W^{**}, which is compared with the actual wage W_i of individual i. Our earlier analysis suggested that the perceived entitlement would be based on the expectation of achieving a level of money wages which would not only compensate for the expected rise in prices (and probably even exceed it) but also ensure that the individual was able to maintain the desired relationship between his wage and the wages of reference groups. A sense of relative deprivation would be created if either of these conditions failed to hold, and the perceived entitlement fell short of the actual wage. This does not tell us anything, however, about the *strength* of feeling of relative deprivation. Generally it might be expected that as the gap between the actual wage and the perceived entitlement increased, so too would the sense of relative deprivation – whether linearly or not, only empirical research will show.

Runcimen (1966), as we saw earlier, noted that relative deprivation might vary in magnitude, frequency and degree. The magnitude of relative deprivation (M) he defined as, 'the extent of the difference between the desired situation and that of the person desiring it (as he sees it).' Similarly, the frequency of relative deprivation (F) was defined as the proportion of the group feeling it, and the degree of relative deprivation (D) as the intensity with which it was felt. The variable M, it should be stressed, is the *perceived* magnitude of inequality, and as such may, or may not, coincide with the actual inequality. The inequalities, moreover, may not only be inequalities of income, but may also include other forms of inequality in society, many of them stemming from inequalities of income. It may be expected, therefore, that inequalities of income will be among the foremost inequalities giving rise to feelings of relative deprivation.

Taking the simplest case of a single group (x) with one reference group, the sum of relative deprivation for all individuals in the group with respect to the kth inequality may be written as:

$$RD_x(M^k) = D_1^k(M_1^k, G) + D_2^k(M_2^k, G) + \ldots + D_n^k(M_n^k, G)$$

$$= \sum_{i=1}^{n} D_i^k\ (M_i^k, G) \qquad (4.10)$$

where M_i^k is the perceived magnitude of relative deprivation of the ith individual with respect to the kth inequality, D_i^k is the degree of relative deprivation of the ith individual with respect to the kth inequality, G is the reference group and n is the number in the group, of N individuals, who consider themselves deprived.

Equation 4.10 expresses the fact that RD is determined by D, which in turn is said to be a function of M, on the grounds that there seems likely to be a positive relationship between the two, with the intensity of feeling of relative deprivation increasing as the magnitude of deprivation increases – M is not treated as having an independent effect on RD, since it only influences RD via D (a point which does not emerge from Runciman's discussion of relative deprivation). The frequency of relative deprivation has been taken into account by assuming that the total number in the group (N) is constant. The frequency of relative deprivation (F) is then n/N and, as N is constant, $n \alpha F$.

Summing over all inequalities (1, 2, ... k) and weighting them to allow for the fact that their influence on relative deprivation is likely to differ, we get:

$$RD_x = \lambda_1 RD(M^1, G) + \lambda_2 RD(M^2, G) + \ldots + \lambda_k RD(M^k, G)$$

$$= \sum_{k=1}^{k} \lambda_k RD(M^k, G); \text{ where } \lambda_i \gtreqless \lambda_j,\ i \neq j. \quad (4.11)$$

Where there are several reference groups ($G_1, G_2 \ldots G_n$) the same principles apply. The sum of relative deprivation for the kth inequality is

$$RD_x(M^k) = D_1^k(M_1^k, \underline{G}) + D_2^k(M_2^k, \underline{G}) + \ldots + D_n^k(M_1^k, \underline{G})$$

$$= \sum_{i=1}^{n} D_i^k(M_i^k, \underline{G}) \quad (4.12)$$

where $\underline{G} = G_1, G_2, \ldots G_n$.

Summing over all inequalities and weighting them arithmetically

$$RD_x = \sum_{k=1}^{k} \lambda_k RD(M^k, \underline{G}); \text{ where } \lambda_i \gtreqless \lambda_j,\ i \neq j. \quad (4.13)$$

Unless a sense of relative deprivation leads to actions which have economic consequences, it will be a matter of no more than general interest to economists. It was suggested in Baxter (1973), however, that feelings of relative deprivation could have a variety of economic effects. Strikes, go-slows, lack of effort, opposition to change and a general unwillingness to cooperate might all arise from feelings of grievance associated with relative deprivation. To the extent that these cause a loss of output, they are also likely to result in increased unit costs, and therefore have inflationary consequences.

Where feelings of relative deprivation arise from inequalities in pay, there may be even more important implications for inflation. Should the wage of an individual, or group, fall short of the perceived entitlement, one could expect pressure from employees to increase their wage until W** had been obtained. Their ability to press successfully for higher wages will depend upon their bargaining power. Here we are in danger of turning full-circle. If bargaining-power depends only upon economic circumstances, such as the pressure of demand for labour, then it might be argued that, even if our analysis helps improve our understanding of the way in which the labour market works, it is of little consequence for improving our control over the economy, in particular over pay, since the key variables remain what they have always been. It really boils down to a question of whether increased dissatisfaction with pay, as expressed in terms of relative deprivation, could result in a rise in pay greater than that which would normally take place in the economic circumstances prevailing. Can it be demonstrated, in other words, that relative deprivation is capable of exerting an *independent* effect on pay?

The various forms of possible disruption to production outlined earlier constitute a form of power, in so far as they involve costs to the employer (and perhaps also to employees) who will wish to avoid them, if possible. Baxter (1980) also identified a number of other ways in which employees could increase their bargaining power in negotiations, independently of market forces. Power is a complex subject, with numerous dimensions, about which a great deal has been written without a clear consensus emerging as to its precise nature, or even the best means of subjecting it to analysis. One approach which does seem especially appropriate for present purposes, however, is that of the latent power theorists, who focus attention primarily on the bases, or sources, of power commanded by groups in society, and endeavour to identify the underlying power of these groups and their potential for achieving given ends, if necessary in conflict with other groups.

Bierstedt (1950), one of the principal advocates of this approach, has identified three sources of latent power: number of people, social organization and resources. The first two of these we can examine together, as in a bargaining situation in which individual workers join together to represent their interests in negotiations with an employer, the two are already interlinked. Assuming that the employees are represented by a trade union, an increase in the power of the union could come from either an increase in the total number of employees who are members of the union (the proportion of employees unionized remaining unchanged) or it may derive from an increase in the proportion unionized. In the former case, the main benefits seem likely to be associated with economies of scale – there may be no need, for example, for a corresponding increase in the number of union officials – and the greater financial resources made available to the union (there is therefore a link there with the third source of power). A greater degree of unionization, on the other hand, might be expected to augment union power by making it more difficult, in the event of withdrawal of union labour, for an employer to carry out the work with the remaining labour force, or to find sufficient replacements – the more so if the labour is skilled. The accretion of power would tend to be especially great if the unionized sector changed from being a minority to a majority; and generally speaking the greater the majority the greater the authority the union seems likely to wield within the group.

There are also numerous ways in which purely organizational changes might be expected to lead to increased union power. Any changes which gave a union greater cohesion and improved discipline, such as closer contact between members, between members and officials, or better transmission of information between all levels of a union, could, for example, help the union withstand a prolonged strike and make it more difficult for an employer to break a strike by splitting the membership. We have also seen examples of how well-organized picketing, as in the miners' strike of 1974 in the United Kingdom, and the organized canvassing of support from other unions, make it possible to draw on sources of power outside the bargaining unit.

Resources may be of many kinds, economic and non-economic. Although it is likely to be principally the financial resources available to a union which determine its ability to withstand a strike, and therefore the power it wields, access to physical and organizational resources, skills and knowledge may also form some part of a union's power. Moreover, although there may be finite limits to the resources available at any given time, these limits are by no means clearly identifiable, not even the financial ones, and it is most unlikely therefore that a union ever uses its resources to the limits. If we add to potential resources the increased power which may come from greater numbers or improved organization, and the assistance available to a union from other unions or outside bodies, it is clear that unions may have access to considerable reserves of latent power. We may even go so far as to say that the full potential bargaining power of unions is seldom, if ever, exercised, and that there are generally substantial latent reserves of union power in bargaining situations.

In those economic studies of wage determination which have incorporated union power as an explanatory variable, either explicitly or implicitly, the tendency has been to concentrate on one or other, but not all, of the sources of latent power noted above. This is true of perhaps the best-known work in the field, by Hines (1964, 1969) who used the rate of change of the percentage of the labour force unionized as a proxy for union militancy, which, he believed, has a bearing on union bargaining power. This proxy, however, is likely to be an adequate reflection of changes in numbers only, not of changes in organisation or resources. Greater unionization is nevertheless one possible source of additional power, and for the purposes of our argument it is sufficient to demonstrate that, even in unchanged economic circumstances, it is possible for unions to draw on additional reserves of power. These reserves of power are latent, in the sense that they are unlikely to exert their full influence on the bargaining situation unless drawn upon.

If employees (whom we assume for present purposes are members of a union) are able, because of dissatisfaction with their pay, to take steps which increase their bargaining power, what precisely will be the consequences in pay bargaining? Stated simply in terms of Hicks' (1932) model, the origin of many bargaining theories, there would tend to be a greater readiness to strike, as a trade union would be more confident of winning concessions from an employer. The union would also be able to withstand a longer strike, either because of greater cohesion among union members, improved organization or greater resources. In effect, the union's resistance curve would tend to shift upwards to the right. The near-horizontal section of the curve might also lengthen in so far as workers were less willing to accept a pay rise below a certain minimum amount. On the employer's side, assuming he were aware of the dissatisfaction of his employees, the consequent increase in their bargaining power and their greater readiness to strike (if he were not so aware at the outset, he would doubtless become aware as the dispute continued) his concession curve would tend to shift upwards to the left. Concession and resistance curve would then intersect at a wage-rate higher than that determined by the original point of intersection, and union members would benefit to the extent of the difference between the two.

Subsequent developments of Hicks' model have attempted to take into account features of pay bargaining omitted by Hicks, but the basic approach used has generally not altered greatly, and there appears to be no reason why our analysis should not be equally valid in these models. Our conclusion, then, is that if employees feel dissatisfied with their pay they can draw on additional sources of power which enable them to obtain larger increases in pay than would otherwise have been obtained. This does not imply, it should be stressed, that employees are therefore able to demand virtually any increase in pay and be sure of obtaining it. Working in the opposite direction there will still be the forces which govern the response of employers – productivity growth, the labour market situation, profits, etc. – and in any general model of wage determination these must also be taken into account. The main point, however, is that the pay settlement ultimately reached depends upon the relative bargaining powers of the parties involved, and the bargaining power of employees (and for that matter, employers) is not dependent solely on economic circumstances.

If unemployment is not to rise appreciably, the above scenario will also require an accommodative monetary policy. This is likely to be forthcoming. In a democratic society, governments may be prepared for a time to let unemployment rise, even markedly so, but politicians eventually have to face their electorates again – even dictators are not immune from such pressures – and the tendency then is to relax the fiscal and monetary stance. Monetary policy, in other words, inevitably responds to the deep-rooted forces at work in societies. We shall have more to say on this matter in section 5.

A wage spillover process of the sort outlined above can help explain both the continuous upward pressures underlying the long-term rise in money wages, and short-term fluctuations around that trend. It can also help explain both the variations in wage behaviour between countries, and the transmission of inflation between countries. Continuous upward pressure on wages is especially great in circumstances in which pay bargaining groups have incompatible views on appropriate differentials between groups. A simple case is illustrated in Table 4.14. At time t, group x receives a weekly wage of £200, and y a wage of £180. These are shown as the actual wages at time t (W_t). In the opinion of group x, this represents an appropriate pay differential (in the ratio 1:0.9) all things considered, including the relative inputs and outcomes of each group. The desired wage of group x at time t $(W^{**})_t$ is therefore £200. Seen from group y's point of view, however, *parity* of wages is fair, and $(W^{**})_t$ for group y is therefore also £200. If we assume that in time-period t + 1 group y is successful in attaining a wage increase of £20, raising its wage to £200, then for y equity now prevails. Group x will then be unhappy, however, since a wage of £200 for y means that $(W^{**})_{t+1}$ for x has now increased to £222, in order to maintain its view of the appropriate differential. And so the process would continue, with continual leap-frogging, unless consensus between the groups could be achieved or an outside party were to impose a wage on each group.

Table 4.14: Incompatible views on pay differentials

	The equitable pay differential from group x's point of view (£)					
Pay group	W_t	$(W^{**}_x)_t$	W_{t+1}	$(W^{**}_x)_{t+1}$	W_{t+2}	$(W^{**}_x)_{t+2}$
x	200	200	200	222	222	222
y	180	180	200	200	200	200
	The equitable pay differential from group y's point of view (£)					
	W_t	$(W^{**}_y)_t$	W_{t+1}	$(W^{**}_y)_{t+1}$	W_{t+2}	$(W^{**}_y)_{t+2}$
x	200	200	200	200	222	222
y	180	200	200	200	200	222

Even in circumstances in which both groups agree about the appropriate differential, where differentials are adhered to a wage increase for one group would set off a push for a corresponding increase for the other group (assuming they started off from a position in which differentials were appropriate). But at least equilibrium between group wages is possible. It is not possible in the previous example.

It will be apparent from the above examples that, where pay comparisons are made and bargaining groups have notions of appropriate, equitable differentials, *any* wage increase for one group of employees may have repercussions among other pay groups in the labour market – and the larger the pay increase, the greater the likelihood of the repercussions. Where there is consensus about appropriate differentials, however, the effect will tend only to be short-term, since it will eventually peter out once appropriate differentials have been restored. Given, however, that the initial, or primary, pay increase may be set off by a whole host of factors, such as an improvement in productivity in one firm or industry, or a sudden upsurge in profits in one sector, or developments external to an economy affecting only some firms, or a large public sector pay settlement, it is not surprising that wages are in a constant state of ferment, and even what may only be short-term effects when seen in isolation, take on the nature of a constant long-term upward push in wages when taken as a whole. Such a process may be at work even when the labour market as a whole is far from buoyant.

The analysis in the previous sections suggests that there are also other strong reasons for employees to press continually for ever higher incomes. It is, for one thing, an obvious route to greater utility, through high consumption. It is not surprising, therefore, that a number of economists (such as Sargan, 1964 and 1980; Henry, Sawyer and Smith, 1976; and Foster *et al.*, 1984) claim to have found empirical support for the idea of a targeted growth of real wages by employees. There is always the possibility, too, of even greater utility gains if a person can increase his money wages relative to that of other workers, even if in the process prices are forced up faster. If unemployment is thereby increased, it is often among those most vulnerable, and not amongst those doing the original (wage) pushing. Even if the community as a whole loses as a consequence of wage push, there may still be benefits to the individual, or group, from any relative improvement it is possible to achieve in the wage hierarchy.

In the light of the above, our wage equation for the individual employee i (and a similar specification would apply to a group of employees) takes the form

$$\dot{W}_i = f(W^T, \dot{W}_i / \dot{\overline{W}}^e_{r1}, \dot{W}_i / \dot{\overline{W}}^e_{r2}, \ldots \dot{W}_i / \dot{\overline{W}}^e_{rn}, \dot{G}^e_c, \dot{P}^e, x_1 \ldots x_n) \tag{4.14}$$

where W^T is the target growth of money wage rates (which will take account of the expected rate of inflation $\dot{P}^e$), $\dot{W}_i / \dot{\overline{W}}^e_{r1}$ represents the rate of growth of i's money wage relative to the expected rate of growth of money wages in reference group r_1 (and similarly for reference groups $r_2 \ldots r_n$), $\dot{G}^e_c$ is the expected rate of growth of government expenditure as it affects i's spending decisions and utility, $x_1 \ldots x_n$ is a vector of other variables having an influence on $\dot{W}_i$. We assume in equation 4.14 that we start off from a position in which $W_i = W^{**}$. If this were not the case, a catch-up variable would also have to be included.

At the level of the economy as a whole, the aggregate growth of money wages $\dot{W}$ is influenced by the extent to which individuals are dissatisfied with their pay. In effect, we are dealing with the sum of relative deprivation, and our aggregate wage equation for the whole economy would take the form:

$$W = f(W^T, \dot{RD}, \dot{G}_c^e, \dot{P}^e, x_1 \ldots x_n) \tag{4.15}$$

where $\dot{RD}$ is the rate of change of relative deprivation. Since RD is a subjective variable, and not directly measurable, a suitable proxy would have to be devised. One possible means of constructing an appropriate indicator would be to use self-rating scales – as are widely and successfully employed in market research sample surveys – to measure the extent of felt grievance over pay. These scales are open to certain theoretical objections, in that they entail interpersonal comparisons of responses, but they may nevertheless serve a practical purpose if they can be shown to work. Curtin (1977) has in fact demonstrated that such scales can be used successfully to measure feelings about equity and relative deprivation. Use of such scales might well have given a warning of the growing feelings of grievance and frustration during certain periods, including those of government pay constraints. At present governments have little or no knowledge of the changing mood of employees in matters of pay.

We turn, finally, to the international aspects. While the needs of people appear to be much the same, irrespective of country, the local customs and practices may result in very different patterns of wants to satisfy these needs. Perceptions of equity may also differ, and so too many social comparisons, and therefore pay goals. Governments also play very different roles, and economic developments generally do not coincide. The framework of analysis we have developed nevertheless seems of general application. Moreover, despite the many divergencies between countries, the analysis indicates that what happens in one country is still likely to affect others. Wage increases, after all, have an important bearing on prices, and rapid wage and price inflation in one country, especially a major trading country, will feed through to other countries, to the extent that it is not offset by movements in exchange rates. In this era of mass media and foreign travel, what happens in one country frequently influences events in others – social comparisons, after all, are not restricted by national boundaries (this will be even more the case when direct broadcasting by satellite becomes common). To paraphrase an old saying, no country is an island – not in economic terms, at least.

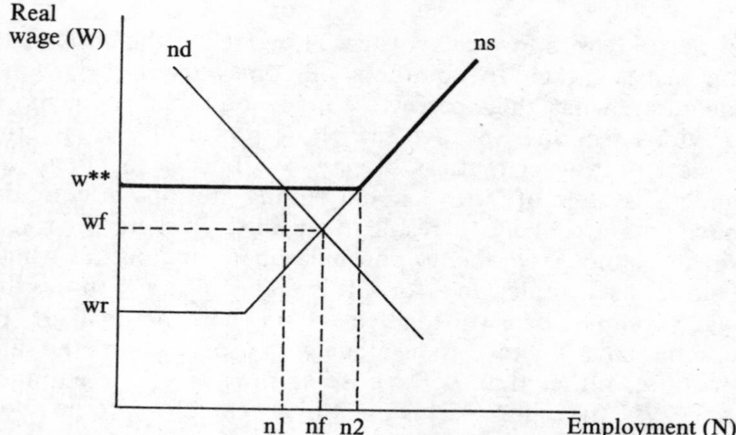

Figure 4.3: Equitable wages and disequilibrium in the labour market

4.3 LABOUR MARKET EQUILIBRIUM AND DISEQUILIBRIUM

The conventional aggregate supply curve of labour is depicted as a function of the real wage, sloping upwards to the right as the real wage increases (Figure 4.3). The empirical evidence in support of this view of the labour supply is by no means wholly convincing, as we saw earlier, and it leaves many questions unanswered. A number of critics, including Keynes (1936), have also questioned the assumption that the labour supply is likely to fall if the real wage is reduced, as the supply curve implies. Table 4.13 showed that a high proportion of female workers are dependent on their earnings from employment for the purchase of basic essentials, and this is likely to be even more the case among males, who tend still to be the principal breadwinners. They cannot therefore simply opt out of employment if their real wage falls: indeed they are likely to want to work more in order to compensate for a fall in real wages.

The fact that many workers are barely able to cover the cost of basic essentials, means that even when the real wage is above the full-employment level (w_f in Figure 4.3) there will be resistance to any attempt to reduce real wages. Another powerful reason for 'sticky wages', however, is the importance employees attach to equitable outcomes from their work, including what they perceive to be equitable payment. In previous sections we have seen how powerful a motivating force equity is in matters of pay. We have also noted that under a system of free wage bargaining, notions of equitable payments are likely to result in upward pressure on wages, since it is not incumbent upon bargainers to consider what a country as a whole can afford. It is in the nature of things that wage comparisons will tend to err on the generous side, i.e. comparisons will tend to be made with those earning the same or more, rather than with those earning less. The equitable wage w^{**} (in Figure 4.3) is most likely therefore, to lie above w_f, and well above w_r, a reservation wage often introduced to take account of the fixed costs of working.

The gist of our analysis, then, is that even if one were to accept the notion of an upward sloping supply curve of labour linked to the growth of real wages, the labour market operates in such a manner that equilibrium, and therefore full employment, is unlikely to be achieved either through general downward adjustments in money wages or through attempts to manipulate relative wages in order to reduce their aggregate level. Moreover, in the absence of any emerging consensus about the equitable wages for different groups of workers, there seems to be every likelihood that labour market disequilibrium will be a continuing feature, even in the long run.

We appear to have moved into another economic era which, while it differs in many important respects from that of the 1920s and 1930s, is also characterized by persistent long-term unemployment on a scale which cannot be dismissed simply as a temporary market aberration. Keynes in his *General Theory* put his finger squarely on one of the sources of the trouble – the importance of relative wages, and what this implies for attempts to reduce real wages (quite apart from possible demand effects) – without, however, attempting to explain the basis of this source of friction. Today, however, thanks to the work of social scientists in a variety of fields, we are much better placed to understand the forces at work.

5 Concluding Comments and Policy Implications

Economics is concerned with the analysis of human behaviour, principally of men and women in their roles as consumers and producers. In order fully to understand the activities of economic agents, however, it is first necessary to have some knowledge and appreciation of human psychology, and of social behaviour, since human beings generally live and work in a social environment. These basic facts of life were well understood by early economists. Unfortunately, in the eighteenth and nineteenth centuries, when economics was still at an early stage of development, psychology and sociology were, if anything, even less well developed. The psychological foundations of early economics were therefore rather rudimentary. Individuals were assumed to be thinking, rational beings, and, as such, consumers were held to be motivated only by the desire to maximise their utility, or satisfaction, and businessmen only by the desire to maximize profit.

While these simple, and simplifying, assumptions might have been all that was possible, given the state of knowledge then prevailing, events have moved on, and knowledge in the fields of psychology and sociology has expanded enormously – even if we still have a long way to go before we can really claim to know 'what makes people tick'. Unfortunately, the main body of economic theory has dismally failed to give due recognition to these achievements in the other social services, and has been content to hold fast to the assumptions about human nature which have served it in the past. The human dimension in economics is now woefully inadequate, however;

so much so, that economics in its present state can hardly claim to be more than a semi-social science.

The central requirement is a fuller, updated view of human motivation. Early on, economists recognized the importance of needs, and needs satisfaction, in motivating people, but instead of pursuing this promising line of enquiry, the emphasis of analysis shifted to utility *per se*, thereby avoiding any requirement to discuss the psychological foundations upon which utility itself rested. This shift in emphasis appears to be one of the principal reasons why the development of the behavioural basis of economics has been so slow, and so stunted.

The problem is not, however, just one of according personal needs a more central role in economic analysis. By limiting the discussion of motivation, economics has also failed to take full account of other powerful motivating forces. Personal notions of equity, for example, are much too important an influence on human behaviour to be ignored, especially in the analysis of wage behaviour. Personal goals are also of crucial importance. With regard to the latter, economics is guilty not just of the sin of neglect, but also of misrepresentation. Goals have been assumed to take only one particular form – and that the most extreme form – of maximization, be it of utility or profits. Furthermore, at the same time as the goal is set it is also assumed that it is fully achieved. The goal is never reassessed, nor the possibility of failure ever countenanced. Man in economics is no ordinary being: he is superman. The maximization assumption, in effect, deals only with special cases which, while of interest as possible goals which might ultimately be striven for – although not everyone would even agree with that – are sufficiently divorced from reality to limit their usefulness.

In the consumer field, it seems sufficient for the purposes of economic analysis simply to assume that the goal of consumers is to satisfy their needs, within the usual income constraint. That certainly implies that consumer behaviour is purposeful, but we need not go so far as to assume a 100 per cent maximization goal, since that is to set an unobtainable objective, implying a form of behaviour on the part of human beings which is, quite simply, inhuman and alien to them. We must also recognize that consumers' goals are likely to change, not remain for ever immutable. If a person finds that his lifestyle is not bringing him happiness – a not uncommon state of affairs – then he may well change it, perhaps spending less on drink and cigarettes, and more on outdoor healthy pursuits – as many have decided to do. Why should it be assumed that only in economic affairs do people behave rationally, when all around there is glaring evidence that human behaviour is far from being wholly rational? The evidence to the contrary is just too overwhelming.

In the case of equity, we have also attempted to spell out more clearly the nature of personal goals. The heart of the matter is that, in the absence of absolute standards by which equity may be judged, individuals are obliged to fall back on their own personal perceptions of equity, and these may disagree with the perceptions of others, and even with reality. We look more fully at the implications of equity goals below.

The motivational influence on individuals of needs satisfaction, equity considerations and goals cannot be considered independently of the social comparisons made by these same individuals. Once again, however, economics has, for the most part, unfortunately restricted its own development by attempting to hold this important social influence at bay, preferring to encompass it in the catch-all variable of changes in 'tastes'. Social comparisons, however, exert far too important an influence on consumer behaviour, and on employees' behaviour, for them to be relegated to the role of a peripheral variable. Much of the behaviour of individuals in the economic sphere simply cannot be explained, or properly understood, unless social comparisons are brought into consideration.

One of the most telling arguments in favour of more fully-developed psychological and social foundations for economics, is that the foundations, by providing a common base, would also provide much firmer links between the different subject areas, and therefore a much more fully integrated whole. It is hoped that the present study has made some progress in demonstrating how the same basic framework of analysis is widely applicable.

Turning to the main policy implications of our analysis, we

saw that money wages are not likely to react to conditions of excess supply in the labour market in the way standard economic theory predicts. We have here a good demonstration of the dangers of ignoring some of the basic social and psychological influences on human behaviour; and therefore of undertaking only a partial analysis of economic problems. Social comparisons and views on equity will provoke strong resistance to any policy which tries to impose unilateral reductions in the money incomes of particular groups of workers. Nor is such resistance likely to mellow with the passage of time. In the United States, unemployment has been at high levels throughout most of the post-war period, yet money wages, and real wages, have risen fairly steadily. In the United Kingdom, unemployment has been on an upward trend throughout the post-war era, and, as in many other countries, is now exceptionally high, yet wages, both in money and real terms, press ever upwards. Waiting for money wages to respond in the predicted fashion is like waiting for Godot. We may pretend that we are waiting in anticipation of a future event, but no one in their hearts really expects that it will come to pass. It is time, therefore, that we bowed to the inevitable, and recognized that the labour market does not function like a commodity market, and that we must therefore seek alternatives to flexible money wages if we are to cure unemployment.

That does not mean to say that wage restraint has no part to play in fostering employment. An unduly rapid growth in unit labour costs relative to competitors is unlikely to make a country's problem of creating additional jobs any easier. What, therefore, of the implications of our analysis for wage restraint? Here again the omens are not good. It is not necessary to find regular spillover patterns in order to demonstrate that wage spillover is a real force in the labour market. Spillover tends to have certain characteristics, as we saw, but the pattern tends to change over time as new wage leaders emerge and old ones becomes followers. Moreover, *any* wage increase, whatever the reason, may have repercussions on wage increases elsewhere in the economy, simply because of the desire of other groups not to suffer a deterioration in their relative wage position. Once again, it is the forces of equity, goals and social comparisons which are at work.

What, then, of the argument that inflation is a monetary problem? This argument hinges largely, it seems, on the important distinction, to which Addison *et al.* (1980) have drawn attention, between the '*proximate*' and '*fundamental*', or ultimate, causes of inflation. The proximate causes of inflation are defined by Addison *et al.* as 'the direct causes of an inflationary situation', while the fundamental causes are, 'those factors which themselves bring about the occurrence of the proximate determinants'. Monetarists are primarily concerned with the proximate causes of inflation, in so far as they attribute inflation to an excessive growth of the money supply. In advancing such a viewpoint, it is not necessary to take a stance on the fundamental causes of inflation, for which a variety of explanations have been offered. One common explanation is 'union pressure', a concept which is often vague and not adequately formulated. Political forces also enter such explanations of inflation. Our own explanation of inflation is also of the fundamental kind, since it rests on the upward pressure on wages caused by social and psychological forces which are deep-seated in human nature.

We can try to deal with these fundamental causes of inflation principally in three ways, it seems. We can pursue the commonly adopted approach which might best be described as 'battening down the hatches'. This entails the use of restrictive fiscal and monetary policies to hold down demand, giving rise to increased unemployment, in an effort to lessen wage and price pressures. The cost of such measures, in terms of lost output, distortions to the market mechanism, and sheer human misery, is high. Above all, however, experience has surely shown that such policies on their own simply do not work, other than for at best a temporary period, since they fail to address the fundamental causes of inflation.

An alternative approach, increasingly popular since it became clear that monetarism alone was insufficient to cure inflation, is to adopt 'supply-side' policies, i.e. policies which will improve the workings of the market system. There is certainly much that can be done to encourage the smooth flow of resources throughout most economies, but even those inclining towards the smoothly functioning free market ideal recognize that they have a long haul ahead, the 'time to be measured by quinquennia or decades, not years' (Friedman, 1977). During this time, major changes will be required in personal attitudes and in institutions.

The third approach, which seems to the writer to hold out the best prospect of success, although once again it offers no simple panacea, is to recognize that it is to the *fundamental* factors underlying inflationary pressures that we must chiefly turn our attention – without, however, ignoring that much else can also be done to improve the functioning of economies. The starting point should be a better appreciation of human needs, since these are among the most potent forces influencing human behaviour. Considerations of equity must also be an integral part of any pay system if it is to endure; and it must be accepted that social comparisons are an essential ingredient of equity, inconvenient though this may be for those responsible for determining pay. People do in general have quite clearly defined ideas about what is equitable, and acceptable, and we ought therefore to consult them more about their views. Attention needs to focus first on those cases where there is obvious disagreement about appropriate differentials, since these give rise to the greatest and most prolonged upwards pressure on wages. As we noted earlier, however, any out-of the-ordinary pay increase is like to have repercussions elsewhere in the pay system, unless other employees can be persuaded that it is justified as a special case. This is likely to require education, and the provision of much more information than is usually made available to employees.

What it boils down to in the end, is that in a democratic society, with an essentially free, or mixed market, economy, curtailing inflationary pay increases requires the development of a consensus about what is fair and reasonable. Such a consensus cannot possibly take account of every single pay scale, or pay award, but it can set the general tone, and provide a background against which individual pay developments may be assessed. Such a system must be flexible, of course, and be able to adapt to changing economic circumstances. Where labour shortages develop, or employees with new technological skills are required, for example, the pay system must be able to respond. The case for different rates of pay should then be made explicitly to other employees, however, not simply assumed.

But how does one build consensus, one might reasonably ask? Our analysis gives some indication of how individuals view the question of equity, and what must therefore be done if this requirement is to be met. Among the other important ingredients of consensus building one could probably also include: information, education, consultation, participation and incentives, and there are doubtless other aspects as well. Such exhortations may sound rather vague and idealistic, but some countries do seem to manage more successfully than others to achieve a consensus over pay. An oft-cited example is Austria; and in the past Sweden and the Netherlands have provided other examples of countries achieving long periods of reasonable accord on pay. It is unfortunate that social scientists do not have their corporate finger on the pulse of such societies, as well as on these where consensus clearly does not prevail, since they could provide us with the evidence we need. Differences between countries must exist, and there must be warning signs of changing views when consensus starts to break down. Greater priority to research of this kind could yield handsome dividends, it seems. Our own prediction is that needs, equity and social comparisons would feature prominently in whatever explanations finally emerged.

The above comments are not intended to rule out more formal government intervention in the pay determination process, where this might be necessary. In any sizeable group of people there are usually some recalcitrant members who do not like abiding by the rules, be they explicit or implicit. If the few become many, or if they are able to exert an undue influence, governments may have no option but to step in.

Prices and incomes policies have gone out of fashion for the present, since the prevailing orthodoxy is that such policies have always failed. Numerous studies have shown that, using past economic relationships as the norm, wage increases have generally only fallen temporarily below normal during 'policy-on' periods, followed by above normal increases during the subsequent 'policy-off' periods, with little long-term departure from expected values. What such studies do not, and cannot, tell us, however, is what would have happened had no policy been in operation. Without them, it is quite possible that circumstances might on occasions have deteriorated much more than they did.

A good example is provided by British experience in 1974–75, following the first large oil price rises, when pay and price increases accelerated alarmingly. Within the space of twelve months, the normal rate of increase of basic hourly wage rates for manual workers increased from 5 per cent to 35 per cent, and claims for 40 per cent increases were being lodged when in mid–1975 a pay policy was introduced. Within two years the rate of pay increase was back down to around 5 per cent, and that with a continued rise in output and very little reduction in the number of employees in employment. By early 1978, the rate of wage increase was accelerating once more, although by mid–1979 there were again signs of deceleration, even if the rate of increase was still around 12 per cent. Are we therefore to conclude that pay policies during the period were a failure? The experience certainly contrasts sharply with that over the years 1979–83, under a different government, when the 'batten down the hatches' approach was adopted, on top of the effects of a world trade recession, to which Britain itself contributed. Inflation was also brought down successfully on this occasion, but at an exceptionally heavy cost in terms of lost output and jobs – GDP in real terms fell by 5 per cent, manufacturing output by as much as 15 per cent, and the number of employees in employment by almost 2 million, or 9 per cent.

The real problem with pay policies is that we are unsure of how best to operate them, other than for limited periods. Tensions inevitably build up, it seems, between bargaining groups, or between bargaining groups and the central authorities. It would take a great deal of space to review the many types of pay policies which have been tried – as well as those suggested, but not yet tried. A central problem appears to be, however, that pay policies have not been able to cater successfully for employees' expectations of equitable treatment. Criteria such as productivity growth, or unit labour cost comparisons, are insufficient on their own, and even these are frequently discarded in favour of naked expediency. We return inevitably to the need for a consensus, and that can only be built upon knowledge about employees' perceptions of equity, and a determination to incorporate these in the pay structure from the ground up.

The implications of our analysis for the prospects of reducing high unemployment in many countries are not very hopeful. One of our main conclusions has been that governments should not place great hopes on money wage flexibility as a means of reducing exceptionally high levels of unemployment. Measures aimed at reducing money wages to an extent sufficient to make any noticeable impact seem doomed to failure, for the sorts of reasons we have outlined. Wage restraint, to be successful, must be greater than that in competitor countries, and with all countries trying to practise restraint, gaining a significant competitive advantage in this manner could take years of effort, and the chances of failure must be high. There is always the possibility of adjustment via relative exchange rate movements, of course, but this generally requires a measure of international cooperation greater than that currently prevailing. Countries with very high levels of unemployment must therefore, it seems, look to other, more radical, solutions for their problem. It is hoped, however, that the present volume makes a positive contribution to the debate.

We conclude by noting that, while we have covered a good deal of ground in the present study, the basic framework we have devised is capable of extension into many other areas of economics. The discussion of needs and equity touches on such other matters as income distribution and sex and racial equality. There are also many other aspects of psychology and sociology, and of other social sciences, which are very relevant to economic affairs, as the work of many writers, like Earl (1983) and Furnham and Lewis (1986), have shown. Attitudes provide one example of another promising area which could be linked to the model used in the present study, although there seems to be less uniformity of view among psychologists about the nature and structure of attitudes, and how they relate to motivation. There is a need for more research in this area, and this is a cry which could be echoed at virtually every stage of analysis in the present study.

On the brighter side, the work cited in the present study also indicates clearly that tremendous strides forward have been made in the social sciences in recent years. It is just a pity that economics has failed to make the fullest possible use of the new findings. It is, in consequence, much the poorer for it. If economics is to become a social science in the fullest sense, it must build on the foundations of psychology and sociology, rather than rely on its own improvisations of these subjects. We might then hope for an economics with a truly human face.

Notes

CHAPTER 2

1. Note how the term 'needs' appears to be used synonymously with 'wants'. The failure to distinguish between the two is quite common in economics writings, yet, as we shall argue later, there is an important distinction between the two.
2. Habitual behaviour, to which some psychologists attach considerable importance, might also in the present context be described as 'non-motivated'.

CHAPTER 3

1. Leibenstein demonstrates that such ideas have a very long lineage indeed.
2. Friedman (1957) notes a family connection between the relative income hypothesis and his own, although it holds only under certain conditions. He explains the connection – a somewhat tenuous one – as follows:

   Suppose that transitory components of income and expenditure average out to zero for any group as a whole. The measured income of consumer units whose measured income is equal to the average for their group then equals their permanent component of income, and their average consumption is, on our hypothesis, equal to k times their income. For units at this position in the measured income scale, the ratio of consumption to income varies from group to group only because of differences in k; there are no differences in the ratio of permanent to measured income to introduce additional variation. Similarly, the mean transitory component of income is positive for incomes above the average and negative for incomes below the average, so that classifying units by their relative position rather than their absolute income at least makes the sign of the transitory component the same for units in the same relative income class but in different groups.

> Under certain conditions, then, our hypothesis predicts that the ratio of measured consumption to measure income is a function of relative income position.

Later, Friedman also notes:

> ... acceptance of the permanent income hypothesis does not imply rejection of relative income as a meaningful and relevant variable. The permanent income hypothesis explains why relative income is meaningful and relevant, ...

CHAPTER 4

1. Martin and Roberts (1984) point out that single persons ought really to be distinguished from those widowed, divorced and separated, since the activity rate for the former is much higher than that for the latter.
2. The reference groups r_1 and r_2 used here áre pay bargaining reference groups, and need not correspond with the reference groups used by consumers. Since income provides a common link between the two sets of reference groups, however, and since reference groups are generally drawn from those with whom individuals associate themselves, the same persons may well feature in both the pay and consumer reference groups used by an individual.

Bibliography

Adams, J.S. (1963) 'Toward an Understanding of Inequity', *Journal of Social Psychology*, *67*, pp. 422–36.

Adams, J.S. (1985) 'Inequity in Social Exchange', in Berkowitz, L. (ed.) (1965) *Advances in Experimental Social Psychology 2*, New York and London, Academic Press.

Addison, J.T. and Burton, J. (1984) 'The Socio-political Analysis of Inflation', *Weltwirtschaftliches Archiv 120*, February, pp. 90–119.

Addison, J.T. and Siebert, W.S. (1979) *The Market for Labor: An Analytical Treatment*, Santa Monica, California, Goodyear Publishing.

Adrian, J. and Daniel, R. (1976) 'Impact of Socioeconomic Factors on Consumption of Selected Food Nutrients in the United States', *American Journal of Agricultural Economics 58*, pp. 31–8.

Albion, M.S. and Farris, P.W. (1981) *The Advertising Controversy: Evidence on the Economic Effects of Advertising*, Boston, Mass., Auburn House.

Alderfer, C.P. (1972) *Existence, Relatedness and Growth: Human Needs in Organisational Settings*, New York, Free Press.

Alexander, K. (1961) 'Market Practices and Collective Bargaining in Automotive Parts', *Journal of Political Economy 69*, No. 1, pp. 15–29.

Annable, J.E. (1977) 'A Theory of Downward-rigid Wages and Cyclical Unemployment', *Economic Inquiry 15*, July, pp. 326–44.

Arrow, K.J. (1951) *Social Choice and Individual Values*, New Haven, Yale University Press.

Arrow, K.J. (1967) 'Values and Collective Decision-Making', in Hook, S. (ed.) *Human Values and Economic Policy*, New York, New York University Press.

Arrow, K.J. (1973) 'Some Ordinalist-Utilitarian Notes on Rawls's Theory of Justice', *Journal of Philosophy 70*, pp. 245–63.

Arrow, K.J. (1985) 'Distributive Justice and Desirable Ends of Economic Activity', pp. 135–56, in Feiwel, G.R. (ed.) *Issues in Contemporary Macroeconomics and Distribution*, London, Macmillan.

Asch, S.E. (1951) 'Effects of Group Pressure Upon the Modification and Distortion of Judgments', in Guetzkow, H. (ed.) *Groups, Leadership and Men*, Pittsburg, Carnegie Press.

Ashenfelter, O.C., Johnson, G.E. and Pencavel, J.H. (1972) 'Trade Unions and the Rate of Change of Money Wages in United States Manufacturing Industry', *Review of Economic Studies 39*, No. 117, pp. 27–54.

Atkinson, A.B. (1972) *Unequal Shares: Wealth in Britain*, London, Allen Lane The Penguin Press.

Atkinson, R.L., Atkinson, R.C., Smith, E.E. and Hilgard, E.R. (1987) *Introduction to Psychology*, New York, Harcourt Brace Jovanovich.

Baumol, W.J. (1967) *Business Behavior, Value and Growth*, New York, Harcourt, Brace and World.

Bausor, R. (1984) 'Toward a Historically Dynamic Economics: Examples and Illustrations', *Journal of Post Keynesian Economics*, Spring 1984, Vol. VI, No. 3.

Baxter, J.L. (1973) 'Inflation in the Context of Relative Deprivation and Social Justice', *Scottish Journal of Political Economy 20*, November, pp. 263–82.

Baxter, J.L. (1980) 'A General Model of Wage Determination', *Bulletin of Economic Research 32*, May, pp. 3–17.

Baxter, J.L. (1987) 'Intervening Variables in Economics: An Explanation of Wage Behaviour', in Earl, P. (ed.) *Psychological Economics: Development, Tensions, Prospects*, Boston/Dordrecht/Lancaster, Kluwer Academic Publishers.

Baxter J.L. and McCormick, B.J. (1984) 'Staying on at School and the Effects of the Current Recession', Study commissioned by the OECD, Paris.

Bearden, W.O. and Etzel, M.J. (1982) 'Reference Group Influence on Product and Brand Purchase Decisions', *Journal of Consumer Research 9*, pp. 183–94.

Becker, G.S. (1965) 'A Theory of the Allocation of Time', *Economic Journal 75*, pp. 493–517.

Becker, G.S. (1975) *Human Capital*, New York, National Bureau of Economic Research/Columbia University Press.

Behrend, H., Knowles, A. and Davies, J. (1970) *Views on Income Differentials and the Economic Situation*, Paper No. 57, Dublin, Economic and Social Research Institute.

Behrend, H. (1984) *Problems of Labour and Inflation*, London, Croom Helm.

Bentham, J. (1789) *An Introduction to the Principles of Morals and Legislation*, reprinted 1982, London and New York, Methuen.

Bentham, J. (1815) *A Table of the Springs of Action*, reprinted in Goldworth, A. (ed.) (1983), *Deontology Together with a Table of the Springs of Action and The Article on Utilitarianism*, Oxford, Clarendon Press.

Bernstein, M. and Crosby, F.J. (1980) 'An Empirical Examination of Relative Deprivation Theory', *Journal of Experimental Social Psychology 16*, pp. 442–56.

Bettman, J.R. (1979) *An Information Processing Theory of Consumer Choice*, Reading, Mass., Addison–Wesley.

Bigelow, H.F. (1942) 'Money and Marriage', in Becker, H. and Hill, R. (eds) *Marriage and the Family*, Boston, Heath, pp. 382–6.

Blaug, M. (1980) *The Methodology of Economics: or How Economists Explain*, Cambridge, Cambridge University Press.

Boland, L.A. (1982) *The Foundations of Economic Method*, London, George Allen and Unwin.

Bolles, R.C. (1975) *Theory of Motivation*, New York, Harper and Row.

Boulding, K.E. (1972) 'Human Betterment and the Quality of Life', pp. 455–70, in Strumpel, B., Morgan, J.N. and Zahan, E., *Human Behavior in Economic Affairs: Essays in Honor of George Katona*, New York, Elsevier.

Bourne, E.S. (1957) 'Group Influences in Marketing and Public Relations', in Likert, R. and Hayes, S.P. (eds) *Some Applications of Behavioral Research*, New York, UNESCO.

Brown, J.A.C. and Deaton, A.S. (1972) 'Models of Consumer Behaviour: a Survey', *Economic Journal 82*, pp. 1145–236.

Brown, W. and Sisson, K. (1975) 'The Use of Comparisons in Workplace Wage Determination', *British Journal of Industrial Relations 13* (March), pp. 25–53.

Burnkrant, R.W. and Cousineau, A. (1975) 'Informational and Normative Social Influence in Buyer Behavior', *Journal of Consumer Research 2* (December), pp. 206–15.

Burton, J. and Addison, J. (1977) 'The Institutionalist Analysis of Wage Inflation: A Critical Appraisal', in Ehrenberg, R.G. (ed.) *Research in Labor Economics*, Vol. 1, Greenwich, Conn., Jai Press.

Caldwell, B.C. (1982) *Beyond Positivism: Economic Methodology in the Twentieth Century*, London, George Allen and Unwin.

Caldwell, B.C. (ed.) (1984) *Appraisal and Criticism in Economics: A Book of Readings*, Boston and London, Allen and Unwin.

Charters, W.W. and Newcomb, T.M. (1952) 'Some Attitudinal Effects of Experimentally Increased Salience of a Membership Group', pp. 415–20, in Swanson, G.E., Newcomb, T.M. and Hartley, E.L. (eds) *Readings in Social Psychology*, New York, Holt.

Cook, T.D., Crosby, F.J. and Hennigan, K.M. (1977) 'The Construct Validity of Relative Deprivation', pp. 307–33, in Suls, J.M. and Miller, R.L. (eds) *Social Comparison Processes: Theoretical and Empirical Perspectives*, New York, Wiley.

Crosby, F.J. (1976) 'A Model of Egoistical Relative Deprivation', *Psychological Review 83*, pp. 85–113.

Crosby, F.J. (1982) *Relative Deprivation and Working Women*, Oxford, Oxford University Press.

Crosby, F.J. and Gonzales-Intal, A.M. (1984) 'Relative Deprivation and Equity Theories: Felt Injustice and the Undeserved Benefits of Others', pp. 141–65, in Folger, R. (1984) *The Sense of Injustice*, New York, Plenum Press.

Cullen, D.E. (1956) 'The Interindustry Wage Structure, 1899–1950', *American Economic Review 46*, pp. 353–69.

Curtin, R.T. (1977) *Income Equity among U.S. Workers: The Bases and Consequences of Deprivation*, New York, Praeger.

Cyert, R.M. and March, J.G. (1963) *A Behavioral Theory of the Firm*, Englewood Cliffs, N.J., Prentice-Hall.

Daniel, W.W. (1975) *The PEP Survey on Inflation*, Broadsheet No. 563, London, Political and Economic Planning.

Davis, J.A. (1959) 'A Formal Interpretation of the Theory of Relative Deprivation', *Sociometry 22*, pp. 280–96.

Deutsch, M. and Gerard, H.B. (1955) 'A Study of Normative and Informational Social Influences upon Individual Judgment', *Journal of Abnormal and Social Psychology 51*, pp. 629–36.

Dow, S.C. and Earl, P.E. (1982) *Money Matters: A Keynesian Approach to Monetary Economics*, Oxford, Martin Robertson.

Duesenberry, J.S. (1949) *Income, Saving and the Theory of Consumer Behaviour*, Cambridge, Mass., Harvard University Press.

Dunlop, J.T. (1950) *Wage Determination under Trade Unions*, Fairfield, N.J., Augustus M. Kelly.

Dunlop, J.T. (1957) 'The Task of Contemporary Wage Theory', in Taylor G.W. and Sisson, F.C. (eds) (1957) *New Concepts in Wage Determination*, New York, McGraw-Hill.

Earl, P.E. (1983) *The Economic Imagination: Towards a Behavioural Analysis of Choice*, Brighton, England, Wheatsheaf Books, and New York, M.E. Sharpe.

Earl, P.E. (1984) *The Corporate Imagination: How Big Companies Make Mistakes*, Brighton, England, Wheatsheaf Books, and New York, M.E. Sharpe.

Earl, P. (1987) *Lifestyle Economics: Consumer Behaviour in a Turbulent World*, Brighton, Wheatsheaf Books.

Eckstein, O. (1968) 'Money Wage Determination Revisited', *Review of Economic Studies 35*, No. 102, pp. 133–43.

Eckstein, O. and Wilson, R.A. (1962) 'The Determination of Money Wages in American Industry', *Quarterly Journal of Economics 76*, No. 3, pp. 379–414.

Edgren, G., Faxén, K. and Odhner, C. (1969) 'Wages, Growth and the Distribution of Income', *Swedish Journal of Economics 71* (September), pp. 133–60.

Edgren, G., Faxén, K. and Odhner, C. (1975) *Wage Formation and the Economy*, London, Allen and Unwin.

Ekelund, R.B. and Herbert, R.F. (1975) *A History of Economic Theory and Method*, New York, McGraw-Hill.

Engel, E. (1875) 'Die Productions–und Consumptions–verhältnisse des Königreichs Sachsen', reprinted in *International Statistical Institute Bulletin 9*, Appendix.

Ferber, R. (1962) 'Research on Household Behavior', *American Economic Review 52*, pp. 19–63.

Ferber, R. (1973) 'Consumer Economics: A Survey', *Journal of Economic Literature 11*, pp. 1303–42.

Festinger, L. (1954) 'A Theory of Social Comparison Processes', *Human Relations 7*, pp. 117–140.

Festinger, L. (1957) *A Theory of Cognitive Dissonance*, Evanston, Ill., Row and Peterson.

Fisher, I. (1930) *The Theory of Interest*, New York, Macmillan.

Fisher, M. (1956) 'Exploration in Savings Behaviour', *Bulletin of the Oxford University Institute of Economics and Statistics 18*, (No. 3), pp. 201–77.

Flanagan, R.J. (1976) 'Wage Interdependence in Unionized Labor Markets', *Brookings Paper on Economic Activity 3*, pp. 635–73.

Ford, J.D. and Ellis, E.A. (1980) 'A Re-examination of Group Influence on Member Brand Preference', *Journal of Marketing Research 17* (February), pp. 125–32.

Foster, N., Henry, S.G.B. and Trinder, C. (1984) 'Public and Private Sector Pay: A Partly Disaggregated Study', *National Institute Economic Review* No. 107 (February), pp. 63–73.

Foster, N., Henry, S.G.B. and Trinder, C. (1986) *Public and Private Sector Pay: Some Further Results*, Discussion Paper No. 267 (November, 1986), Centre for Labour Economics, London School of Economics.

Frank, R.H. (1985) *Choosing the Right Pond: Human Behavior and the Quest for Status*, London and New York, Oxford University Press.

French, J.R. and Raven, B. (1968) 'The Bases of Social Power', pp. 259–69, in Cartwright, D. and Zander, A. (eds) *Group Dynamics: Research and Theory*, New York, Harper and Row.

Freud, S. (1915) 'Instincts and Their Vicissitudes', in *Collected Papers*, Vol, IV, New York, Basic Books.

Friedman, M. (1953) 'The Methodology of Positive Economics', in Friedman, M., *Essays in Positive Economics*, Chicago, Ill., University of Chicago Press.

Friedman, M. (1957) *A Theory of the Consumption Function*, Princeton, NJ, Princeton University Press.

Fritzsche, D.J. (1981) 'An Analysis of the Energy Consumption Patterns by Stage of Family Life Cycle', *Journal of Marketing Research 18* (May), pp. 227–32.

Galbraith, J. and Cummings, L.L. (1967) 'An Empirical Investigation of the Motivational Determinants of Task Performance: Interactive Effects between Instrumentality Valence and Motivation–ability', *Organizational Behavior and Human Performance 2*, pp. 237–57.

Galbraith, J.K. (1969) *The Affluent Society*, 2nd edn., revised, London, Hamish Hamilton.

Galbraith, J.K. (1969) *The New Industrial State*, London, Penguin Books.

Georgescu-Roegen, N. (1954) 'Choice, Expectations and Measurability', *Quarterly Journal of Economics 68*, pp. 503–34.

Georgescu-Roegen, N. (1968) 'Utility', *International Encyclopaedia of the Social Sciences 16*, pp. 236–67, New York, Crowell, Collier and Macmillan.

Ghez, G.R. and Becker, G.S. (1975) *The Allocation of Time and Goods over the Life Cycle*, New York, National Bureau of Economic Research.

Gibson, J.L., Ivancevich, J.M. and Danelly, J.H. (1985) *Organizations: Behavior, Structure, Processes*, Plano, Texas, Business Publications.

Gilbert, M. (1986) *Inflation and Social Conflict: A Sociology of Economic Life in Advanced Societies*, Brighton, Wheatsheaf Books.

Goldthorpe, J.H. (1978) 'The Current Inflation: Towards a Sociological Account', in Hirsch, F. and Goldthorpe, J.H. (eds) *The Political Economy of Inflation*, London, Martin Robertson.

Gordon, B.F. (1966) 'Influence and Social Comparison as Motives for Affiliation', *Journal of Experimental Social Psychology*, Supplement 1, pp. 55–65.

Gordon, J.R. (1983) *A Diagnostic Approach to Organisational Behavior*, Boston, Allyn and Bacon.

Gordon, R.A. (1961) *Business Leadership in the Large Corporation*, Berkeley, University of California Press.

Gordon, R.J. (1981) 'Output, Fluctuations and Gradual Price Adjustment', *Journal of Economic Literature 19* (June), pp. 493–530.

Gossen, H.H. (1854, 1927) *Entwicklung der Geetz des Menschlichen Verkehrs*, Berlin, Prager.

Guillebaud, C.W. (1942) 'The Evolution of Marshall's *Principles of Economics'*, *Economic Journal 52*, pp. 330–49.

Gurr, T.R. (1968a) 'A Causal Model of Civil Strife: A Comparative Analysis Using New Indices', *American Political Science Review 62*, pp. 1104–24.

Gurr, T.R. (1968b) 'Psychological Factors in Civil Violence', *World Politics 20*, pp. 245–78.

Gurr, T.R. (1970) *Why Men Rebel*, Princeton, N.J., Princeton University Press.

Haines, W.W. (1982) 'The Psychoeconomics of Human Needs: Maslow's Hierarchy and Marshall's Organic Growth', *Journal of Behavioral Economics 11* (Winter), pp. 97–121.

Hammond, P. (1985) 'Welfare Economics', pp. 405–34, in Feiwel, G.R., *Issues in Contemporary Microeconomics and Welfare*, London, Macmillan.

Hansen, F. (1969) 'Primary Group Influence and Consumer Conformity', pp. 300–5, in McDonald, P.R. (ed.) *Proceedings of the American Marketing Association's Educators Conference*, Chicago, American Marketing Association.

Harsanyi, J.C. (1953) 'Cardinal Utility in Welfare Economics and in The Theory of Risk-taking', *Journal of Political Economy 61*, pp. 434–5.

Harsanyi, J.C. (1955) 'Cardinal Welfare, Individualistic Ethics, and Interpersonal Comparisons of Utility', *Journal of Political Economy 63*, pp. 309–21.

Hartley, R.E. (1960a) 'Relationships between Perceived Values and Acceptance of a New Reference Group', *Journal of Social Psychology 51*, pp. 181–90.

Hartley, R.E. (1960b) 'Personal Needs and the Acceptance of a New Group as a Reference Group', *Journal of Social Psychology 51*, pp. 349–58.

Hartley, R.E. (1968) 'Personal Characteristics and Acceptance of Secondary Groups as Reference Groups', pp. 247–56, in Hyman, H.H. and Singer, E. (eds).

Heckman, J.J. and MaCurdy, T.E. (1980) 'A Life Cycle Model of Female Labour Supply', *Review of Economic Studies*, XLVII, pp. 47–74.

Hendry, D.F. and Ericsson, N.R. (1983) 'Assertion without Empirical Basis: An Econometric Appraisal of Friedman and Schwartz'

'Monetary trends in . . . the United Kingdom', in *Monetary Trends in the United Kingdom*, Panel Paper No. 22, Bank of England Panel of Academic Consultants.

Herzberg, F., Mausner, B. and Singerman, B.B. (1959) *The Motivation to Work*, New York, Wiley.

Hicks, J.R. (1939, 1946) *Value and Capital: An Inquiry into Some Fundamental Principles of Economic Theory*, Oxford, Clarendon Press.

Hicks, J.R. and Allen, R.G.D. (1934) 'A Reconsideration of the Theory of Value', *Economica*, New Series l, pp. 52–76, 196–219.

Hirsch, F. (1977) *Social Limits to Growth*, London, Routledge and Kegan Paul.

Hirschleifer, J. (1985) 'The Expanding Domain of Economics', *American Economic Review 75*, pp. 53–68.

Hisrich, R.D. and Peters, M.P. (1974) 'Selecting the Superior Segmentation Correlate', *Journal of Marketing 38* (July), pp. 60–3.

Homans, G.C. (1961) *Social Behavior: Its Elementary Forms*, New York, Harcourt Brace.

Houthakker, H.S. (1957) 'An International Comparison of Household Expenditure Patterns Commemorating the Centenary of Engel's Law', *Econometrica 25*, pp. 532–51.

Howard, J.A. (1963) *Marketing: Executive and Buyer Behavior*, New York, Columbia University Press.

Hutchison, T.W. (1953) *A Review of Economic Doctrines, 1870–1929*, Oxford, Clarendon Press.

Hyman, H.H. (1942) 'The Psychology of Status', *Archives of Psychology*, No. 269, pp. 5–38, 80–6.

Hyman, H.H. and Singer, E. (1968) *Readings in Reference Group Theory and Research*, London, Collier-Macmillan.

Jackson, D., Turner, H.A. and Wilkinson, R. (1975) *Do Trade Unions Cause Wage Inflation?*, Cambridge, Cambridge University Press.

James, W. (1890) *Principles of Psychology*, New York, Holt.

Jevons, W.S. (1879) *The Theory of Political Economy*, reprinted 1970, Harmondsworth, Middlesex, Penguin Books.

Johnson, G.E. (1977) 'The Determination of Wages in the Union and Non-Union Sectors', *British Journal of Industrial Relations 15*, pp. 211–25.

Jones, A. (1973) *The New Inflation: The Politics of Prices and Incomes*, London, André Deutsch and Penguin.

Joshi, H., Layard, R. and Owen, S. (1981) *Female Labour Supply in Post-war Britain: A Cohort Approach*, Discussion Paper no. 79, Centre for Labour Economics, London School of Economics.

Kahneman, D. and Tversky, A. (1979) 'Prospect Theory: An Analysis of Decision under Risk', *Econometrica 47*, No. 2, pp. 263–91.

Kahneman, D., Slovic, P. and Tversky, A. (eds) (1982) *Judgement under Uncertainty: Heuristics and Biases*, Cambridge, Cambridge University Press.

Katona, G. (1951) *Psychological Analysis of Economic Behavior*, New York, McGraw-Hill.

Kay, N.M. (1982) *The Evolving Firm: Strategy and Structure in Industrial Organization*, London, Macmillan.

Keat, P.G. (1960) 'Long Run Changes in the Occupational Wage Structure, 1900–1956', *Journal of Political Economy 68*, pp. 584–600.

Kelly, H.H. (1952) 'Two Functions of Reference Groups', pp. 410–14, in Swanson, G.E., Newcomb, T.M. and Hartley, E.L. (eds) *Readings in Social Psychology*, New York, Holt, Rinehart and Winston.

Kelly, G.A. (1955) *The Psychology of Personal Constructs*, New York, Norton.

Kelly, G.A. (1963) *A Theory of Personality*, New York, Norton.

Keynes, J.M. (1936) *The General Theory of Employment, Interest and Money*, London, Macmillan.

Keynes, J.M. (1972) *Collected Writings of John Maynard Keynes*, Vol. IX, *Essays in Persuasion*, London, Macmillan.

Killingsworth, M.R. (1983) *Labour Supply*, Cambridge, Cambridge University Press.

Kirkpatrick, E.L., Cowles, M. and Tough, R. (1934) 'The Life Cycle of the Farm Family in Relation to its Standard of Living', *Research Bulletin* No. 21, Maddison, Wisc., University of Wisconsin Agricultural Experiment Station.

Klineberg, O. (1980) 'Human Needs: A Social-Psychological Approach', Lederer, K. (ed) (1980), pp. 19–35.

Knowles, K.G.J.C. and Robinson, D. (1962) 'Wage Rounds and Wage Policy', *Bulletin of the Oxford University Institute of Economics and Statistics 24*, No. 2, pp. 269–329.

Knowles, K.G.J.C. and Thorne, E.M.F. (1961) 'Wage Rounds, 1948–1959', *Bulletin of the Oxford University Institute of Economics and Statistics 23*, No. 1, pp. 1–26.

Kotlikoff, L.J. and Summers, L.H. (1981) 'The Role of Intergenerational Transfers in Aggregate Capital Accumulation', *Journal of Political Economy 89*, pp. 706–32.

Lancaster, K.J. (1966) 'A New Approach to Consumer Theory', *Journal of Political Economy 74*, pp. 132–57.

Lancaster, K.J. (1971) *Consumer Demand: A New Approach*, New York, Columbia University Press.

Lancaster, K.J. (1974) *Introduction to Modern Economics*, Chicago, Rand McNally.

Landy, F.J. (1985) *Psychology of Work Behavior*, Homewood, Ill., Dorsey Press.

Lansing, J.B. and Kish, L. (1957) 'Family Life Cycles as an Independent Variable', *American Sociological Review 22* (October), pp. 512–19.

Lansing, J.B. and Morgan, J.N. (1955) 'Consumer Finances over the Life Cycle', pp. 36–51, in Clark, L.H. (ed.) *Consumer Behavior 2*, New York, New York University Press.

Latané, B. (1966) 'Studies in Social Comparison: Introduction and Overview', *Journal of Experimental Social Psychology*, Supplement 1, pp. 1–5.

Lawler, E.E. (1971) *Pay and Organizational Effectiveness: A Psychological View*, New York, McGraw-Hill.

Lawler, E.E. (1973) *Motivation in Work Organizations*, Monterey, California, Brooks/Cole.

Lederer, K. (ed) (1980) *Human Needs: A Contribution to the Current Debate*, Cambridge, Mass., Oelgeschlager, Gunn and Hain.

Leibenstein, H. (1976) *Beyond Economic Man: A New Foundation for Microeconomics*, Cambridge, Mass., Harvard University Press.

Lessig, V.P. and Park, C.W. (1978) 'Promotional Perspectives of Reference Group Influence: Advertising Implications', *Journal of Advertising* (now *International Journal of Advertising*) *7*, pp. 41–7.

Levinson, H.M. (1960) 'Pattern Bargaining: A Case Study of the Automobile Workers', *Quarterly Journal of Economics 74*, No. 2, pp. 296–317.

Levinson, H.M. (1962) *Collective Bargaining in the Steel Industry: Pattern Setter or Pattern Follower?*, Ann Arbor, Chicago Institute of Industrial Relations.

Lewin, K. (1935) *A Dynamic Theory of Personality*, New York, McGraw-Hill.

Lewin, K. (1938) *The Conceptual Representation and the Measurement of Psychological Forces*, Durham, N.C., Duke University Press.

Locke, E.A. (1968) 'Toward a Theory of Task Motivation and Incentives', *Organizational Behavior and Human Performance 3*, pp. 157–89.

Locke, E.A. (1969) 'Purpose Without Consciousness: A Contradiction', *Psychological Reports 25*, pp. 991–1009.

Locke, E.A. (1970) 'Job Satisfaction and Job Performance: A

Theoretical Analysis', *Organizational Behavior and Human Performance 5*, pp. 484–500.

Locke, E.A. (1975) 'Personal Attitudes and Motivation', *Annual Review of Psychology 26*, pp. 457–80.

Locke, E.A., Saari, L.M., Shaw, K.H. and Latham, G.P. (1981) 'Goal Setting and Task Performance: 1969–1980', *Psychological Bulletin 90* (No. 1), pp. 125–52.

Locks, M.O. (1955) 'The Influence of Pattern-Bargaining on Manufacturing Wages in the Cleveland, Ohio Market, 1945–1950', *Review of Economics and Statistics 37*, No. 1, pp. 70–6.

Loomis, C.P. (1936) 'The Study of the Life Cycle of Families', *Rural Sociology 1*, pp. 180–99.

Lutz, M.A. and Lux, K. (1979) *The Challenge of Humanistic Economics*, Menlow Palm, California, Benjamin/Cummings.

McCarthy, W.E.J., O'Brien, J.S. and Dowd, V.G. (1975) *Wage Inflation and Wage Leadership: A Study of the Role of Wage Bargains in the Irish System of Collective Bargaining*, Dublin, Economic and Social Research Institute.

McDougall, W. (1908) *An Introduction to Social Psychology*, London, Methuen.

McGuire, W.J. (1976) 'Some Internal Psychological Factors Influencing Consumer Choice', *Journal of Consumer Research 2* (March), pp. 302–19.

McLelland, D. (1961) *The Achieving Society*, Princeton, N.J., D. Van Nostrand.

Maher, J.E. (1961) 'The Wage Pattern in the United States, 1946–1957', *Industrial and Labor Relations Review 15*, No. 1, pp. 3–20.

Mallman, C.A. and Marcus, S. (1980) 'Logical Clarifications in the Study of Needs', in Lederer, K. (ed.) (1980), pp. 163–85.

Marris, R. (1964) *The Economic Theory of 'Managerial' Capitalism*, London, Macmillan.

Marshall, A. (1961) *Principles of Economics* (9th edn.), London, Macmillan.

Martin, J. and Roberts, C. (1984) *Women and Employment: A Lifetime Perspective*, London, Her Majesty's Stationery Office.

Maslow, A.H. (1970) *Motivation and Personality*, New York, Harper and Row.

Mehra, Y.P. (1976) 'Spillovers in Wage Determination in U.S. Manufacturing Industries', *Review of Economics and Statistics 58* (August), pp. 300–12.

Menger, C. (1950) *Principles of Economics: First General Part* (edited by Dingwall, J. and Hoselitz, B.F.), Glencoe, Ill., Free Press.

Merton, R.K. and Kitt, A.S. (1950) 'Contributions to the Theory of Reference Group Behaviour', pp. 40–105, in Merton, R.K. and

Lazarsfeld, P.F. (eds) *Continuities in Social Research: Studies in the Scope and Method of "The American Soldier"*, Glencoe, Ill., Free Press.

Merton, R.K. and Rossi, A.K. (1968) 'Contributions to the Theory of Reference Group Behavior', reprinted in Hyman, H.H. and Singer, E. (1968).

Miner, J.B. (1985) *Theories of Organizational Behavior*, Hinsdale, Ill., Dryden Press.

Mitchell, D.J.B. (1980a) *Unions, Wages and Inflation*, Washington, D.C., The Brookings Institution.

Mitchell, D.J.B. (1980b) 'Union/Non-Union Wage Spillovers: A Note', *British Journal of Industrial Relations 18*, pp. 372–6.

Modigliani, F. and Brumberg, R. (1952) 'Utility Analysis and Aggregate Consumption Functions: An Attempt at Integration', reprinted in Abel, A. (ed.) *The Collected Papers of Franco Modigliani*, Vol. 2 (1980), Cambridge, Mass., MIT Press.

Modigliani, F. (1986) 'Life Cycle, Individual Thrift, and the Wealth of Nations', *American Economic Review 76* (June), pp. 297–313.

Morgan, J.N. (1978) 'Multiple Motives, Group Decisions, Uncertainty, Ignorance and Confusion: A Realistic Economics of the Consumer Requires Some Psychology', *American Economic Review*, Papers and Proceedings 68 (May), pp. 58–63.

Morris, N. and Preston, I. (1986) 'Inequality, Poverty and the Redistribution of Income', *Bulletin of Economic Research 38* (No. 4), pp. 277–344.

Moschis, G.P. (1976) 'Social Comparison and Informal Group Influence', *Journal of Marketing Research 13* (August), pp. 237–44.

Murphy, P.E. and Staples, W.A. (1979) 'A Modernized Family Life Cycle', *Journal of Consumer Research 16* (June), pp. 12–22.

Newcomb, T.M. (1943) *Personality and Social Change*, New York, Dryden Press.

Newman, D.K. and Day, D. (1975) *The American Energy Consumer*, Cambridge, Mass., Ballinger.

O'Brien, T.V., Tapia, H.S. and Brown, T.L. (1977) 'The Self-Concept in Buyer Behavior', *Business Horizons* (October), pp. 65–71.

OECD (1965) *Wages and Labour Mobility*, Paris, Organisation for Economic Co-operation and Development.

Ofshe, R. (1972) 'Reference Conflict and Behavior', pp. 88–116, in Berger, J., Zelditch, M. and Anderson, B. *Sociological Theories in Progress*, Boston, Houghton Mifflin.

Orton, E. (1976) 'Changes in the Skill Differential: Union Wages in Construction, 1907–1972', *Industrial and Labor Relations Review 30*, pp. 16–24.

Park, C.W. and Lessig, V.P. (1977) 'Students and Housewives: Differences in Susceptibility to Reference Group Influence', *Journal of Consumer Research 4* (September), pp. 102–9.

Parsons, T. (1931–32) 'Wants and Activities in Marshall', *Quarterly Journal of Economics 46*, pp. 101–40.

Patchen, M. (1961) *The Choice of Wage Comparisons*, Englewood Cliffs, N.J., Prentice-Hall.

Petri, H.L. (1981) *Motivation: Theory and Research*, Belmont, California, Wadsworth.

Pissarides, C.A. (1981) 'Staying on at School in England and Wales', *Economica 48* (November), pp. 345–63.

Plowman, D., Siebert, C.D. and Zaidi, M.A. (1986) 'Market and Spillover Forces in Wage Award Determination in Australia', *Applied Economics 18*, pp. 191–203.

Pollis, N.P. (1968) 'Reference Group Re-examined', *British Journal of Sociology 19*, pp. 300–7.

Porter, L.W. and Lawler, E.E. (1968) *Managerial Attitudes and Performance*, Homewood, Ill., Irwin-Dorsey.

Pritchard, R.D. (1969) 'Equity Theory: A Review and Critique', *Organizational Behavior and Human Performance 4*, pp. 176–211.

Raiffa, H. (1968) *Decision Analysis: Introductory Lectures on Choice Under Uncertainty*, Reading, Mass., Addison-Wesley.

Rawls, J. (1971) *A Theory of Justice*, Cambridge, Mass., Harvard University Press.

Reingen, P.H., Foster, B.L., Brown, J.J. and Seidman, S.B. (1984) 'Brand Congruence in Interpersonal Relations: A Social Network Analysis', *Journal of Consumer Research 11* (December), pp. 771–83.

Reynolds, F.D. and Wells, W.D. (1977) *Consumer Behavior*, New York, McGraw-Hill.

Rizzo, E. and Vinacke, E. (1975) 'Self-actualization and the Meaning of Critical Experience', *Journal of Humanistic Psychology 15*, pp. 19–30.

Robinson, O. and Wallace, J. (1984) 'Growth and Utilisation of Part-time Labour in Great Britain', *Employment Gazette*, pp. 391–7, London, HMSO.

Rodgers, R.H. (1962) *Improvements in the Construction and Analysis of Family Life Cycle Categories*, unpublished PhD. thesis, University of Minnesota.

Rolle, E. (1973) *A History of Economic Thought*, London, Faber.

Rosen, S. (1969) 'Trade Union Power, Threat Effects and the Extent of Organisation', *Review of Economic Studies 36*, No. 106, pp. 185–96.

Ross, A.M. (1948) *Trade Union Wage Policy*, Berkeley and Los

Angeles, University of California Press.

Ross, A.M. (1957) 'The External Wage Structure', in Taylor G.W. and Pierson, F.C. (eds) *New Concepts in Wage Determination*, New York, McGraw-Hill.

Routh, G. (1980) *Occupation and Pay in Great Britain 1906–79*, London, Macmillan.

Rowntree, B.S. (1903) *Poverty: A Study of Town Life*, London, Macmillan.

Runciman, W.G. (1966) *Relative Deprivation and Social Justice*, Henley, Routledge and Kegan Paul.

Ryan, T.A. (1970) *Intentional Behavior: An Approach to Human Motivation*, New York, Ronald Press.

Sargan, J.D. (1971) 'A Study of Wages and Prices in the U.K., 1949–1968', in Johnson, H.G. and Nobay, A.R. (eds) *The Current Inflation*, London, Macmillan.

Sawyer, M.C. (1979) *Theories of the Firm*, London, Weidenfeld and Nicolson.

Sayles, L.R. (1958) *Behavior of Industrial Work Groups: Production and Control*, New York, Wiley.

Schachter, S. (1968) 'Deviation, Rejection and Communication', pp. 165–81, in Cartwright, D. and Zander, A. (eds) *Group Dynamics: Research and Theory*, New York, Harper and Row.

Schmidt, F.L. (1973) 'Implications of a Measurement Problem for Expectancy Theory Research', *Organizational Behavior and Human Performance 10*, pp. 243–51.

Schmit, R.L. (1972) *The Reference Other Orientation: An Extension of the Reference Group Concept*, Carbondale, Southern Illinois University Press.

Scitovsky, T. (1976) *The Joyless Economy*, New York, Oxford University Press.

Scitovsky, T. (1987) 'Growth in the Affluent Society', *Lloyds Bank Review*, No. 163 (January), pp. 1–14.

Seltzer, G. (1951) 'Pattern Bargaining and the United Steel Workers', *Journal of Political Economy 59*, No. 4, pp. 319–31.

Seltzer, G. (1961) 'The United Steelworkers and Unionwide Bargaining', *Monthly Labor Review 84* (February), pp. 129–36.

Sen, A. (1973) *On Economic Inequality*, Oxford, Clarendon Press.

Shackle, G.L.S. (1972) *Epistemics and Economics*, Cambridge, Cambridge University Press.

Sherif, M. (1936) *The Psychology of Social Norms*, New York, Harper and Row.

Sherif, M. (1953) 'The Concept of Reference Groups in Human Relations', pp. 203–31, in Sherif, M. and Wilson, M.O. (eds) *Group Relations at the Crossroads*, New York, Harper.

Shostrom, E. (1964) 'An Inventory for the Measurement of Self-actualization', *Educational and Psychological Measurement 24*, pp. 207–16.

Simon, H.A. (1955) 'A Behavioral Model of Rational Choice', *Quarterly Journal of Economics 69* (February), pp. 99–118.

Simon, H.A. (1956) 'Rational Choice and the Structure of the Environment', *Psychological Review 63* (March), pp. 129–38.

Simon, H.A. (1957) *Models of Man, Social and Rational: Mathematical Essays on Rational Human Behavior in a Social Setting*, New York, Wiley.

Simon, H.A. (1976) 'From Substantive to Procedural Rationality', pp. 129–48, in Latsis, S.J. (ed.) *Method and Appraisal in Economics*, Cambridge, Cambridge University Press.

Simon, H.A. (1979) 'Rational Decision Making in Business Organizations', *American Economic Review 69* (September), pp. 493–512.

Simon, H.A. (1983) 'Alternative Visions of Rationality', pp. 3–35, in *Reason in Human Affairs*, Oxford, Basil Blackwell.

Sims, J.T. (1971) 'Comparison of Consumer Behavior Conformity and Independence between Blacks and Whites: An Exploratory Study', pp. 76–81, in Gardner, D.M. (ed.) *Proceedings of the Second Annual Conference*, Chicago, Association for Consumer Research.

Solow, R.M. (1979) 'Alternative Approaches to Macroeconomic Theory: A Partial View', *Canadian Journal of Economics 12* (August), pp. 339–55.

Solow, R.M. (1980) 'On Theories of Unemployment', *American Economic Review 70* (March), pp. 1–11.

Sorokin, P.A., Zimmerman, C.C. and Galpin, C.J. (1931) *A Systematic Source-book in Rural Sociology 2*, Minneapolis, University of Minnesota Press.

Stafford, J.E. (1966) 'Effects of Group Influences on Consumer Brand Preferences', *Journal of Marketing Research 3* (February), pp. 68–75.

Stafford, J.E. and Cocanougher, A.B. (1977) 'Reference Group Theory', Ch. 16 in Ferber, R. (ed.) *Selected Aspects of Consumer Behavior*, Washington, DC, Government Printing Office.

Steers, R.M. and Porter, L.W. (1987) *Motivation and Work Behavior*, New York, McGraw-Hill.

Stewart, F. (1985) *Planning to Meet Basic Needs*, London, Macmillan.

Stone, J.R.N. (1954) *The Measurement of Consumers' Expenditure and Behaviour in the United Kingdom, 1920*–1938, Vol. 1, Cambridge, Cambridge University Press.

Stouffer, S.A., Suchman, E., De Vinney, L., Star, S. and Williams, R. (1949) *The American Soldier 1: Adjustment During Army Life*, Princeton, N.J., Princeton University Press.

Strotz, R.H. (1957) 'The Empirical Implications of a Utility Tree', *Econometrica 25*, pp. 269–80.

Strotz, R.H. (1959) 'The Utility Tree – A Correction and Further Appraisal', *Econometrica 27*, pp. 482–89.

Suls, J.M. and Miller, R.L. (1977) *Social Comparison Processes: Theoretical and Empirical Perspectives*, Washington, Hemisphere Publishing.

Thurow, L.C. (1969) 'The Optimum Lifetime Distribution of Consumption Expenditures', *American Economic Review 59*, pp. 324–30.

Thurow, L.C. (1983) *Dangerous Currents: The State of Economics*, Oxford, University Press.

Tobin, J. (1967) 'Life Cycle Saving and Balanced Growth', in Fellner, W. *et al.*, *Ten Economic Studies in the Tradition of Irving Fisher*, New York, Wiley.

Tobin, J. (1972) 'Inflation and Unemployment', *American Economic Review 62* (March), pp. 1–8.

Tolman, E.C. (1932) *Purposive Behavior in Animals and Men*, New York, Appleton-Century.

Trevithick, J. (1976) 'Money Wage Inflexibility and the Keynesian Labour Supply Function', *Economic Journal 86* (June), pp. 327–32.

Turner, H.A. and Jackson, D. (1969) 'On the Stability of Wage Differentials and Productivity-Based Wage Policies: An International Analysis', *British Journal of Industrial Relations 7*, No. 1, pp. 3–18.

Turner, H.A. and Jackson, D. (1970) 'On the Determination of the General Wage Level: A World Analysis – or "Unlimited Labour Forever"', *Economic Journal 80* (December), pp. 827–49.

Turner, R.H. (1955) 'Reference Groups of Future-oriented Men', *Social Forces 34*, pp. 130–6.

Tversky, A. and Kahneman, D. (1974) 'Judgement under Uncertainty: Heuristics and Biases', *Science 185*, pp. 1124–31.

Venkatesan, M. (1966) 'Experimental Study of Consumer Behavior Conformity and Independence', *Journal of Marketing Research 3*, pp. 384–7.

Vickrey, W.S. (1945) 'Measuring Marginal Utility by Reactions to Risk', *Econometrica 13*, pp. 319–33.

Vickrey, W.S. (1960) 'Utility, Strategy and Social Decision Rules', *Quarterly Journal of Economics 74*, pp. 507–35.

Vroman, S. (1980) 'Union/Non-Union Spillovers', *British Journal of*

Industrial Relations 18, pp. 369–71.

Vroman, S. (1982) 'The Direction of Wage Spillovers in Manufacturing', *Industrial and Labor Relations Review 36* (October), pp. 102–12.

Vroom, V.H. (1964) *Work and Motivation*, New York, Wiley.

Wachter, M.L. (1970) 'Relative Wage Equations for U.S. Manufacturing Industries 1947–1967', *Review of Economics and Statistics 52*, No. 4, pp. 405–10.

Wachter, M.L. (1974) 'Cost-Push Inflation and Relative Wages', *American Economic Review 64*, No. 3, pp. 482–91.

Wagner, J. and Hanna, S. (1983) 'The Effectiveness of Family Life Cycle Variables in Consumer Expenditure Research', *Journal of Consumer Research 10*, pp. 281–91.

Wagner, J. and Sherman, H. (1983) 'The Effectiveness of Family Life Cycle Variables in Consumer Expenditure Research', *Journal of Consumer Research 10* (December), pp. 281–91.

Walras, L. (1926) *Elements of Pure Economics*, translated by Jaffé, W. (1977), Fairfield, N.J., Augustus M. Kelley.

Walster, E., Walster, G.W. and Berscheid, E. (1973) 'New Directions in Equity Research', *Journal of Personality and Social Psychology 25*, pp. 151–76.

Warr, P. (1976) 'Theories of Motivation', in Warr, P. (ed.) *Personal Goals and Work Design*, London, Wiley.

Weik, K.E. (1966) 'The Concept of Equity in the Perception of Pay', *Administrative Science Quarterly 11*, pp. 414–39.

Wells, W.D. and Gubar, G. (1966) 'Life Cycle Concept in Marketing Research', *Journal of Marketing Research 3*, pp. 355–63.

Wheeler, L. and Zuckerman, M. (1977) 'Commentary', in Suls, J.M. and Miller, R.L. (eds) *Social Comparison Processes: Theoretical and Empirical Perspectives*, New York, Wiley.

White, B.B. (1978) 'Empirical Tests of the Life Cycle Hypothesis', *American Economic Review 68* (no. 4), pp. 547–60.

Williamson, O.E. (1964) *The Economics of Discretionary Behavior: Managerial Objectives in a Theory of the Firm*, Englewood Cliffs, N.J., Prentice-Hall.

Witt, R.E. (1969) 'Informal Social Group Influence on Consumer Brand Choice', *Journal of Marketing Research 6* (November), pp. 473–6.

Witt, R.E. and Bruce, G.D. (1970) 'Purchase Decisions and Group Influence', *Journal of Marketing Research 7* (November), pp. 533–5.

Wood, A. (1978) *A Theory of Pay*, Cambridge, Cambridge University Press.

Acknowledgements

The author wishes to thank the following for permission to reproduce material included in the book: Richard D. Irwin Inc. for Figure 2.3; the American Economic Association and L. Thurow for Figure 3.2; the National Bureau of Economic Research and G. R. Ghez and G. S. Becker for Figure 3.3; the University of Chicago Press and L. J. Kotlikoff and L. H. Summers for Figure 3.4; The Controller of HM Stationery Office for Figure 4.2 and Tables 4.5–4.9, 4.11 and 4.13; Basil Blackwell for material from J. L. Baxter, 'A General Model of Wage Determination', *Bulletin of Economic Research*, 32 (1980).

Name Index

Subject Index